RAINFED AGRICULTURE AND WATERSHED MANAGEMENT

AS PER LATEST ICAR SYLLABUS

MR. DEVANG SHRIVAS

Made with ♥ on the Notion Press Platform
www.notionpress.com

To
My Beloved Mother, Mrs. Sunita Shrivas
whose unconditional love, strength, and sacrifices have been the
foundation of all my achievements. Your unwavering faith in me has been
my greatest motivation.

And to
My Brother, Deependra Shrivas
whose constant support, encouragement, and quiet belief in my dreams
have inspired me to keep moving forward.

This book is a small tribute to your love, patience, and presence in my life.

With all my heart,
— Devang Shrivas

Contents

Preface

Rainfed agriculture remains the backbone of food production in many developing countries, including India, where nearly two-thirds of cultivated land depends solely on monsoon rains. However, with the increasing unpredictability of climate patterns, declining soil health, and pressure on water resources, the need for sustainable and climate-resilient farming practices has never been greater.

This book, Rainfed Agriculture and Watershed Management: Principles, Practices, and Innovations, is born out of an academic passion and practical concern for improving the productivity, sustainability, and resilience of farming systems in water-scarce regions. It is designed to serve as a comprehensive resource for students, researchers, teachers, and practitioners in the fields of Agronomy, Agricultural Extension, Environmental Science, and Rural Development.

The book is structured into ten well-researched chapters, beginning with the fundamentals of soil and water conservation and extending to advanced topics such as climate-smart agriculture, emerging technologies, and policy frameworks for rainfed farming. Each chapter integrates theoretical insights with field-level examples, case studies, and references to recent research findings. Particular emphasis has been given to student-centric learning, including simplified explanations, bullet points, and the integration of current schemes and educational policies like NEP 2020.

This book was also inspired by my experience in the B.Ed. program and classroom research on student engagement and attention span, where I explored innovative teaching strategies. The pedagogical approach used throughout this book reflects those learnings—making technical content accessible, relatable, and practical.

I am deeply grateful to my mentors, faculty members, and peers whose guidance enriched this work. Special thanks are due to the students and researchers whose responses and participation informed many of the discussions presented in the chapters. I also acknowledge the role of digital tools and open-access journals that supported my evidence-based writing process.

It is my hope that this book contributes meaningfully to the ongoing dialogue on sustainable agriculture, and that it empowers future educators, agronomists, and policy-makers to innovate with empathy and scientific rigor.

— Devang Shrivas

Ph.D Scholar, Ravindranath Tagore University, Raisen, Madhya Pradesh (M.P.)

11-04-2025

Acknowledgements

First and foremost, I express my deepest gratitude to the Almighty for granting me the strength, perseverance, and clarity of mind to undertake and complete this book.

I am sincerely thankful to my teachers and mentors, whose insightful guidance and constant encouragement have been instrumental in shaping the content and direction of this work. Their dedication to teaching and research continues to inspire me every day. Whose academic wisdom and constructive feedback helped refine each chapter of this book.

I am also grateful to the authors and researchers whose works I have drawn upon and cited throughout the book. Their commitment to open knowledge sharing has made this learning journey deeply rewarding.

A warm thank you goes to my family and friends, whose patience, emotional support, and belief in me gave me the strength to work through long hours and tight deadlines. Their encouragement was my quiet source of strength.

Lastly, I appreciate the technical tools and platforms—especially Google Forms, citation managers, and AI-based assistants—that streamlined the research and writing process. The integration of traditional research methods with modern tools has been a learning experience in itself.

This book is a humble contribution to the field of agricultural science and education, and I hope it serves as a useful reference for students, educators, and professionals working toward a more sustainable and climate-resilient future.

— Devang Shrivas

Ph.D Scholar, Ravindranath Tagore University, Raisen, Madhya Pradesh (M.P.)

11-04-2025

Prologue

In a world increasingly defined by climate uncertainty and resource scarcity, the need for sustainable agricultural practices has never been more pressing. Rainfed agriculture, which sustains the livelihoods of millions of smallholder farmers across India and the Global South, is particularly vulnerable to the vagaries of rainfall, soil degradation, and dwindling water resources. Yet, within these challenges lie opportunities—opportunities to innovate, adapt, and transform farming into a resilient, science-backed, and people-centered endeavor.

This book emerges from both academic inquiry and a personal desire to contribute meaningfully to the field of sustainable agriculture. What began as a study project during my teacher education journey gradually evolved into a broader exploration of key topics such as soil and water conservation, watershed development, student attention span in agricultural classrooms, climate resilience, and policy-driven solutions. These diverse themes are woven together with the aim of offering not just theoretical knowledge, but actionable insights.

The chapters in this book are structured to reflect the practical needs of students, researchers, and early-career educators. Whether you're a teacher-in-training seeking pedagogical relevance, a student of agriculture trying to make sense of complex systems, or a practitioner searching for ground-level innovations, this book has something for you. It is rooted in real-world examples, enriched by field-based data, and informed by the latest research and policies like the National Education Policy 2020 and global sustainability frameworks.

This prologue is not just a preface to the chapters ahead—it is an invitation. An invitation to question existing methods, to reimagine the way we teach and practice agriculture, and to embrace interdisciplinary solutions that are inclusive, innovative, and impactful. As you turn the pages of this book, may you find not only knowledge but inspiration to act—because the future of agriculture lies in what we choose to learn, share, and do today.

— Devang Shrivas

Ph.D Scholar, Ravindranath Tagore University, Raisen, Madhya Pradesh (M.P.)

11-04-2025

CHAPTER ONE

FUNDAMENTALS OF RAINFED AGRICULTURE

1.1 OVERVIEW OF RAINFED AGRICULTURE

Indian agriculture is a risky endeavor during the monsoon season, making water a crucial resource for sustainable development. Freshwater resources are essential for the life of humans and the flora and fauna on Earth. Plant cells and tissues contain 80-90% water by weight, affecting their physiological processes. The variable global distribution of annual average rainfall contributes to disparities in agriculture production and socio-economic conditions. Over half of the earth's land surfaces receive less than 500mm annual precipitation, requiring reclaimed land through dry farming practices. Areas with 500-750mm rainfall also require dry farming measures for successful crop production.

India's annual average rainfall distribution is highly variable and irregular, with wide spread variations among meteorological subdivisions. The spatial distribution varies from 100mm/annum in Rajasthan to 11000mm/annum in Cherrapunji in Meghalaya. Agriculture uses almost 85% of the country's water, with 92 and 33 million hectares receiving less than 750mm rainfall annually.

Agriculture is a crucial part of the Indian economy, contributing 25% of the national gross product. Rainfed lands account for 70% of agriculture, contributing 44% to food production and supporting 40% of the human and

60% of livestock population. Despite the full irrigation potential being used, half of the cultivated land remains rainfed. About 30% of the country is drought-prone and suffers from critical water shortages. The rainfed agro-ecosystem covers 90 million ha of net cultivated area, distributed unequally among states. In Assam, Gujarat, Himachal Pradesh, Karnataka, Kerala, Madhya Pradesh, Maharashtra, and Rajasthan, more than 70% of the net cultivated area is rainfed. Crop production in rainfed areas is risky due to uncertainties in rainwater availability and swings in monsoon rainfall patterns. The coefficient of variation in monsoon rainfall in these areas ranges from 50-55 to 20-30%.

Rainfed agriculture relies heavily on water, which is the most scarce resource. Inefficient use of water leads to inefficient inputs. Water resource management focuses on developing new water resources and utilizing existing ones, particularly based on indigenous systems. Rainfall can be intercepted by vegetation, infiltrated into the ground, flowed over land, evaporated, or evaporated. Soil acts as a reservoir for water entering the soil, and water in the soil is always transitory. Rainfed areas can be made more productive and profitable by adopting improved rainwater conservation and harvesting technologies and agricultural production technologies.

The fundamental problems Of dry farming are:-

- Choice of crops capable of growth under moisture stress conditions and
- Crop management for proper utilization Of stored soil moisture.

- Retention of the moisture in the soil until it is needed by the plants;
- Prevention of direct evaporation of soil moisture during the growing season;

- Storage in the soil of a small annual rainfall;
- Regulation of the amount of water drawn from the soil by plants;

Dry farm problems arise from the relationship between crops and arid lands. Some plants are drought-resistant, some are drought-tolerant, and some have a deep root system or waxy layer for survival. Proper seeding, tillage, nutrient management, plant population, weed control, and mid-season correction are essential for efficient use of conserved moisture in dry farming.Area under dry land is likely to a change according to definition and irrigation facilities developed from time to time. Areas receiving annual rainfall between lees than 750 mm is known as dry farming tracts zones.There are about 105 districts under this category but 18 of these districts have good irrigation facilities. Therefore dry farming tract comprises 87 districts spread over Andrapradesh, Gujart, Haryana, Punjab, Karnataka, MP, Maharashtra, Rajastan, Tamilnadu and Uttar Pradesh

Dryland agriculture, often used synonymously with dry farming, famming, and rainfed farming, is crucial for meeting future food needs. This farming method involves cultivating crops entirely under rainfed conditions, which can be challenging due to the intensity and frequency of rainfall. Despite the use of all water resources for irrigation, about half of the cultivated area remains rainfed, making it a significant challenge for future food production.

1.1.1 . Definition

"Rainfed agriculture refers to the cultivation of crops relying solely on natural precipitation without any form of supplementary irrigation. This system depends entirely on local climate conditions, particularly rainfall patterns, making it susceptible to variability in productivity."

"The Food and Agriculture Organization (FAO) defines rainfed agriculture as the practice of growing crops solely with water obtained from direct rainfall. It highlights that the timing and success of such agriculture are governed by the region's natural rainfall distribution."

"An agricultural system where rainfall is the only water source, distinguishing it from irrigated agriculture which uses artificial water applications. This reliance exposes it to substantial inter-annual and intra-seasonal yield variability."

"A type of agricultural practice that operates without supplementary irrigation, depending entirely on precipitation. This form of agriculture is subject to the risks associated with uneven rainfall distribution, making it less predictable than irrigated systems."

"In India, rainfed agriculture is described as the cultivation of crops in areas without irrigation facilities. It encompasses significant portions of the country, especially semi-arid and arid zones, where seasonal rainfall plays a crucial role in determining crop type and yield potential."

1.2 CLASSIFICATION OF RAINFED AGRICULTURE

Rainfed agriculture refers to farming that relies primarily on rainfall for water, rather than irrigation. The types of rainfed agriculture are classified based on the amount of annual rainfall in the region, the length of the growing season, and the moisture stress conditions that crops are likely to face. Here's a detailed explanation of each type:

1. Dry Farming

- **Definition:** Dry farming is the cultivation of crops in areas with very low annual rainfall, typically less than 750 mm.
- **Challenges:** Due to the limited rainfall, these regions often experience severe moisture stress, leading to frequent crop failure. Prolonged dry spells are common during the crop growing season, which significantly impacts crop survival and yields.
- **Growing Season:** These areas are considered arid, with a short growing season—typically less than 75 days—during which there is sufficient soil moisture to support plant growth.
- **Agricultural Practices:** Moisture conservation techniques are essential in dry farming to ensure successful crop production. Practices include:

  - **Mulching:** Covering the soil with organic or inorganic materials to reduce water evaporation.
  - **Contour Plowing:** Plowing along the contours of the land to slow down water runoff and increase soil moisture retention.
  - **Minimum Tillage:** Reducing the disturbance of soil to minimize moisture loss.

- **Typical Crops:** Hardy, drought-resistant crops like millets (e.g., pearl millet), sorghum, and pulses (e.g., pigeon pea) are common in dry farming systems.

2. Dryland Farming

- **Definition:** Dryland farming involves growing crops in areas with moderate annual rainfall, typically more than 750 mm but still subject to occasional dry spells.

- **Growing Season and Moisture Stress:** These are semi-arid regions with a growing season lasting between 75 and 120 days. Although prolonged dry spells can occur, crop failure is less frequent compared to dry farming areas.
- **Agricultural Practices:** While moisture conservation is still important, the emphasis here is on managing periods of moisture scarcity during the growing season rather than an overall lack of moisture. Practices include:

  - **Intercropping:** Growing two or more crops together to maximize resource use and minimize risk.
  - **Crop Rotation:** Alternating different types of crops across seasons to preserve soil fertility and moisture.
  - **Early Maturing Varieties:** Using crop varieties with shorter growth cycles to take advantage of the available moisture before it becomes scarce.

- **Typical Crops:** In dryland farming, crops include grains like wheat and maize, and legumes like chickpeas, which can withstand moderate water scarcity.

3. Rainfed Farming

- **Definition:** Rainfed farming is practiced in regions with high annual rainfall, generally above 1,150 mm, where soil moisture is not a limiting factor during the crop growth period.
- **Growing Season and Moisture Levels:** These are humid regions with a long growing season—typically more than 120 days—during which crops experience minimal moisture stress. In fact, excessive moisture or waterlogging can be more of a concern than water scarcity.
- **Agricultural Practices:** In rainfed farming, emphasis is often placed on draining or managing excess water rather than conserving it. Key practices include:

  - **Drainage Systems:** Installing drainage canals or using raised beds to prevent waterlogging and ensure adequate root aeration.
  - **Soil Fertility Management:** Applying balanced fertilizers to counteract nutrient leaching due to high rainfall.

- ◦ **Erosion Control:** Preventing soil erosion caused by heavy rains using terraces, bunds, or grass strips.

- **Typical Crops:** Crops with high water requirements, such as rice, sugarcane, and certain fruits and vegetables, are commonly grown in rainfed farming regions.

1.3 SCOPE OF RAINFED AGRICULTURE

Rainfed agriculture, which relies primarily on natural rainfall for crop growth, holds a critical role in global food security, especially in regions with limited access to irrigation. Its scope encompasses a wide range of aspects, including its environmental, economic, and social implications, as well as its challenges and opportunities. Here are some key points that would highlight the scope of rainfed agriculture:

1. **Global Importance and Contribution to Food Security**

    1. Role in Food Production: Rainfed agriculture accounts for a significant portion of the world's food production, especially in developing countries where over half of the agricultural land is rainfed. In India, for instance, rainfed farming supports a substantial part of staple food production, especially cereals, pulses, and oilseeds.
    2. Role in Rural Livelihoods: Many rural communities rely on rainfed agriculture as their primary source of income and employment. Understanding its scope helps in recognizing its influence on poverty reduction, rural development, and food security.

2. **Ecological and Environmental Significance**

    1. Biodiversity Conservation: Rainfed systems often incorporate a variety of crops, trees, and other plant species, supporting biodiversity and promoting ecosystem resilience.
    2. Soil and Water Conservation: Rainfed agriculture, with proper management, can contribute to soil conservation, water infiltration, and retention, reducing soil erosion and promoting

sustainable land use.

3. Climate Resilience: Rainfed agriculture systems are key to promoting climate-resilient farming. They play a significant role in adapting to climate variability by using drought-resistant crops and conservation techniques.

3. Challenges and Constraints

1. Dependence on Weather Patterns: The success of rainfed agriculture is inherently linked to rainfall distribution and intensity, making it vulnerable to climate change effects such as droughts, erratic rainfall, and extreme weather.
2. Soil Degradation and Low Productivity: Many rainfed areas face issues of soil erosion, low soil fertility, and reduced water-holding capacity, leading to lower productivity compared to irrigated systems.
3. Technological and Knowledge Gaps: The scope includes identifying ways to overcome these challenges through research and technology, including soil conservation, water harvesting, and improved crop varieties.

4. Water Management and Conservation

1. Water Harvesting and Efficient Utilization: Innovations in water harvesting, soil moisture management, and efficient water use are crucial to rainfed systems. This section of the book could explore a range of methods such as micro-catchment systems, traditional water conservation practices, and modern water-saving techniques.
2. Watershed Management: Watershed development is integral to rainfed agriculture, promoting better resource management and sustainable development. A discussion on the principles, components, and benefits of watershed management provides an expanded view of sustainable practices in rainfed regions.

5. Potential for Technological Innovation

1. Drought-Resistant Crop Varieties and Genetic Improvements: Advances in plant breeding and biotechnology, which can produce crops better suited for low-water environments, are critical for enhancing productivity in rainfed areas.
2. Agroforestry and Mixed Farming Systems: Integrating trees and crops can improve soil quality, enhance water conservation, and provide additional income sources.
3. Digital Tools for Climate Adaptation: The use of remote sensing, precision agriculture, and forecasting tools to monitor rainfall, soil moisture, and drought conditions can enhance the adaptability and resilience of rainfed agriculture.

6. Economic and Policy Aspects

1. Policies for Supporting Rainfed Farmers: This section would discuss the importance of targeted policies, subsidies, and financial aid that support rainfed farmers in adopting sustainable practices and mitigating risks.
2. Market Opportunities for Rainfed Crops: Many rainfed crops have high market value, and with proper support, farmers can access better markets, both locally and globally. Promotion of indigenous, drought-resistant, and nutritionally rich crops can add economic value and diversify income streams.

7. Sustainability and Future Prospects

1. Achieving Sustainable Development Goals (SDGs): Rainfed agriculture can play a significant role in achieving SDGs, particularly those related to hunger, poverty, and environmental sustainability.
2. Potential for Research and Development: There is a scope for ongoing research in agronomic practices, crop adaptation, and community-based approaches to make rainfed agriculture more productive, resilient, and sustainable.
3. Climate Change Adaptation: This area of study is essential to developing policies, practices, and innovations that will help rainfed farmers adapt to the uncertainties of climate change.

IMPORTANCE OF RAINFED AGRICULTURE

Rainfed agriculture, which relies on rainfall rather than irrigation, is essential to food security, rural livelihoods, and environmental sustainability, especially in developing countries where access to irrigated water systems may be limited. Here's a breakdown of its key roles and contributions:

1. Food Security

- **Essential Source of Food**: Rainfed agriculture is vital for feeding millions globally, particularly in countries with restricted irrigation infrastructure. For instance, in India, around 60% of the country's cereal output comes from rainfed areas, which underscores its role in national food supply.
- **Diverse Crop Production**: Rainfed regions produce a variety of crops, including cereals, pulses, and oilseeds, which contribute to a balanced diet. This diversity in crop production helps in meeting nutritional needs for local populations.

2. Climate Resilience

- **Adaptation to Climate Change**: With climate change causing more unpredictable rainfall patterns, rainfed agriculture offers a model of resilience. It inherently relies on sustainable methods that adapt to local conditions, such as crop rotation, conservation tillage, and use of drought-resistant crops.
- **Mitigating Climate Risks**: By diversifying crop choices and managing water efficiently, rainfed farmers can reduce the risks associated with extreme weather, such as droughts and floods. These adaptive strategies help maintain productivity even under erratic climatic conditions, ensuring a stable food supply.

3. Rural Livelihoods

- **Economic Backbone for Rural Areas**: In many developing regions, rainfed agriculture is a primary source of income and employment, directly supporting rural economies. It enables farmers, laborers, and small-scale producers to sustain themselves through crop cultivation, livestock, and sometimes integrated agro-forestry systems.

- **Supporting Diverse Livelihoods**: Rainfed agriculture is not limited to crop production. It also sustains livestock rearing, where animals graze on fallow fields, and agro-forestry, which provides additional income through tree crops and forest products.

4. Adaptive Practices in Rainfed Agriculture

- **Innovative Water Management**: Rainfed farmers often employ traditional and modern methods to maximize water availability, including rainwater harvesting, contour bunding, and soil moisture conservation techniques. These practices capture and store rainfall, making it available for crops during dry periods.
- **Efficient Crop Management**: By using techniques such as mixed cropping and selecting drought-resistant or early-maturing varieties, farmers can reduce water dependency and optimize crop yield. These adaptive measures enable them to better manage limited rainfall resources.

Characteristics of Rainfed Agriculture

1. **Unreliable and Limited Rainfall:** Rainfed crops often suffer from unpredictable weather, such as a late start to the monsoon season, extended dry spells, or an early end to the rains, impacting growth cycles.
2. **Extreme Climate Risks:** These areas face various climatic threats like drought, flooding, or waterlogging, as well as frost damage, which can cause partial or complete crop failure.
3. **Irregular Soil Surfaces:** Soil erosion due to wind and water is common, leading to the formation of rills and gullies. Many farmers lack the resources for land leveling, resulting in uneven soil surfaces that affect crop establishment.
4. **Extensive Farming Practices:** Due to limited irrigation, farming in dryland areas is extensive rather than intensive, often requiring larger plots to achieve minimal productivity.

5. **Larger Field Sizes:** Without irrigation, smaller plots are less practical. Farmers generally use larger field sizes, which are easily recognized as typical rainfed areas.

6. **Limited Crop Variety:** Drought-tolerant crops are commonly cultivated, leading to uniform cropping across the area. Growth is often limited, making it clear these are rainfed regions.

7. **Lower Crop Yields:** Due to economic limitations, farmers in dryland areas often cannot apply adequate inputs or high-yielding seeds, resulting in lower productivity.

8. **Weak Market Demand:** Since most farmers grow the same crops that mature simultaneously, market saturation occurs, driving prices down and reducing income for the farmers.

9. **Economic Hardships for Farmers and Poor Livestock Health:** Farmers often struggle financially due to low returns, and livestock health suffers due to limited feed and fodder resources.

10. **Widespread Nutritional Deficiencies:** An abundance of low-calorie food and a lack of vegetables, fruits, and dairy products in diets can lead to deficiencies in essential nutrients, contributing to malnutrition and related health issues in the population.

CHAPTER TWO

HISTORICAL CONTEXT AND DEVELOPMENT

2.1 HISTORY OF RAINFED AGRICULTURE IN INDIA

Rainfed agriculture, a practice deeply intertwined with India's agrarian history, has been a lifeline for millions of people. This system, reliant solely on natural rainfall, has shaped the country's agricultural landscape and cultural heritage.

The roots of rainfed agriculture in India trace back to ancient civilizations like the Indus Valley Civilization, where sophisticated water management systems and agricultural practices were employed. Over centuries, indigenous communities developed ingenious techniques to maximize crop yields in the face of unpredictable rainfall. Traditional practices like crop rotation, mixed cropping, and intercropping were widely used to optimize resource utilization and mitigate risks.

The advent of the Green Revolution in the mid-20th century, while primarily focused on irrigated agriculture, also brought advancements in seed technology, fertilizers, and pest control to rainfed areas. However, the benefits were often limited due to the constraints of water availability.

In recent decades, climate change has posed significant challenges to rainfed agriculture in India. Increasing temperatures, erratic rainfall patterns, and prolonged droughts have exacerbated the vulnerability of rainfed farmers. To address these challenges, a renewed focus is being placed on climate-resilient agriculture, sustainable water management, and community-based approaches to watershed development.

TRADITIONAL RAINFED PRACTICES IN INDIA

Traditional rainfed agriculture is crucial for livelihood security in India, as 56% of the country's cultivated area relies on rainfall. This sector contributes 40% of India's food production and supports 60% of the livestock population. Despite advances in irrigation, a significant portion of the country still relies on rainfed farming, meeting 40% of long-term foodgrain demand.

Traditional rainfed agriculture faces challenges such as low productivity levels, particularly in dry regions. Despite significant productivity gains since the 1960s, rainfed crop yields have stagnated, often higher than national averages. Mismatches in development strategies and intensive agriculture in unsuitable dry regions have led to issues like groundwater depletion. Policy shifts, such as agricultural liberalization, have negatively impacted rainfed crops, changing growth patterns and creating disparities between irrigated and rainfed areas. These trends underscore the need for development strategies considering both internal and external challenges.

Traditional rainfed agriculture in India has evolved over centuries, with farmers adapting to the region's variable climate and limited water resources. These practices are based on local knowledge, agro-ecological conditions, and sustainable resource management, aimed at maximizing productivity while minimizing risk. Below are some key traditional rainfed practices commonly found in India:

1. Mixed Cropping

- **Description**: Farmers plant a variety of crops in the same field, such as cereals, legumes, and oilseeds, to reduce risk from unpredictable rainfall. This method ensures some level of harvest even if one crop fails.
- **Example**: A combination of crops like **sorghum (jowar), pearl millet (bajra),** and pulses such as **gram (chana)** or **moong** is typical in dry regions.

2. Crop Rotation

- **Description**: This practice involves growing different crops in succession on the same plot of land, which helps improve soil health, control pests, and reduce the risk of disease buildup.
- **Example**: In many rainfed areas, farmers rotate between **legumes** (which fix nitrogen in the soil) and **cereals** like **wheat**, **rice**, or **maize**.

3. Agroforestry

- **Description**: Integrating trees with crops is common in rainfed areas to reduce soil erosion, improve soil fertility, and provide shade and fodder. Trees also help conserve moisture and regulate local microclimates.
- **Example: Tamarind, Neem**, and **Acacia** trees are often planted alongside crops in dry regions.

4. Rainwater Harvesting

- **Description**: In areas with unpredictable rainfall, traditional methods like **johads, khalis**, and **ponds** are used to collect and store rainwater for use during dry spells.
- **Example**: The **Johad** is a traditional water harvesting structure found in Rajasthan, designed to collect rainwater, recharge groundwater, and store water for irrigation.

5. Terracing and Contour Plowing

- **Description**: In hilly regions, farmers build terraces along contours to slow down the movement of rainwater, reduce soil erosion, and conserve moisture. Contour plowing is used to follow the natural shape of the land.
- **Example**: In the **Western Ghats** and **Himalayan foothills**, terraces are a common practice.

6. Low-Input and Organic Farming

- **Description**: Traditional rainfed farming systems are usually low-input, relying on organic methods such as **composting, green manuring**, and the use of **farmyard manure** (FYM) to maintain soil fertility and minimize the dependence on chemical fertilizers.

- **Example**: **Vermicomposting** and the use of cow dung and urine as organic fertilizers are common in dryland farming.

7. Dryland Crop Varieties

- **Description**: Farmers often use drought-resistant, hardy varieties that can withstand periods of water scarcity. These varieties are well-adapted to the local climatic conditions and require minimal water.
- **Example**: **Millets** like **finger millet (ragi), pearl millet (bajra)**, and **sorghum** are popular in dryland areas due to their ability to thrive on minimal rainfall.

8. Soil Moisture Conservation

- **Description**: To retain moisture, farmers use various techniques like **mulching, deep plowing**, and **ridge planting** to minimize evaporation and improve water retention in the soil.
- **Example**: In regions like **Madhya Pradesh** and **Rajasthan, mulching with crop residues** or dry grass is a common practice to prevent soil drying out.

9. Indigenous Seed Saving

- **Description**: Farmers save seeds from each season's crop for future planting, using varieties that have been passed down through generations. This helps maintain biodiversity and ensures the availability of locally adapted seeds.
- **Example**: **Indigenous varieties of rice, pulses**, and **millets** are commonly saved and exchanged among farming communities.

10. Livestock Integration

- **Description**: Livestock plays a crucial role in traditional rainfed farming systems, providing manure for soil enrichment, fodder for the family, and a buffer against crop failure.
- **Example**: **Cattle, goats**, and **sheep** are integrated into the farming system for draft power, manure, and milk production.

11. Water-Saving Techniques

- **Description**: In regions with scarce water resources, farmers employ methods like **irrigation from wells** or small canals during critical growing periods, ensuring crops receive adequate water.
- **Example: Wells** or **hand pumps** are commonly used in the **dry regions of Gujarat, Madhya Pradesh**, and **Rajasthan** to provide supplementary irrigation during drought periods.

These traditional practices, while often low-tech and resource-efficient, are critical for maintaining food security, enhancing resilience to climate change, and sustaining agricultural productivity in India's rainfed regions. Many of these methods also have environmental benefits, such as maintaining soil fertility, conserving water, and protecting biodiversity.

EVOLUTION OF AGRICULTURAL POLICIES AND PROGRAMS

The evolution of agricultural policies and programs in India reflects the country's changing priorities and responses to various challenges faced by the agricultural sector over the years. India's agricultural policy development can be understood in different phases, from the pre-Independence period to the present, each marked by distinct policies and programs aimed at ensuring food security, improving productivity, and addressing rural poverty.

1. Before Independence Period (Until 1947)

- **Focus**: During British rule, agriculture was largely ignored, and policies primarily aimed at revenue extraction rather than development.
- **Land Tenure Systems**: Systems like the **Zamindari** and **Ryotwari** were established, which often placed heavy tax burdens on farmers and limited land ownership rights.
- **Export of Cash Crops**: Policies encouraged the cultivation of cash crops (such as cotton, tea, and indigo) for export, which led to food shortages in some regions.

2. After Independence to the Green Revolution (1947–1960s)

- **Initial Focus on Food Security and Land Reforms**: India's first agricultural policies after Independence focused on food self-sufficiency, land redistribution, and improving the livelihoods of small farmers.
- **Land Reform Acts**: These acts sought to abolish the Zamindari system, redistribute land, and secure tenancy rights, but implementation varied by state.
- **Community Development Programs**: Introduced in the 1950s, these programs aimed to modernize rural areas through infrastructural development and community involvement.
- **Five-Year Plans**: The government introduced Five-Year Plans, starting with the **First Plan (1951–56)**, which allocated significant resources to agriculture and irrigation.

3. Green Revolution Era (1960s–1970s)

- **Introduction of High-Yielding Varieties (HYVs)**: To address food shortages, the government introduced HYV seeds for wheat and rice, especially in northern states, significantly boosting productivity.
- **Intensification of Inputs**: Use of chemical fertilizers, pesticides, and mechanization increased, along with improved irrigation facilities.
- **Impact**: The Green Revolution led to self-sufficiency in food grains, especially wheat, but created regional imbalances and environmental issues.
- **Institutional Support**: Organizations like the **Food Corporation of India (FCI)** and **Agricultural Prices Commission** (now the Commission for Agricultural Costs and Prices, or CACP) were established to ensure fair prices for farmers and maintain food buffer stocks.

4. Diversification and Expansion of Support (1980s–1990s)

- **Broad-Based Agricultural Development**: Programs like the **Integrated Rural Development Program (IRDP)** focused on poverty alleviation and provided subsidies for assets to rural households.
- **National Bank for Agriculture and Rural Development (NABARD)**: Established in 1982 to provide credit and financial support for agricultural development and rural infrastructure.

- **Emphasis on Oilseeds and Pulses**: Initiatives like the **Technology Mission on Oilseeds and Pulses** aimed at reducing dependence on imports by increasing the production of oilseeds and pulses.

5. Post-Liberalization Period (1990s–2000s)

- **Economic Reforms and Agricultural Market Liberalization**: With economic liberalization in 1991, India opened up its economy, impacting agriculture. Policies aimed to reduce subsidies, deregulate the agricultural sector, and encourage private sector investment.
- **WTO and Global Integration**: India's entry into the **World Trade Organization (WTO)** in 1995 required reforms in agricultural trade policies, particularly regarding tariffs, subsidies, and export-import regulations.
- **National Agricultural Policy (2000)**: This policy aimed to achieve 4% agricultural growth per annum through diversification, modernization, and sustainable practices.
- **Focus on Rural Credit and Insurance**: Programs like the **Kisan Credit Card Scheme** were introduced to improve access to credit. The **National Agricultural Insurance Scheme (NAIS)** aimed to protect farmers against crop losses due to natural disasters.

6. National Mission Approach and Modernization (2000s–2010s)

- **National Food Security Mission (NFSM)**: Launched in 2007, NFSM focused on increasing the production of rice, wheat, and pulses to ensure food security.
- **Rashtriya Krishi Vikas Yojana (RKVY)**: Introduced in 2007, RKVY aimed to incentivize states to increase investment in agriculture.
- **National Horticulture Mission (NHM)**: This mission focused on promoting horticulture crops, enhancing post-harvest management, and expanding export opportunities.
- **Mahatma Gandhi National Rural Employment Guarantee Act (MGNREGA)**: Launched in 2005, MGNREGA provided employment opportunities in rural areas, which indirectly benefited agriculture by improving rural infrastructure and income security.
- **Sustainable Agriculture Initiatives**: Policies promoting organic farming, soil health cards, and integrated pest management emerged to address

the environmental impacts of the Green Revolution.

7. Recent Reforms and Digital Transformation (2010s–Present)

- **Pradhan Mantri Krishi Sinchai Yojana (PMKSY)**: Focused on "Har Khet Ko Pani" (water for every field) and "Per Drop More Crop," this program aims to improve irrigation efficiency and water management.
- **Soil Health Card Scheme (2015)**: This program provides farmers with soil health cards to encourage soil testing and promote balanced fertilizer use.
- **Pradhan Mantri Fasal Bima Yojana (PMFBY)**: Launched in 2016, PMFBY provides affordable crop insurance to farmers against crop loss due to natural disasters.
- **E-NAM (National Agriculture Market)**: Launched in 2016, this online trading platform connects farmers, traders, and buyers across India, improving price transparency and market access.
- **Agri-Export Policy (2018)**: This policy focuses on increasing India's agricultural exports to $60 billion by 2022, promoting value addition, and creating export-oriented infrastructure.
- **Farm Laws and Reforms (2020)**: The controversial 2020 farm laws aimed at reforming agricultural marketing, contract farming, and removing restrictions on storage. Despite potential benefits, they faced opposition and were repealed in 2021.

8. Current Focus and Emerging Trends

- **Climate-Resilient Agriculture**: Policies now emphasize climate adaptation with programs like the **National Mission for Sustainable Agriculture (NMSA)** and **Paramparagat Krishi Vikas Yojana (PKVY)** for organic farming.
- **Digital Agriculture**: There is a growing focus on digital tools, precision agriculture, and AgriTech solutions to enhance productivity, market access, and weather forecasting.
- **Agri-Entrepreneurship and Start-Up Promotion**: Initiatives to promote agri-businesses and start-ups are gaining attention, with incubation centers and funding support to drive innovation in agriculture.
- **Doubling Farmers' Income (DFI) by 2022**: Though ambitious, this goal has driven numerous interventions in input cost reduction, market

reforms, crop diversification, and value chain development.

This highlights key milestones that contributed to the evolution of agricultural policies, rainfed farming and watershed development efforts in India.

1880

First Famine Commission

Established by the British Empire to suggest ways to offset the adverse effects of recurring droughts.

1920

Scarcity Track Development

Prioritized by the Royal Commission on Agriculture to address drought-affected areas.

1923

Dry Farming Research Station (Manjari)

Set up in Pune to focus on drought-prone regions.

1933

Dry Farming Research Stations (Bijapur, Solapur)

Established to support dryland farming techniques.

1934

Dry Farming Research Stations (Hagari, Raichur)

New research stations established for dry farming.

1935

Dry Farming Research Station (Rohtak)

Created in Punjab to aid dryland agriculture.

1942

Bombay Land Development Act

Enacted to support land management and drought resilience.

1944

Monograph on Dry Farming

Published by Kanitker, focusing on dryland agriculture techniques.

1950

All India Coordinated Research Project for Dryland Agriculture (AICRPDA)

Launched to advance research in dryland farming across India.

1953

Central Soil Conservation Board

Formed to coordinate soil conservation efforts nationwide.

1955

Dry Farming Demonstration Centers

Established to promote dryland farming practices among farmers.

1959

Central Arid Zone Research Institute (CAZRI)

Set up in Jodhpur for research on arid and semi-arid regions.

1962-63

Soil Conservation Work in Catchments of River Valley Projects (RVP)

Centrally Sponsored Scheme launched to manage soil and water conservation in river valley catchments.

1970

AICRPDA Expansion

Extended to 23 centers across various agro-climatic zones in India.

1972

International Crop Research Institute for Semi-Arid Tropics (ICRISAT)

Established in Hyderabad to address semi-arid tropical agriculture challenges.

1973-74

Drought Prone Area Programme (DPAP)

Initiated to promote economic development and drought-prone area management through soil and moisture conservation.

1976

Soil Conservation Research Centers

Eight centers established under Central Soil and Water Conservation across locations like Dehradun, Chandigarh, and Bellary.

1977

First Krishi Vigyan Kendra (KVK)

Launched at Hayatnagar to extend agricultural research to the community.

1977-78

Desert Development Programme (DDP)

Aimed to minimize adverse effects of drought and desertification through reforestation.

1980-81

Integrated Watershed Management in Flood Prone Rivers (FPR)

Ministry of Agriculture scheme focused on flood-prone river catchment areas.

1980

Successful Watershed Initiatives

Fully treated watersheds, such as Sukhomajri in Haryana and Ralegaon Siddhi in Maharashtra, demonstrated success.

1982-83

Water Harvesting Technology Promotion

Launched by Ministry of Agriculture in 19 rainfed locations to promote water conservation.

1983

AICRP on Agro-meteorology

Started to enhance localized weather forecasting for agriculture.

1983

47 Model Watersheds by ICAR

Initiated by ICAR to demonstrate watershed management practices.

1985

Central Research Institute for Dryland Agriculture (CRIDA)

Founded in Hyderabad to specialize in dryland agriculture research.

1986

National Watershed Development Project for Rainfed Areas (NWDPRA)

Launched in 15 states to enhance productivity in rainfed regions.

1990

Integrated Watershed Development Institutionalization

NWDPRA launched across 99 districts in 16 states, institutionalizing integrated watershed management.

1992

Indo-German Watershed Development Programme

Implemented by NABARD and WOTR to rehabilitate micro-watersheds for sustainable livelihoods using a participatory approach.

2009

Integrated Watershed Management Programme (IWMP)

Consolidated IWDP, DPAP, and DPP with a cluster approach by MoRD focusing on 1000 to 5000 ha micro-watersheds.

2.2 DEVELOPMENT OF WATERSHED PROGRAMS

The recognition of the importance of rainfed agriculture and the challenges it faces led to the development of various watershed development programs in India. These programs, such as the National Watershed Development

Project for Rainfed Areas (NWDPRA), Drought Prone Areas Programme (DPAP), Integrated Watershed Management Programme (IWMP), Mission Kakatiya, and Jal Shakti Abhiyan, aim to conserve water, improve soil health, and enhance agricultural productivity in rainfed areas.

These initiatives focus on a wide range of activities, including soil and water conservation, afforestation, development of minor irrigation sources, sustainable land use practices, and capacity building of local communities. For example, the NWDPRA promotes the construction of check dams, farm ponds, and other water harvesting structures to capture and store rainwater. The DPAP focuses on drought-prone areas, implementing measures to improve soil moisture retention, reduce runoff, and enhance crop productivity. The IWMP takes a holistic approach to watershed management, considering ecological, social, and economic factors. It promotes integrated watershed management practices, such as agroforestry, sustainable agriculture, and community-based natural resource management. Mission Kakatiya, a flagship program of the Telangana government, aims to restore and rejuvenate traditional water bodies, including tanks and lakes, to improve irrigation and groundwater recharge. Jal Shakti Abhiyan is a nationwide campaign launched by the Government of India to conserve water, rejuvenate traditional water bodies, and promote water conservation practices.While these programs have made significant strides, challenges such as inadequate funding, lack of technical expertise, and poor implementation often hinder their full potential.

INTRODUCTION TO WATERSHED CONCEPTS IN INDIA

Watershed management in India is a vital approach to managing natural resources, focusing on sustainable use and conservation of water, soil, and other resources within a watershed area. A watershed, or drainage basin, is defined as an area of land that channels rainfall and runoff to a common outlet, such as a river, lake, or reservoir. Watershed management in India has evolved to address pressing environmental challenges, particularly in rainfed and drought-prone regions, as well as in areas affected by soil erosion, deforestation, and desertification.

India's agriculture depends heavily on monsoon rains, with a significant portion of cultivated land falling under rainfed areas that are vulnerable to irregular rainfall and drought. This dependency, combined with an increasing population and demand for food, has driven the need for effective watershed management practices. The concepts of watershed management focus on water conservation, soil conservation, afforestation, and sustainable agricultural practices that together help to enhance land productivity, stabilize rural incomes, and mitigate the impacts of drought.

Objectives of Watershed Management

The primary objectives of watershed management in India include:

1. **Soil and Water Conservation**: Preventing soil erosion and conserving water resources within a defined area.
2. **Water Resource Development**: Enhancing water availability through rainwater harvesting, check dams, and storage structures.
3. **Sustainable Agriculture**: Increasing agricultural productivity while promoting soil health and resource efficiency.
4. **Afforestation and Biodiversity Conservation**: Promoting vegetation cover and conserving local flora and fauna to maintain ecological balance.
5. **Livelihood Improvement**: Ensuring long-term livelihood options for communities dependent on land and water resources, especially in rural areas.
6. **Community Participation and Empowerment**: Involving local communities in planning, implementing, and managing watershed activities.

Key Components of Watershed Management

1. **Soil Conservation Measures**: Techniques like contour bunding, terracing, and vegetative barriers are used to reduce soil erosion and enhance moisture retention.
2. **Water Conservation and Harvesting**: Structures such as check dams, percolation tanks, and rainwater harvesting systems are established to capture and store runoff, making water available for agriculture and domestic needs.

3. **Crop and Land Management**: Improved farming practices, crop rotation, and intercropping are promoted to maintain soil fertility and optimize water use.
4. **Reforestation and Vegetative Cover**: Planting trees and vegetation helps to reduce surface runoff, protect soil, and recharge groundwater.
5. **Community Involvement**: Watershed management emphasizes a participatory approach, where local communities actively engage in planning and implementing initiatives to ensure sustainability.

The concept of watershed management gained traction in India during the 1980s with the launch of various national-level programs, such as the Drought Prone Area Programme (DPAP), the Desert Development Programme (DDP), and the Integrated Watershed Management Programme (IWMP). These programs were designed to address the unique challenges of drought, soil degradation, and water scarcity in different regions. The National Watershed Development Programme for Rainfed Areas (NWDPRA), launched in 1990, institutionalized watershed management by covering 99 districts in 16 states, focusing on resource conservation, water harvesting, and livelihood support for rural communities.

Watershed management has shown notable success in regions like Sukhomajri in Haryana and Ralegaon Siddhi in Maharashtra, where effective watershed interventions transformed degraded land into productive fields, increased water availability, and significantly improved the local ecosystem. These projects demonstrated the benefits of community-driven approaches, showing that sustainable watershed management could achieve long-term gains in agricultural productivity and rural livelihoods.

In recent years, the Integrated Watershed Management Programme (IWMP), launched in 2009, has consolidated several earlier programs, adopting a holistic approach that involves micro-watershed management on a cluster basis. This program emphasizes the need for scientific planning, community involvement, and use of advanced technologies like remote sensing for better monitoring and impact assessment. The recent focus is also on integrating watershed management with climate resilience strategies to address new challenges posed by climate change.

In conclusion, watershed management in India has evolved from initial soil conservation efforts to a comprehensive, multi-sectoral approach aimed at ensuring water security, sustainable agriculture, and rural development.

By managing watersheds effectively, India can mitigate the impacts of climate variability, support rural livelihoods, and promote the sustainable use of natural resources.

KEY WATERSHED DEVELOPMENT MILESTONES

The development of watershed policies and programs in India reflects a gradual but steady recognition of the importance of sustainable water, soil, and forest management, particularly in rural, rainfed, and drought-prone areas. Watershed development in India has gone through various stages, with each phase contributing unique policies and programs that shaped India's approach to soil conservation, moisture retention, and community-based natural resource management.

1. Early Efforts and Soil Conservation Initiatives (Pre-1960s)

- **Focus:** Initial efforts were primarily aimed at soil conservation and reducing erosion in catchment areas.
- **Central Soil Conservation Board (1953):** Established to address soil erosion and implement soil conservation measures across the country.

2. Centrally Sponsored Schemes and Focus on Catchment Areas (1960s–1970s)

- **1962-63:***Soil Conservation Work in the Catchments of River Valley Projects (RVP)* launched as a centrally sponsored scheme to focus on soil conservation efforts in river valley project catchments.
- **1973-74:***Drought Prone Area Programme (DPAP)* initiated to promote economic development and mainstream drought-prone areas through soil and moisture conservation techniques.

3. Expanding Focus to Desertification and Integrated Management (1970s–1980s)

- **1977-78:***Desert Development Programme (DDP)* launched to mitigate the adverse effects of drought and desertification, primarily through reforestation in arid regions.
- **1980-81:** The Ministry of Agriculture started the *Integrated Watershed Management in the Catchments of Flood-Prone Rivers (FPR)*, emphasizing

soil conservation in flood-prone regions.

- **1980:** Successful community-based watershed management examples like Sukhomajri in Haryana and Ralegaon Siddhi in Maharashtra highlighted the potential of local engagement and watershed management in rural development.

4. Institutionalizing Watershed Management and Community Involvement (1980s–1990s)

- **1982-83:** Ministry of Agriculture launched a scheme for propagating water harvesting/conservation technologies in rainfed areas, covering 19 identified locations.
- **1990:***National Watershed Development Programme for Rainfed Areas (NWDPRA)* institutionalized the concept of integrated watershed management across 99 districts in 16 states.
- **1992:***Indo-German Watershed Development Programme* by NABARD and the Watershed Organisation Trust (WOTR) emphasized rehabilitation of micro-watersheds and natural resource regeneration using a participatory approach.

5. Consolidation and Scale-Up of Watershed Programs (2000s–Present)

- **2009:***Integrated Watershed Management Programme (IWMP)* consolidated DPAP, DDP, and IWDP into a single program focusing on a cluster-based approach for micro-watersheds (1,000–5,000 ha). The program adopted a comprehensive strategy targeting soil conservation, water resource development, and sustainable agriculture.

Each phase in the evolution of watershed development policies in India marked a step towards a more sustainable and community-focused approach, integrating soil and water conservation with broader goals of rural development, climate adaptation, and sustainable livelihoods.

2.3 KEY POLICIES AND INSTITUTIONAL FRAMEWORKS

India has developed a range of policies, programs, and institutional frameworks specifically designed to support rainfed agriculture, a vital sector that caters to a large portion of the country's rural population. Given the unique challenges faced by rainfed areas, including unpredictable rainfall, limited irrigation facilities, and frequent droughts, these initiatives aim to improve agricultural productivity, ensure water availability, and promote sustainable resource management.

1. **Integrated Watershed Management Program (IWMP) (2009)**

   - **Objective:** Launched by the Ministry of Rural Development (MoRD), IWMP is designed to promote sustainable watershed development across rainfed areas, ensuring soil and water conservation, enhancing crop productivity, and improving livelihood opportunities for rural communities.
   - **Approach:** Focuses on a cluster of micro-watersheds (1,000–5,000 ha) and involves community participation to ensure sustainable outcomes.

2. **National Mission for Sustainable Agriculture (NMSA) (2014)**

   - **Objective:** Part of the National Action Plan on Climate Change (NAPCC), NMSA promotes sustainable agriculture practices, particularly in rainfed areas, to enhance resilience to climate variability.
   - **Key Programs:** Soil Health Card Scheme, micro-irrigation facilities, and crop diversification to improve water-use efficiency and adapt agriculture to climatic changes.

3. **Pradhan Mantri Krishi Sinchai Yojana (PMKSY) (2015)**

   - **Objective:** PMKSY aims to expand irrigation coverage and improve water-use efficiency in rainfed areas with a focus on "Per Drop More Crop."
   - **Components:** Includes the watershed development component, Har Khet Ko Pani (water for every field), which promotes water conservation, rainwater harvesting, and efficient irrigation practices.

4. Rashtriya Krishi Vikas Yojana (RKVY)

- **Objective:** RKVY provides financial support to state governments for agricultural development projects, including those focused on rainfed agriculture.
- **Key Focus Areas:** Encourages crop diversification, efficient water use, and infrastructure development to improve the resilience of rainfed farming.

5. National Rainfed Area Authority (NRAA) (2006)

- **Objective:** NRAA was established to provide technical and policy support for the effective implementation of rainfed agriculture programs. It also coordinates research and development efforts across agencies working in this sector.
- **Mandate:** Provides expertise on sustainable land and water management practices, with a special focus on rainfed regions, and advises states on policy and program design.

6. Watershed Development Fund (WDF) by NABARD

- **Objective:** Managed by the National Bank for Agriculture and Rural Development (NABARD), WDF finances watershed projects in rainfed areas and promotes natural resource management to enhance agricultural productivity.
- **Approach:** Engages local communities in watershed activities to improve water resources and reduce soil degradation.

7. Paramparagat Krishi Vikas Yojana (PKVY)

- **Objective:** Promotes organic farming practices in rainfed areas, reducing dependency on chemical inputs and enhancing soil health for sustainable agricultural productivity.
- **Focus:** Encourages traditional farming practices, supports organic certification, and improves farmers' access to organic markets.

8. Mahatma Gandhi National Rural Employment Guarantee Act (MGNREGA)

- ○ **Relevance to Rainfed Agriculture:** Provides rural employment opportunities in rainfed areas by funding water conservation, drought-proofing, and watershed development activities, which indirectly support agriculture by enhancing soil moisture and availability of water resources.

Each of these initiatives and institutions plays a critical role in supporting rainfed agriculture, focusing on sustainable water management, soil conservation, climate adaptation, and community involvement, ensuring a resilient agricultural framework across India's diverse rainfed landscapes.

CHAPTER THREE

SOIL AND CLIMATIC CONDITIONS IN RAINFED REGIONS

3.1 SOIL AND CLIMATE CHARACTERISTICS IN RAINFED AREAS

India, a country with diverse agro-ecological zones, heavily relies on rainfed agriculture, especially in its arid and semi-arid regions. These regions, characterized by unpredictable rainfall, poor soil quality, and high temperatures, present significant challenges to sustainable agriculture. Understanding the specific soil and climatic conditions of these areas is essential for developing effective strategies to improve crop productivity and resilience.

Soil Conditions:

Rainfed soils in India often have low organic matter content, reducing fertility and water-holding capacity. Poor soil structure leads to low infiltration rates and increased runoff. Essential nutrients like nitrogen, phosphorus, and potassium are deficient, limiting crop growth and yield. Additionally, salinity and sodicity in some regions can adversely affect plant growth.

- **Low Organic Matter Content:** Many rainfed soils in India are characterized by low organic matter content, which reduces their fertility and water-holding capacity.
- **Poor Soil Structure:** The structure of rainfed soils is often poor, leading to low infiltration rates and increased runoff.
- **Nutrient Deficiencies:** These soils are often deficient in essential nutrients like nitrogen, phosphorus, and potassium, limiting crop growth and yield.
- **Salinity and Sodicity:** In some regions, rainfed soils suffer from salinity and sodicity, which can adversely affect plant growth.

Climatic Conditions:

Rainfed regions face unpredictable rainfall, high temperatures, low relative humidity, and a short growing season, which can lead to increased evapotranspiration, water stress, and reduced crop growth. These factors can exacerbate the impact of high temperatures on crop water use and limit the time available for crop development.

- **Unpredictable Rainfall:** Rainfall in rainfed regions is highly variable, with frequent droughts and occasional floods.
- **High Temperatures:** High temperatures, especially during the growing season, can lead to increased evapotranspiration and water stress.
- **Low Relative Humidity:** Low relative humidity exacerbates the impact of high temperatures on crop water use.
- **Short Growing Season:** The growing season in many rainfed regions is short, limiting the time available for crop growth and development.

Challenges:

Rainfed regions often experience low productivity due to poor soil quality, unpredictable rainfall, and high temperatures. This can lead to crop failures, economic losses for farmers. Soil degradation, including erosion, nutrient depletion, and salinization, further reduces long-term productivity. Low incomes from rainfed agriculture contribute to rural poverty and migration, further exacerbating the issue.

- **Low Productivity:** The combination of poor soil quality, unpredictable rainfall, and high temperatures often results in low crop yields in rainfed regions.
- **Risk of Crop Failure:** Unpredictable rainfall and extreme weather events can lead to crop failures, causing significant economic losses for farmers.
- **Soil Degradation:** Erosion, nutrient depletion, and salinization further degrade the quality of rainfed soils, reducing their long-term productivity.
- **Livelihood Insecurity:** Low and uncertain incomes from rainfed agriculture contribute to rural poverty and migration.

This chapter delves into the unique characteristics of Indian rainfed regions, highlighting the key factors influencing crop growth and yield, and exploring innovative approaches to address the challenges posed by these conditions.

SOIL TYPES AND THEIR PROPERTIES

1. Alfisols (Red Soil)

- **Characteristics:** Alfisols, commonly referred to as red soils, are generally light-textured soils with low moisture-holding capacity but high water intake. Rainwater quickly infiltrates, saturating the soil profile and reducing surface runoff, which leads to minimal soil erosion (approximately 3.05 tons/ha/year). However, soil crusting is a prevalent issue, especially in low rainfall areas.
- **Challenges in Crop Production:**

  - Poor crop stand due to crusting and rapid drying of the surface.
  - Low moisture storage capacity and unreliable water supply due to shallow soil depth.
  - Low soil fertility, limited in organic matter and essential nutrients such as calcium.
  - Soil degradation due to erosion and crusting.

- **Geographical Area:** Covers approximately 20% of India, primarily in Tamil Nadu, Karnataka, and parts of Andhra Pradesh.
- **Rainfall Range:** 750-2000 mm.

2. Vertisols (Black Soil)

- **Characteristics**: Known as black cotton soil, Vertisols have a high clay content (30-70%) and are well-suited for moisture retention due to their high water-holding capacity. The soil exhibits swelling and shrinking properties, leading to poor permeability and low infiltration rates, resulting in significant surface runoff and soil loss (about 68.5 tons/ha/year). Cracks develop during the Rabi season, which impacts flowering in crops.
- **Challenges in Crop Production**:

  - Limited soil moisture content for tillage.
  - Tendency to waterlogging and poor tractability.
  - Low fertility, especially in nitrogen and phosphorus, leading to soil degradation from erosion and salt accumulation.

- **Geographical Area**: Encompasses about 22% of India, covering parts of Maharashtra, Madhya Pradesh, Gujarat, and Karnataka.
- **Rainfall Range**: 500-1500 mm.

3. Inceptisols and Entisols (Alluvial Soils)

- **Characteristics**: Alluvial soils (Entisols and Inceptisols) are loamy sand or sandy loam, with high depth but low clay content, offering water-holding up to 200 mm per meter of soil profile. They have poor nutrient-holding capacity, with a low clay fraction and nutrient availability.
- **Challenges in Crop Production**:

  - Low water-holding capacity and nutrient status.
  - Land degradation due to soil erosion.

- **Advantages**: Easily managed for crop production, allowing for monsoon cropping in low-rainfall areas and double cropping in high-rainfall regions.
- **Geographical Area**: Covers about 21% of India, mainly along the Indo-Gangetic plains.
- **Rainfall Range**: Variable, supporting intensive agricultural activities.

4. Submontane Soil

- **Characteristics**: Medium-textured with moderate depth and clay content, submontane soils have high moisture retention capacity (300 mm/m profile). These soils are low in nitrogen but have medium levels of other nutrients, although phosphorus may be limited for high-yield systems.
- **Challenges in Crop Production**:

  - Nutrient deficiencies, particularly nitrogen and phosphorus, for intensive agriculture.

- **Advantages**: Double cropping is possible due to the high moisture retention and rainfall.
- **Distribution**: Found in the foothills of the Himalayas, the Western Ghats, and parts of the Eastern Ghats.

5. Sierozemic (Arid Soil)

- **Characteristics**: Arid soils (Sierozemic) are light-textured with low moisture-holding capacity (about 150 mm water per meter). They are commonly shallow due to calcium carbonate accumulation and are highly alkaline.
- **Challenges in Crop Production**:

  - Low water-holding and nutrient capacity, with frequent crusting issues.
  - Salinity in the subsoil layer often limits crop growth.

- **Agricultural Potential**: Mostly suitable for monsoon cropping; however, in areas with deeper profiles, some post-monsoon cropping is also possible.
- **Distribution**: Found in arid regions such as Rajasthan, parts of Gujarat, and southern Haryana.

6. Laterite Soil

- **Characteristics**: Laterite soils develop in high rainfall areas and are leached of bases, making them acidic (pH 5.0 to 6.0). They are well-drained but have low water-holding capacity. They are generally low in nitrogen and potassium and are often deficient in phosphorus.
- **Challenges in Crop Production**:

  - Low fertility due to nutrient leaching, requiring regular fertilization.

- **Agricultural Potential**: Suitable for plantation crops like coffee, tea, cashew, and certain fruits with soil amendments.
- **Distribution**: Found in regions such as the Western Ghats, Eastern Ghats, and parts of the northeastern states.

7. Forest and Hill Soils

- **Characteristics**: These soils are typically loamy to sandy loam, formed under dense forest cover in high-rainfall areas. They vary in depth and texture and are often acidic with moderate organic matter.
- **Challenges in Crop Production**:

  - Erosion due to high slopes and rainfall.
  - Limited nutrient availability, particularly phosphorus.

- **Agricultural Potential**: Used for growing tea, spices, and temperate fruits, requiring erosion control and organic amendments.
- **Distribution**: Found in the hilly and forested areas of the Himalayas, Western Ghats, and Northeastern India.

8. Saline Alkali Soils

- **Characteristics**: These soils contain high salt levels, with an alkaline pH, often affecting the physical and chemical properties of the soil. They are commonly known as kharland soils in certain regions and have poor drainage.
- **Challenges in Crop Production**:

  - Excessive salt content affects plant growth and soil health.

- **Agricultural Potential**: Suitable for salt-tolerant crops like barley, certain grasses, and other halophytes. Soil reclamation techniques, such as gypsum application and improved drainage, can help restore productivity.
- **Distribution**: Predominantly found in coastal areas of Maharashtra, including districts like Ratnagiri, Raigad, Thane, and Palghar.

3.2 CLIMATE PATTERNS AND SEASONAL VARIABILITY IN RAINFED ZONES

Weather is a critical factor influencing crop growth and yield, directly and indirectly affecting physiological, biological, and environmental conditions. The principal weather elements impacting crops include precipitation, temperature, humidity, wind, solar radiation, dew, fog, and frost. Here is an expanded overview of these elements:

1. Precipitation

- **Characteristics of Rainfall**: Rainfall in rainfed regions is often uncertain and erratic, especially in arid and semi-arid areas, where it can be insufficient, unevenly distributed, and marked by frequent dry spells and breaks.
- **Influence on Yield**: Crop yields largely depend on precipitation, with yields rising when rainfall exceeds a minimum threshold needed for maturity. However, excessive rainfall can also reduce yields due to waterlogging and nutrient leaching, which can be detrimental in semi-arid climates where water is a limited resource.

2. Temperature

- **Temperature Variability**: Temperature greatly influences physiological processes in plants. Low temperatures limit nutrient uptake as water becomes tightly bound to soil particles, making absorption difficult, and may result in nutrient deficiencies.
- **High and Low Temperature Effects**: High temperatures lead to chlorophyll loss, causing chlorosis or yellowing of leaves, and excessive transpiration, which can result in leaf scorch. Conversely, low temperatures can inhibit water uptake, restricting plant growth and slowing biological processes essential for crop development.

3. Humidity

- **Relative Humidity Levels**: In dryland regions, relative humidity is typically low (20-30% at midday), while humid regions experience higher relative humidity (60-70%).
- **Implications for Crop Growth**: Low humidity increases transpiration and crop water demand, while high humidity may prevent effective pollen dispersion from anthers, reducing pollination success. Additionally, high humidity increases the risk of pest and disease incidence, both of which can impact yields. Very high or very low humidity can reduce grain yields due to plant stress and water imbalance.

4. Winds

- **Effects of Wind**: Wind accelerates transpiration and evaporation, which can lead to water stress in plants. Strong winds can also cause lodging in herbaceous plants, soil erosion, and may uproot crops when accompanied by rain.
- **Specific Wind Effects**: Hot, dry winds can reduce photosynthesis, affecting plant growth, while cold winds can cause chilling injuries. In extreme cases, hot, dry winds or wind erosion can lead to irreversible crop damage, affecting productivity.

5. Solar Radiation

- **Radiation Levels**: In arid regions, clear skies allow high solar energy input, which is essential for photosynthesis and provides thermal energy necessary for physiological functions.
- **Positive and Negative Impacts**: While solar radiation drives photosynthesis and growth, excessive radiation can increase evapotranspiration, intensifying water demand. The balance between sunlight and water availability is crucial for optimal crop productivity.

6. Dew

- **Dew as Moisture Source**: Dew contributes minimally to the water needs of most crops, but it can be beneficial under water-stressed conditions, especially in areas with low rainfall. In some crops, dew can temporarily relieve water stress and support minor growth functions.

7. Fog

- **Effects of Fog**: Fog influences plant growth by increasing air humidity, wetting plant surfaces, and providing soil surface moisture. In high-humidity environments, fog may also inhibit sunlight penetration, potentially limiting photosynthesis. However, the added moisture can be beneficial in regions with frequent droughts or low rainfall.

8. Frost

- **Impact of Frost in Warm Regions**: In typically warm areas, unexpected frosts can cause significant crop damage, as crops adapted to these climates are often sensitive to low temperatures. Frost damage is particularly harmful during sensitive stages, such as flowering, potentially leading to crop failure.

3.3 Soil and Water Conservation Techniques

Soil and water are essential resources that must be conserved carefully to maintain a high standard of living. The increasing population pressure has led to the dominance of intensive agriculture, which has resulted in land degradation and large-scale water logging. To address this issue, it is crucial to follow appropriate soil and moisture conservation practices along with integrated nutrient supply systems for improving soil fertility and crop productivity on a sustained basis.

In India, where droughts and floods cause chronic food scarcity, adequate soil conservation programs not only increase crop yield but also prevent further deterioration of land. Traditional/local knowledge, or indigenous technical knowledge (ITK) or Indigenous and Local Knowledge (ILK), is a sum total of knowledge accumulated over generations through observation, experimentation, and handling of old people's experiences and wisdom in various areas of human behavior.

ITK is a people-derived science representing creativity, innovations, and skills, and pertains to various cultural norms, social roles, or physical conditions. It is not a static body of wisdom but consists of dynamic insights and techniques that are changed over time through experimentation and adoption to environmental and socio-economic changes. Traditional knowledge and practices have their own importance as they have stood the test of time and have proved efficacious to the local people. Some of these traditional practices include crop production, mixed farming, water harvesting, conservation of forage, combined production system, biodiversity conservation, forestry, and domestic energy.

There are many indigenous techniques for conserving natural resources, and there is a need to integrate these practices along with conventional soil and water conservation measures for promoting sustainable development of agriculture. Incorporating these ITKs would ensure sustainability of different eco-systems, befitting the man-animal-plant-land-water complex in each watershed. Documentation of ITKs on soil and water conservation will form a basis for formulating coordinated research programs for validation and refinement of ITKs on soil and water conservation.

In India, a detail study of Indigenous Technical Knowledge (ITK) on soil and water conservation in rainfed areas was taken up through a National Agricultural Technology Project (NATP) entitled "Documentation & Analysis of Indigenous Methods of In-situ Moisture Conservation and Runoff Management" at the Central Research Institute for Dryland Agriculture (CRIDA) in early 2000.

Principles of soil conservation

The principles of soil conservation focus on protecting soil from degradation, enhancing its fertility, and promoting sustainable agricultural productivity. Soil conservation is essential in maintaining soil health, structure, and function, particularly in areas prone to erosion, nutrient depletion, or salinization. Key principles include:

1. Preventing Soil Erosion

- **Contour Ploughing**: Contour ploughing is a sustainable farming technique that involves tilling and cultivating land along its natural contours, rather than up and down slopes. This practice is especially beneficial in hilly or sloping areas, where it significantly reduces soil erosion and conserves water. By following the contour lines, the speed of water runoff is reduced, minimizing soil erosion and promoting water infiltration. This leads to improved soil moisture, enhanced fertility, and higher crop yields. India, with its diverse topography, has widely adopted contour ploughing as a sustainable agricultural practice, particularly in regions prone to soil erosion.

- **Terracing**: Terracing involves creating step-like formations on steep slopes to slow down water flow and minimize soil erosion. By dividing steep slopes into a series of level or gently sloping terraces, the velocity of water runoff is reduced, preventing the soil from being washed away. This practice not only conserves soil but also improves water infiltration, allowing for better moisture retention and plant growth. Terracing is a sustainable agricultural practice that has been used for centuries to cultivate steep slopes and protect valuable topsoil.
- **Strip Cropping**: Strip cropping involves planting alternating strips of different crops, such as grass or legumes alongside grains. This practice slows down water movement across the land, trapping sediment and preventing soil erosion. The different crops in the strips have varying root depths and growth habits, which help to improve soil structure, increase organic matter, and reduce the risk of pest and disease outbreaks. By diversifying the landscape, strip cropping creates a more complex ecosystem that can better withstand environmental stresses and maintain soil health.

2. Maintaining Soil Fertility

- **Crop Rotation**: Crop rotation involves planting different crops in a field in a sequential pattern. This practice helps to improve soil fertility, reduce pest and disease problems, and maintain soil health. By rotating crops with different nutrient requirements, farmers can prevent the depletion of specific nutrients in the soil. Additionally, crop rotation disrupts the life cycles of pests and diseases, reducing their populations and minimizing the need for chemical pesticides. This sustainable practice contributes to long-term soil health and agricultural productivity.
- **Cover Cropping**: Planting cover crops, such as legumes, is a valuable practice that adds organic matter to the soil, improves its structure, and enhances fertility. Legumes, in particular, have the ability to fix nitrogen from the atmosphere, reducing the need for synthetic fertilizers. When

planted between main crops or during off-seasons, cover crops protect the soil from erosion, prevent weed growth, and suppress pests. By diversifying the plant community, cover crops promote biodiversity and contribute to a more sustainable agricultural system.

- **Nutrient Management**: Nutrient management involves the careful application of fertilizers to meet the specific needs of crops while minimizing environmental impact. By using fertilizers judiciously and applying organic amendments like compost or manure, farmers can enhance soil fertility without causing nutrient runoff or pollution. This practice helps to maintain soil health, reduce the need for chemical fertilizers, and protect water bodies from nutrient pollution.

3. Improving Soil Structure

- **Reduced Tillage (Conservation Tillage)**: Reduced tillage, also known as conservation tillage, involves minimizing soil disturbance during cultivation. By reducing the number of tillage operations, this practice helps to maintain soil structure, reduce erosion, and conserve soil moisture. Reduced tillage also promotes the growth of beneficial soil organisms, which contribute to soil health and fertility. By minimizing the disturbance to the soil, farmers can reduce the loss of organic matter and nutrients, leading to more sustainable agricultural practices.
- **Mulching**: Mulching involves covering the soil surface with organic or inorganic materials to conserve soil moisture, reduce erosion, and improve soil health. Mulch can be made from various materials such as straw, leaves, wood chips, or plastic. By covering the soil, mulch helps to reduce evaporation, maintain soil temperature, and suppress weed growth. Additionally, as the mulch decomposes, it adds organic matter to the soil, improving its structure and fertility. Mulching is a valuable practice for both home gardens and agricultural fields, as it can help to conserve water, reduce labor, and promote sustainable agriculture.
- **Organic Amendments**: Adding organic amendments like compost, green manure, and other organic materials is a crucial practice for improving soil health and fertility. These organic materials enhance soil structure, increase water-holding capacity, and promote the growth of beneficial soil organisms. By incorporating organic matter into the soil, farmers can improve nutrient cycling, reduce the need for chemical fertilizers, and create a more sustainable agricultural system.

4. Managing Water Efficiently

- **Water Harvesting**: Water harvesting is a crucial practice for capturing and storing rainwater, ensuring its availability for crops during dry periods. By constructing structures like check dams, farm ponds, or rainwater harvesting pits, farmers can collect and store rainwater, reducing reliance on traditional irrigation systems. This practice helps to conserve water, improve soil moisture, and enhance crop productivity, especially in regions with erratic rainfall patterns. Water harvesting is a sustainable approach to managing water resources and mitigating the impacts of drought..

- **Efficient Irrigation**: Efficient irrigation techniques, such as drip or sprinkler irrigation, are essential for minimizing water waste and preventing soil erosion. Drip irrigation delivers water directly to the plant roots, reducing evaporation and runoff. Sprinkler irrigation applies water to the soil surface in a controlled manner, minimizing water loss. By using these efficient irrigation methods, farmers can conserve water, improve water use efficiency, and reduce the risk of soil erosion and salinization. Additionally, these techniques can help to improve crop yields and quality.

- **Grassed Waterways**: Grassed waterways are natural or man-made channels established with suitable vegetation to safely transport concentrated runoff from the catchment. These channels are designed to prevent soil erosion by slowing down the water flow and allowing it to infiltrate into the soil gradually. The vegetative cover, usually consisting of grasses or other erosion-resistant plants, binds the soil together, protecting it from the erosive forces of water. Grassed waterways are an effective and sustainable solution for managing runoff and conserving soil, particularly in hilly or sloping areas.

5. Promoting Vegetative Cover

- **Permanent Vegetative Cover**: Maintaining a permanent vegetative cover, such as grasses or trees, in sensitive areas is a crucial soil conservation practice. This cover stabilizes the soil, prevents erosion, and enhances biodiversity. The roots of these plants bind the soil together, reducing the impact of wind and water erosion. Additionally, permanent vegetation helps to regulate soil moisture, improve soil fertility, and create a favorable habitat for beneficial insects and other organisms. By implementing permanent vegetative cover, we can protect our valuable soil resources and ensure a sustainable future.

- **Agroforestry** Agroforestry, the practice of integrating trees with crops and livestock, offers numerous benefits for soil health and environmental sustainability. By strategically planting trees within agricultural landscapes, farmers can improve soil structure, reduce erosion, enhance water retention, and increase biodiversity. The shade provided by trees can protect crops from harsh sunlight and extreme temperatures, while their roots help to stabilize the soil and prevent erosion. Additionally, agroforestry systems can contribute to carbon sequestration, improving air quality and mitigating climate change.

- **Reforestation and Afforestation**: Reforestation and afforestation are crucial practices for restoring degraded lands and protecting the environment. By planting trees in areas that have lost forest cover, we can restore soil health, improve water retention, and prevent landslides and erosion. Trees help to stabilize the soil, reduce runoff, and improve air quality. Additionally, forests provide habitat for wildlife, contribute to biodiversity, and play a vital role in mitigating climate change. By investing in reforestation and afforestation efforts, we can ensure a sustainable future for our planet.

6. Managing Salinity and Acidity

- **Soil Amendments**: Applying lime to acidic soils is an effective way to neutralize the soil pH and improve its fertility. Lime, primarily composed of calcium carbonate, reacts with soil acidity, increasing the pH level and making essential nutrients like phosphorus more available to plants. By neutralizing acidity, lime also improves soil structure and water-holding capacity, leading to healthier plant growth and higher yields. Regular lime application is crucial for maintaining optimal soil pH and ensuring sustainable agricultural practices.

- **Drainage Management**: Drainage management is crucial for maintaining soil health and preventing salt buildup in the root zone, especially in areas with high salinity. By installing drainage systems, such as tile drains or surface drains, excess water can be removed from the soil, reducing the concentration of salts. Proper drainage also helps to maintain optimal soil moisture levels, preventing waterlogging and promoting plant growth. By implementing effective drainage management practices, farmers can improve soil quality, enhance crop yields, and protect their land from salinization.

- **Selection of Crops-** Selecting salt-tolerant or acid-tolerant crops is a crucial strategy for ensuring higher productivity and preventing further soil degradation in affected areas. By choosing crop varieties that are well-adapted to specific soil conditions, farmers can minimize yield losses and maintain soil health. Some examples of salt-tolerant crops include barley, wheat, and certain varieties of rice, while acid-tolerant crops may include blueberries, azaleas, and camellias. By carefully selecting appropriate crops, farmers can optimize production and protect their land from the adverse effects of soil salinity and acidity.

7. Encouraging Sustainable Land Use

- **Integrated Land Use Planning**: Integrated land use planning involves adopting practices that are suited to the specific conditions of each piece of land. This approach maximizes productivity while protecting soil and other natural resources. By carefully considering factors such as slope, soil type, and climate, land managers can make informed decisions about the best land use practices. For example, in non-arable areas, it may be more sustainable to use the land for grazing or forestry rather than intensive agriculture. By implementing integrated land use planning, we can ensure the long-term health and productivity of our land resources.
- **Preventing Overgrazing**: Preventing overgrazing is crucial for maintaining healthy ecosystems and sustainable agriculture. By managing livestock carefully, farmers can avoid overgrazing, which can lead to soil compaction, erosion, and vegetation loss. Implementing rotational grazing, where livestock are moved to different pastures to allow for recovery, can help to distribute grazing pressure and prevent overgrazing. Additionally, adjusting stocking rates to match the carrying capacity of the land can help to minimize the impact of grazing on the environment. By adopting sustainable grazing practices, farmers can protect the land and ensure the long-term viability of their operations.
- **Manage Traffic Farming**: Controlled traffic farming is a sustainable agricultural practice that involves limiting heavy machinery to specific paths within a field. By restricting the movement of heavy equipment to designated traffic lanes, farmers can minimize soil compaction, reduce

erosion, and improve soil structure. Controlled traffic farming also helps to conserve fuel and reduce labor costs. By adopting this practice, farmers can enhance soil health, increase crop yields, and protect the environment.

TECHNIQUES FOR PREVENTING EROSION AND RETAINING SOIL MOISTURE

A. Agronomical (Cultural) Practices:

1. **Strip Cropping**: This involves planting different crops in alternating strips along the contour of the land. The strips act as barriers to wind and water, reducing soil erosion and improving soil structure.
2. **Tillage**: Tillage practices, such as plowing or harrowing, are used to prepare the soil for planting. Conservation tillage methods, such as minimum or no-till farming, reduce soil disturbance, prevent erosion, and improve water retention.
3. **Fallowing**: This is the practice of leaving the land unplanted for a period to allow it to restore its fertility. It helps in breaking the erosion cycle and conserving moisture, especially during dry periods.
4. **Mulching**: Applying a layer of organic or inorganic material to the soil surface helps to retain moisture, suppress weeds, and reduce soil erosion. Mulching also regulates soil temperature and improves fertility.
5. **Use of Antitranspirants**: Antitranspirants are chemicals that reduce the loss of water through transpiration. These are applied to crops to help conserve soil moisture during dry spells and improve crop productivity under water stress conditions.
6. **Crop Rotation**: Rotating different crops in a planned sequence helps maintain soil fertility, control pests and diseases, and prevent soil degradation. It can also improve soil structure and moisture retention.
7. **Contour Cultivation**: This practice involves plowing along the contours of the land to reduce water runoff and soil erosion. Contour farming improves water infiltration, reduces soil displacement, and helps conserve moisture.
8. **Cover Management**: Growing cover crops, such as legumes or grasses, between main crops helps prevent soil erosion, enhance organic matter content, and improve soil structure. Cover crops also help in moisture

conservation.

9. **Planting of Grasses for Stabilizing Bunds**: Grasses are planted along bunds (embankments) to stabilize them and reduce the risk of erosion. The grass roots help bind the soil together and provide ground cover.

10. **Planting of Trees and Afforestation**: Establishing trees and afforestation projects helps protect soil from wind and water erosion, increases organic matter in the soil, and improves water retention.

11. **Selection of Suitable Cropping and Alternate Land Use Systems**: Choosing crops that are well-adapted to the local climate and soil conditions, along with the use of alternate land-use systems (e.g., agroforestry), can significantly reduce soil erosion and improve sustainability.

12. **Micro-Watersheds**: Dividing large watersheds into smaller units (micro-watersheds) for more targeted management of water resources and soil conservation. This approach ensures that water is managed more efficiently, reducing runoff and soil erosion.

B. Mechanical Practices:

1. **Contour Bunding**: Bunds are embankments constructed along the contours of sloped lands to slow down water runoff, reduce soil erosion, and trap soil particles.

2. **Graded Bunding or Channel Terraces**: This involves creating graded bunds or terraces with a slight slope to channel water off the land slowly, preventing erosion and improving water infiltration.

3. **Compartmental Bunding**: Dividing a large field into smaller sections with bunds to control water flow and prevent soil erosion in individual sections.

4. **Bench Terracing**: Creating flat, step-like platforms along slopes to reduce water flow speed, improve soil moisture retention, and control erosion.

5. **Puerto Rican Type Bench Terracing**: A variation of bench terracing that is characterized by wide, flat steps that reduce the risk of erosion and increase water retention.

6. **Conservation Bench Terracing (CBT)**: This method combines terracing with water conservation techniques, such as integrating small check dams or catchment systems to capture and slowly release water.

7. **Broad Base Terracing**: Creating wide, stable terraces with broad bases that can hold more water and reduce the risk of erosion. These terraces are designed to withstand heavy rainfall and maintain soil structure.
8. **Zing Terracing**: A specific type of terracing where the terraces are built with slightly sloping channels for water runoff management, ideal for areas prone to heavy rainfall.
9. **Broad Bed Furrow System**: This involves creating broad, raised beds separated by furrows to promote efficient water drainage and reduce soil erosion in regions with poor drainage.
10. **Trenching (CCF - Conservation of Critical Areas)**: This practice involves creating trenches in eroded or critical areas to capture water, reduce runoff, and prevent further soil erosion.
11. **Gully and Nalla Control**: Managing and controlling the erosion of gullies and small stream courses (nallas) by creating check dams or reinforcing the banks with vegetation to prevent further soil loss.
12. **Control of Stream and River Banks**: Stabilizing riverbanks or stream courses with vegetation, geotextiles, or structures like gabions to reduce bank erosion and maintain water quality.
13. **Dead Furrow**: Creating a furrow at the base of embankments or terraces that serves to collect and redirect water, helping to prevent erosion and retain soil moisture.
14. **Sub-Soiling**: Deep plowing or tilling below the surface to break compacted soil layers, improve water infiltration, and enhance root growth, particularly in areas with hardpans or compacted soils.

3.3 ROLE OF VEGETATION IN SOIL STABILITY

Vegetation plays an essential role in maintaining soil stability in rainfed regions, especially in areas prone to erosion due to variable and often intense climatic conditions. In these areas, the presence of vegetation not only helps in soil retention but also enhances the overall resilience of the ecosystem. Here's a closer look at how vegetation contributes to soil stability in rainfed regions:

1. Root System

- **Anchoring Soil Particles**: Plant roots act as natural anchors, binding soil particles together and preventing them from being easily detached and transported by wind or water. This anchoring effect is critical in preventing soil erosion, particularly in rainfed areas that experience intense rainfall or strong winds.

- **Soil Structure Improvement**: The root systems of plants create natural channels and pores in the soil as they grow and decompose. These channels improve soil structure, allowing for better water infiltration and reducing the likelihood of surface runoff. The enhanced soil structure also facilitates root penetration for subsequent crops, supporting sustainable agricultural practices.

2. Interception of Rainfall

- **Reducing Rainfall Impact**: Plant canopies intercept raindrops before they hit the ground, softening the impact on the soil surface. This interception minimizes the direct force of raindrops, which can otherwise cause soil particles to dislodge and compact, leading to surface crusting and increased susceptibility to erosion.
- **Protection Against Soil Compaction**: By buffering the soil surface from the impact of heavy rainfall, vegetation helps prevent soil compaction. Compacted soil is less permeable and more prone to runoff, which can exacerbate erosion issues in rainfed regions.

3. Reducing Runoff

- **Slowing Water Flow**: Vegetation acts as a natural barrier to water flow, slowing down the movement of rainwater over the soil surface. This slowing effect allows water more time to infiltrate into the soil rather than contributing to surface runoff, which is a primary cause of soil erosion.
- **Increasing Infiltration**: The root channels created by vegetation allow rainwater to penetrate the soil more efficiently. These root-induced pathways reduce surface runoff, enhance soil moisture, and help recharge groundwater. In rainfed regions, where water availability is often limited, this increased infiltration is crucial for maintaining soil moisture and supporting crop growth.

4. Soil Moisture Retention

- **Reducing Evaporation**: Vegetation provides shade to the soil surface, lowering soil temperature and reducing evaporation rates. By retaining soil moisture, vegetation helps to support crop growth during dry spells, which are common in rainfed regions.
- **Improving Water-Holding Capacity**: Organic matter from decaying plant residues enhances the soil's ability to retain moisture. This organic matter increases the soil's water-holding capacity, ensuring that crops have access to moisture even during periods of low rainfall.

5. Soil Fertility

- **Nutrient Cycling**: As plants grow, die, and decompose, they release organic matter and essential nutrients back into the soil. This natural cycle of nutrient release enriches the soil, improving its fertility and supporting sustainable crop production. The addition of organic matter also enhances soil structure, making it less prone to erosion.
- **Nitrogen Fixation**: Leguminous plants, such as beans and peas, play an additional role by fixing atmospheric nitrogen in the soil. This biological nitrogen fixation is crucial in rainfed areas, where farmers may have limited access to fertilizers. By enriching the soil with nitrogen, these plants improve fertility and reduce the need for chemical inputs.

6. Wind Erosion Control

- **Windbreaks**: Trees and shrubs act as natural windbreaks, reducing wind speed near the soil surface. This reduction in wind velocity minimizes the force exerted on the soil, decreasing the likelihood of wind erosion. In regions where wind erosion can be severe, establishing vegetation as windbreaks protects valuable topsoil and enhances long-term soil productivity.

Vegetation is a vital component of soil stability in rainfed regions, where the ecosystem relies heavily on natural processes to sustain soil health and productivity. By anchoring soil particles, intercepting rainfall, reducing runoff, conserving moisture, enhancing fertility, and controlling wind erosion, vegetation helps create a resilient landscape that can withstand the challenges of a rainfed climate. Sustainable management practices that encourage vegetation cover can lead to improved soil health, reduced erosion, and enhanced productivity in rainfed agricultural systems.

53

CHAPTER FOUR

DROUGHT AND ITS IMPLICATIONS

Drought is one of the most devastating natural disasters, significantly impacting agriculture, water resources, ecosystems, and livelihoods worldwide. It is characterized by prolonged periods of deficient precipitation, leading to water scarcity, reduced soil moisture, and decreased agricultural productivity. Unlike other natural disasters, drought develops gradually and can persist for months or even years, making its onset and impacts challenging to predict and manage effectively.

The implications of drought extend far beyond immediate water shortages. In agriculture, drought stress reduces crop yields, affects soil health, and increases the vulnerability of farming communities. It also disrupts hydrological cycles, leading to declining groundwater levels, shrinking reservoirs, and increased competition for water resources. Moreover, the socio-economic consequences of drought include food insecurity, economic losses, migration, and conflicts over water access. Climate change further exacerbates drought frequency and severity, posing significant challenges for sustainable water and land management.

This chapter explores the causes, types, and effects of drought while highlighting its implications for agriculture, ecosystems, and human societies. Additionally, it discusses mitigation strategies, adaptive measures, and policy interventions that can help build resilience against drought. Understanding drought dynamics is crucial for developing sustainable solutions to mitigate its adverse effects and ensure water security in a changing climate.

4.1 Concept of Drought

Drought is generally understood as a temporary scarcity of water in a particular region, primarily caused by insufficient precipitation. This shortage affects vegetation, river flow, water supply, and human consumption.

Causes of Drought

Droughts can result from various natural and anthropogenic factors:

Natural Causes:

- **Variability in Weather Patterns**: Weather patterns are inherently variable, influenced by complex natural processes. These fluctuations can cause significant periods of reduced or erratic rainfall, which in turn affects water availability for agriculture, ecosystems, and other sectors dependent on consistent weather patterns. Such variations can be unpredictable and often result in droughts or other adverse conditions for prolonged periods, contributing to stress on the environment and economy.

- **Climate Phenomena**: Major climate events, such as El Niño and La Niña, can have profound effects on global weather patterns. El Niño, characterized by warmer-than-usual sea surface temperatures in the Pacific Ocean, tends to disrupt weather patterns, often causing drier conditions in some regions and excessive rainfall in others. Conversely, La Niña, which is the opposite of El Niño and involves cooler-than-usual ocean temperatures, can also lead to shifts in rainfall patterns and temperature variations, leading to droughts or flooding, depending on the region. These phenomena can significantly alter seasonal weather expectations and cause widespread environmental and socio-economic challenges.

Human-Induced Causes:

- **Deforestation and Land Degradation**: The clearing of forests and destruction of natural vegetation severely impacts the environment by reducing the land's ability to retain moisture. Vegetation plays a crucial role in maintaining soil moisture by absorbing and storing water. When forests are removed, this vital function is lost, leading to dry, less fertile soils. This, in turn, amplifies the effects of drought, as the landscape becomes more vulnerable to extended periods of low rainfall, further worsening water scarcity.

- **Unsustainable Water Use:** The over-extraction of groundwater, often driven by agriculture and urban demands, coupled with poor water management practices, significantly depletes available water resources. When groundwater is overused beyond its natural replenishment rate, it leads to a depletion of aquifers, reducing water availability for communities and ecosystems. Inefficient water usage, such as irrigation practices that waste large amounts of water, can further exacerbate the impact of drought, making it harder to adapt to periods of water scarcity.

- **Climate Change:** Human-induced climate change is increasingly recognized as a key factor in the intensification of droughts worldwide. Rising global temperatures, altered precipitation patterns, and shifting weather systems contribute to more frequent and severe droughts. These changes are particularly evident in regions that are already prone to dry conditions, where prolonged droughts are becoming more common and intense, threatening agricultural productivity, water resources, and overall resilience to climate variability.

Definition of Drought:

Drought is a complex environmental phenomenon with varying definitions across disciplines. It is generally understood as an extended period of water scarcity due to inadequate rainfall, but its impacts extend beyond mere precipitation deficits. Below is a comprehensive exploration of different definitions of drought based on research and expert perspectives:

a. Traditional Definition:

"Historically, drought has been described as a prolonged period with little or no rainfall, resulting in water shortages." This conventional understanding focuses solely on precipitation levels but does not account for the broader climatic, hydrological, and socio-economic factors influencing drought conditions. Over time, researchers have recognized that drought is a multidimensional issue involving interactions between weather patterns, water resources, and human activities.

b. Ramdas (1960):

"According to Ramdas (1960), drought occurs when seasonal rainfall falls short by more than twice the average deviation." This definition introduces a quantitative approach, emphasizing the statistical assessment of rainfall deficits rather than relying on subjective observations. By setting a threshold for deviation from normal precipitation levels, this criterion helps in identifying drought conditions in specific regions.

c. American Meteorological Society:

"The American Meteorological Society defines drought as an extended period of unusually dry weather that significantly disrupts the hydrological balance in the affected area." This definition highlights the prolonged nature of drought and its consequences on water availability, including reduced surface water levels, groundwater depletion, and ecosystem imbalances.

d. Agricultural Perspective:

"From an agricultural standpoint, drought is seen as a sustained lack of soil moisture that negatively impacts plant growth." This form of drought occurs when soil water availability is insufficient to meet crop water requirements, leading to stress, reduced yields, and potential crop failures. Agricultural drought is a major concern for food security, as it disrupts farming systems and can result in economic losses for farmers.

e. Irrigation Commission of India:

"The Irrigation Commission of India defines drought as a condition where annual rainfall falls below 75% of the normal level." This definition provides a precise threshold for categorizing drought in regions reliant on consistent rainfall for agriculture and water supply. It is particularly relevant for drought-prone areas where deviations in rainfall patterns can have significant consequences for livelihoods and ecosystems.

Current Statistics on Drought:

According to the **World Meteorological Organization (WMO) 2024 Report**, global droughts have increased by **29% in frequency over the last 50 years** due to climate change. In India, the **2023 IMD Report** states that **approximately 40% of the country is susceptible to drought**, with states like Maharashtra, Rajasthan, and Karnataka frequently experiencing severe conditions.

Classification of Drought

Droughts are complex environmental phenomena that can be categorized based on their duration, severity, and impact on different sectors. The classification of drought helps in understanding its causes and consequences, enabling better preparedness and mitigation strategies.

Below is a detailed breakdown of drought types based on duration and impact.

1. Classification Based on Duration

The length and persistence of drought vary by region and climatic conditions. Based on their duration, droughts are classified into the following types:

a. Permanent Drought

Permanent droughts are characteristic of desert ecosystems, where extremely low rainfall and high temperatures create naturally arid conditions. In such regions, native vegetation has evolved to survive with minimal water availability. Agricultural activities are not feasible without artificial irrigation systems that supply water throughout the year.

b. Seasonal Drought

This type of drought is common in regions with well-defined rainy and dry seasons, particularly in arid and semi-arid climates. Seasonal droughts occur when rainfall is restricted to specific months, leading to prolonged dry periods. Farmers in these areas must strategically select crop varieties and planting schedules to align with the rainy season, ensuring optimal growth and yield.

c. Contingent Drought

Contingent droughts are unpredictable and occur due to unexpected failures in rainfall patterns. These droughts can arise in any climatic zone but are particularly common in humid and sub-humid regions, where rainfall fluctuations are irregular. Such droughts are usually short-lived but can have severe localized impacts on water availability, agriculture, and livelihoods.

d. Invisible Drought

Unlike other types of droughts, invisible drought does not result from an absolute lack of rainfall but occurs when water loss due to evapotranspiration exceeds the available soil moisture. Even with frequent precipitation, the rapid loss of moisture through evaporation and plant transpiration can lead to water stress in crops, ultimately reducing yields. This phenomenon is more common in humid regions where temperatures and evaporation rates are high.

2. Classification Based on Impact

Droughts can also be categorized based on the sectors they affect, as outlined by the **National Commission on Agriculture (1976):**

a. Meteorological Drought

Meteorological drought occurs when a region receives significantly less rainfall than its historical average over a specific period—be it a month, a season, or an entire year. This deviation from normal precipitation levels disrupts the hydrological cycle, reducing water availability for various uses.

b. Atmospheric Drought

This form of drought is characterized by extremely low humidity, often accompanied by strong, dry winds. These conditions can lead to temporary wilting in plants, even if the soil contains adequate moisture. Atmospheric drought typically affects plant health and growth by increasing evapotranspiration, leading to higher water stress in vegetation.

c. Hydrological Drought

When a meteorological drought persists over an extended period, it can lead to hydrological drought. This results in significant reductions in surface and groundwater levels, causing drying up of rivers, reservoirs, lakes, and water tanks. Hydrological drought has far-reaching consequences, affecting irrigation systems, drinking water supplies, hydroelectric power generation, and industrial water use.

d. Agricultural Drought (Soil Moisture Drought)

Agricultural drought arises when there is an imbalance between soil moisture levels and the water needs of crops. This occurs when rainfall is insufficient, unevenly distributed, or poorly timed relative to crop growth stages. As soil moisture declines, plants experience water stress, leading to reduced yields or complete crop failure. The severity of agricultural drought depends on factors such as soil type, crop variety, and the timing of rainfall deficits.

4.2 IMPACT OF WATER DEFICIT ON CROP GROWTH

Water availability is a crucial factor affecting plant growth, development, and overall productivity. A water deficit, commonly referred to as drought stress, occurs when plants experience limited water supply, disrupting physiological, morphological, and biochemical processes. The severity of the impact depends on factors such as **crop species, growth stage, soil properties, and duration of stress.** This section elaborates on the effects of water deficits on crops, with a focus on physio-morphological changes and their influence on yield and quality.

Physio-Morphological Effects of Water Deficit on Plants
Physiological Effects of Drought Stress on Plants

Drought stress causes significant disruptions in the physiological processes of plants, leading to reduced growth and productivity. Some key physiological responses to water scarcity include:

a. Stomatal Closure and Reduction in Photosynthesis

- One of the plant's immediate responses to water scarcity is the closure of stomata, the small pores on leaves. This action helps conserve water by reducing transpiration (the loss of water vapor). However, stomatal closure also restricts the intake of carbon dioxide (CO_2) from the atmosphere, which is essential for photosynthesis.
- As a result, photosynthesis is compromised, leading to a decrease in the production of carbohydrates, which are crucial for the plant's growth and development. This reduction in photosynthesis directly hampers biomass accumulation, affecting overall plant health and yield.
- When stomata remain closed for extended periods, leaf temperature increases, which may induce oxidative stress and damage to cell structures, further worsening the plant's health.

b. Impaired Water and Nutrient Uptake

- A water deficit affects the plant's ability to take up essential nutrients from the soil. Water serves as the medium for nutrient transport to the plant roots, and without sufficient moisture, nutrient uptake is limited.
- This leads to deficiencies in critical nutrients such as nitrogen, phosphorus, and potassium, which are vital for enzymatic processes and overall plant metabolism. These deficiencies further hinder the plant's ability to grow and produce, as nutrients are essential for cellular functions and energy production.

c. Alterations in Hormonal Balance

- Drought stress triggers an increase in the production of **abscisic acid (ABA)**, a plant hormone that plays a crucial role in signaling stomatal closure and reducing cell expansion to help conserve water.
- Concurrently, the production of growth-promoting hormones like **cytokinins** and **auxins** decreases under water stress, resulting in stunted growth and reduced cell division.

- As drought conditions worsen, the plant also produces increased levels of **ethylene**, a hormone that accelerates the senescence (aging) of leaves. This leads to premature leaf death, further limiting the plant's ability to carry out photosynthesis and reducing overall productivity.

Morphological Effects

Drought stress induces several morphological adaptations in plants that help them conserve water and improve survival under water-limited conditions. These changes are crucial for minimizing water loss and ensuring the plant's ability to endure harsh conditions.

a. Reduction in Leaf Area and Growth

- Water stress limits the expansion and division of plant cells, leading to smaller leaves. In response, plants may develop thicker cuticles (the waxy outer layer of the leaves), which helps reduce water loss by minimizing evaporation.
- To further reduce water loss, some plants undergo leaf rolling or wilting. This process decreases the surface area exposed to direct sunlight, thus reducing the rate of transpiration. By limiting water loss through the leaves, plants conserve vital water resources.

b. Root System Modifications

- To adapt to water scarcity, many plants exhibit changes in their root systems, such as increased root length and deeper penetration into the soil. This adaptation allows plants to access water from deeper soil layers that are less affected by surface drought conditions.
- However, in extreme drought situations, root growth can also be inhibited due to soil compaction and a lack of essential nutrients. Compacted soils make it difficult for roots to grow freely, which can hinder the plant's ability to access both water and nutrients, further stressing the plant.

c. Decreased Biomass Accumulation

- Due to reduced photosynthesis and nutrient uptake during drought stress, the overall accumulation of dry matter (biomass) is limited. This results in shorter plant height, fewer tillers (side shoots), and a reduction in leaf biomass.

- In addition to growth limitations, many crops experience delayed flowering and poor fruit or seed set under drought conditions. These factors significantly impact plant productivity, leading to lower yields and reduced reproductive success, which ultimately affects agricultural output.

2. Influence of Drought on Crop Yield and Quality

Drought has significant implications for agricultural productivity, affecting both the **quantity and quality** of crop yields.

Impact on Crop Yield

Drought stress significantly reduces agricultural productivity by impairing grain and seed development. Water scarcity during key growth stages, such as flowering and grain filling, disrupts essential physiological processes, leading to lower yields across different crop types.

- **Reduced Grain and Seed Production:**

  - Insufficient water availability during flowering and grain-filling stages affects pollen viability and fertilization, resulting in incomplete grain development and seed abortion.
  - This leads to a considerable decline in overall yield, particularly in crops that are highly sensitive to water stress.

- **Yield Loss Varies by Crop Type:**

  - **Cereal Crops (Wheat, Rice, Maize):** Reduced photosynthesis under drought conditions limits carbohydrate production, leading to poor grain filling and lower yields.
  - **Leguminous Crops (Soybean, Chickpea):** Drought stress hampers pod formation and decreases seed weight, significantly reducing productivity.
  - **Root Crops (Potato, Carrot):** Limited water availability restricts tuber formation, resulting in smaller and fewer tubers, ultimately lowering marketable yield.

Impact on Crop Quality

Drought stress not only affects crop yield but also alters the quality of agricultural produce, influencing its nutritional value, chemical composition, and post-harvest characteristics.

- **Nutritional Composition Alterations:**

  - Water scarcity disrupts the synthesis of essential macronutrients, leading to changes in protein, starch, and lipid content in grains and fruits.
  - In cereal crops, drought conditions often result in reduced protein levels, affecting grain quality and nutritional value.
  - Oilseed crops experience alterations in oil composition, including changes in fatty acid profiles, which can impact their suitability for industrial and dietary use.

- **Increased Accumulation of Secondary Metabolites:**

  - Under drought stress, plants produce higher amounts of secondary metabolites such as phenolics, flavonoids, and antioxidants as defense mechanisms against oxidative stress.
  - While this can enhance the medicinal and antioxidant properties of certain crops, excessive accumulation may reduce digestibility and palatability, making them less suitable for consumption.

- **Post-Harvest Quality Issues:**

  - Water deficits during crop growth affect fruit size, sugar accumulation, and overall texture, leading to lower market value.
  - In grains, drought stress can impair milling and baking properties, making them less desirable for processing industries and reducing their economic significance.

3. Strategies to Mitigate the Impact of Water Deficit

To mitigate the adverse effects of drought and ensure long-term agricultural sustainability, several adaptive strategies can be implemented:

1. **Development of Drought-Resistant Crop Varieties**

- Breeding and genetic engineering approaches can be used to develop crop cultivars with enhanced drought tolerance.
- Key traits include deeper root systems for better water uptake, improved water-use efficiency, and resilience to stress-induced damage.

2. Efficient Water Management

- Adoption of **drip irrigation** and **precision irrigation techniques** helps optimize water use by delivering moisture directly to plant roots.
- **Rainwater harvesting** systems can be utilized to store and utilize water during dry periods.
- **Soil moisture conservation techniques**, such as contour farming and cover cropping, help reduce evaporation and enhance water retention in the soil.

3. Application of Bio-Stimulants

- The use of **plant growth regulators** (e.g., abscisic acid, cytokinins) can help plants better cope with drought stress.
- **Microbial inoculants**, such as mycorrhizal fungi and plant growth-promoting rhizobacteria (PGPR), enhance nutrient and water uptake, improving drought tolerance.

4. Soil Health Improvement

- Incorporating **organic matter** through compost and green manure enhances soil structure and moisture-holding capacity.
- **Mulching** helps reduce evaporation, regulate soil temperature, and improve soil moisture retention.
- **Minimum tillage** practices prevent excessive soil disturbance, reducing water loss and maintaining soil microbial activity essential for plant health.

4.3. COPING MECHANISMS AND PLANT ADAPTATION TO WATER SCARCITY

Water scarcity is a major environmental challenge that limits plant growth and agricultural productivity worldwide. Drought stress occurs when water availability is insufficient to meet a plant's physiological requirements, affecting **photosynthesis, nutrient uptake, and overall plant health**. To survive under these harsh conditions, plants have evolved **complex adaptive mechanisms** that allow them to conserve water, optimize its usage, and maintain cellular functions.

These adaptations are broadly classified into three categories:

1. **Morphological adaptations** – Structural modifications in roots, leaves, and stems.
2. **Physiological adaptations** – Mechanisms involving stomatal regulation, osmotic adjustments, and biochemical responses.
3. **Genetic and metabolic adaptations** – Activation of drought-resistant genes and metabolic pathways that enhance water-use efficiency.

MORPHOLOGICAL ADAPTATIONS TO DROUGHT
1. ROOT SYSTEM ADAPTATIONS

Roots play a crucial role in water absorption and uptake from the soil. Drought-adapted plants develop **modifications in root architecture** to improve water acquisition efficiency:

- **Deep Root Systems:** Certain plants extend their roots deeper into the soil to reach underground moisture reserves. Examples include **pigeon pea (Cajanus cajan), sorghum (Sorghum bicolor), and date palm (Phoenix dactylifera).**
- **Increased Root Hair Density:** Root hairs enhance water absorption by increasing surface area. Drought-resistant crops like **wheat, maize, and sunflower** exhibit a greater number of root hairs under water-limited conditions.
- **Fibrous Root Systems:** Some plants develop **highly branched fibrous roots** to maximize water absorption from the upper soil layers, a common feature in grasses and cereal crops.

2. LEAF AND CANOPY ADAPTATIONS

Leaves are the primary site of transpiration, and plants exhibit several modifications to **minimize water loss:**

- **Leaf Rolling and Folding:** Certain plants roll their leaves inward to **reduce surface area exposed to sunlight**, minimizing transpiration. This response is commonly observed in **rice, maize, and sugarcane.**
- **Thick Cuticle Layer:** Some plants develop a **waxy coating (cuticle) on their leaves** to prevent excessive water loss. Examples include **olive trees (Olea europaea) and cacti (Cactaceae).**
- **Reduced Leaf Area and Leaf Shedding:** Many drought-tolerant plants **drop older leaves** or reduce their leaf size during dry periods to conserve water. **Neem (Azadirachta indica)** and **Acacia species** use this strategy effectively.

3. STEM AND STORAGE ADAPTATIONS

- **Succulence:** Some plants store water in their **stems and leaves**, allowing them to survive prolonged droughts. Examples include **aloe vera, agave, and baobab trees.**
- **Sunken Stomata and Trichomes:** Certain plants develop **deeply embedded stomata and hairy (trichome-covered) surfaces** to reduce transpiration, commonly seen in desert-adapted species like **rosemary (Rosmarinus officinalis) and sage (Salvia officinalis).**

PHYSIOLOGICAL ADAPTATIONS TO WATER SCARCITY
1. STOMATAL REGULATION AND TRANSPIRATION CONTROL

One of the most effective physiological responses to drought is **stomatal closure.** Stomata are tiny pores on the leaf surface that regulate gas exchange and transpiration. During drought stress:

- **Plants close their stomata to prevent excessive water loss.**
- **Abscisic acid (ABA), a plant hormone, signals stomatal closure** when water availability is low.
- Drought-tolerant crops like **pearl millet, sorghum, and cowpea** show enhanced ABA production to manage water loss.

2. OSMOTIC ADJUSTMENT AND WATER RETENTION

Osmotic adjustment is a vital mechanism that helps plants **maintain water balance within cells** under drought conditions:

- **Accumulation of osmolytes (compatible solutes):**

  - Proline, glycine betaine, sugars, and polyols help retain cellular water and protect proteins from dehydration.
  - **Leguminous crops (e.g., chickpea, soybean) and sugarcane** use this adaptation effectively.

- **Water Storage in Tissues:**

  - Succulent plants store water in vacuoles to survive prolonged dry periods.
  - **Cacti and Agave species** are excellent examples.

3. PHOTOSYNTHETIC ADAPTATIONS AND METABOLIC CHANGES
Plants alter their photosynthesis process to **improve water-use efficiency (WUE):**

- **C4 Photosynthesis:**

  - Some crops (e.g., maize, sugarcane, sorghum) follow the **C4 pathway,** which is more water-efficient than the C3 pathway.

- **Crassulacean Acid Metabolism (CAM) Pathway:**

  - Succulent plants like **pineapple and agave** use the CAM pathway, where stomata open at night to reduce daytime water loss.

GENETIC AND BIOCHEMICAL ADAPTATIONS TO DROUGHT
1. DROUGHT-RESPONSIVE GENES AND MOLECULAR MECHANISMS
Modern research has identified several **drought-resistant genes** that enhance plant survival under water stress:

- **DREB (Dehydration-Responsive Element Binding) genes** activate drought tolerance pathways.

- **AREB (ABA-Responsive Element Binding) proteins** regulate stomatal closure and osmotic adjustment.
- **Late Embryogenesis Abundant (LEA) proteins** help protect cell membranes from dehydration damage.

2. ROLE OF PHYTOHORMONES IN DROUGHT TOLERANCE

Plant hormones play a critical role in regulating drought response:

- **Abscisic Acid (ABA):** Signals stomatal closure and induces drought-resistant genes.
- **Cytokinins:** Delays leaf senescence and sustains photosynthesis.
- **Ethylene:** Regulates stress responses, although excess ethylene can accelerate leaf drop.

BREEDING AND AGRICULTURAL STRATEGIES FOR DROUGHT RESISTANCE

1. DEVELOPMENT OF DROUGHT-RESISTANT CROP VARIETIES

Plant breeders use **traditional breeding and genetic engineering** to develop drought-tolerant crops:

- **Hybrid maize (Zea mays) varieties with deeper roots.**
- **Drought-resistant rice (Oryza sativa) cultivars using DREB genes.**
- **Drought-tolerant wheat with enhanced osmolyte accumulation.**

2. WATER-SAVING AGRONOMIC PRACTICES

- **Mulching:** Reduces soil evaporation and retains moisture.
- **Drip Irrigation:** Supplies water directly to roots, improving water-use efficiency.
- **Conservation Tillage:** Enhances soil moisture retention.

CHAPTER FIVE

SOIL AND WATER CONSERVATION TECHNIQUES

Conserving soil and water is essential for maintaining agricultural output, protecting the environment, and guaranteeing food security, especially in areas that receive rainfall and have erratic water supplies. Significant obstacles to sustainable agriculture are presented by the deterioration of soil and water resources due to nutrient depletion, erosion, and wasteful water usage. Reducing these problems and advancing long-term agricultural sustainability need the implementation of efficient conservation techniques. It refers to methods and techniques that are used to prevent soil erosion, improve soil fertility, and maximize water use efficiency. These methods are intended to improve the sustainable use of natural resources, stop soil deterioration, and lessen water runoff. The fundamental ideas include preserving ground cover, enhancing soil composition, and controlling water flow to promote infiltration and lessen erosion.

Soil erosion is a critical concern in agriculture, leading to the loss of topsoil, which is rich in organic matter and nutrients essential for crop growth. Erosion diminishes soil fertility, reduces agricultural productivity, and can lead to sedimentation in waterways, affecting aquatic ecosystems. Practices such as contour farming, terracing, and the use of cover crops are effective in reducing soil erosion by slowing water flow and increasing water infiltration into the soil. For instance, contour farming involves plowing along the natural contours of the land, which helps in reducing runoff and preventing soil loss. Water is a critical input in agriculture, and its efficient use is vital for crop production, especially in areas reliant on rainfall. Techniques such as rainwater harvesting, efficient irrigation methods like drip and sprinkler systems, and the construction of check dams contribute to water conservation by capturing and efficiently utilizing available water resources. These methods not only enhance water availability for crops but also aid in groundwater recharge and reduce dependency on erratic rainfall patterns.

Traditional soil and water conservation practices have been employed for centuries across various regions. In India, for example, structures like 'johads' in Rajasthan and 'kuls' in Himachal Pradesh have been used to harvest and manage water resources effectively. These indigenous methods demonstrate the importance of local knowledge in resource conservation. Modern approaches, such as conservation tillage and agroforestry, integrate scientific research with traditional practices to enhance conservation outcomes. Conservation tillage, which includes minimal soil disturbance, helps maintain soil structure, reduce erosion, and improve water retention.

The Loess Plateau project in China serves as a notable example of large-scale soil and water conservation efforts. Initiated to combat severe soil erosion and restore degraded land, the project implemented measures like banning deforestation, promoting terracing, and encouraging sustainable land use practices. These efforts led to increased vegetation cover and improved agricultural productivity, demonstrating the effectiveness of integrated conservation strategies.

In the United States, the adoption of prairie strips—bands of native grasses and wildflowers integrated into croplands—has shown significant benefits in reducing soil erosion, improving water infiltration, and providing habitats for pollinators. Research indicates that implementing prairie strips can reduce soil erosion by up to 95%, highlighting their potential as a conservation practice.

5.1 Principles of Soil Conservation

Soil conservation is a set of management strategies aimed at preventing soil degradation, preserving soil fertility, and enhancing agricultural sustainability. The primary principles of soil conservation involve controlling erosion, maintaining soil structure, and optimizing water retention to ensure long-term productivity.

Soil conservation is a comprehensive approach involving various management strategies to protect soil resources from degradation, maintain its fertility, and support long-term agricultural productivity. As soil is a non-renewable resource on a human timescale, its conservation is critical for sustaining food production, ensuring ecosystem stability, and mitigating climate change effects.

The degradation of soil occurs due to multiple factors, including erosion (by wind and water), depletion of organic matter, compaction, salinization, and chemical contamination. If left unchecked, these issues can lead to reduced crop yields, loss of biodiversity, and increased vulnerability to climate extremes such as droughts and floods.

To combat soil degradation and promote sustainable land use, soil conservation practices focus on three fundamental principles:

Erosion Control

Soil erosion is a critical environmental and agricultural challenge that leads to the degradation of land productivity, threatening food security and ecosystem stability. It occurs when soil particles are detached and transported by natural forces such as wind and water. The severity of soil erosion depends on factors like rainfall intensity, soil type, vegetation cover, topography, and land management practices.

Erosion primarily affects the **topsoil layer**, which is rich in organic matter, essential nutrients, and beneficial microorganisms that support plant growth. The loss of topsoil results in **reduced soil fertility, lower water-holding capacity, increased runoff, and disruption of soil structure**. If left unchecked, soil erosion can lead to **desertification, sedimentation of water bodies, and reduced agricultural productivity**.

To mitigate soil erosion, **effective conservation strategies** must be implemented. These strategies focus on minimizing runoff, enhancing soil stability, and protecting soil from erosive forces such as rainfall, surface water flow, and strong winds.

1. Minimizing Runoff and Water Erosion

Water erosion is one of the most significant forms of soil degradation, particularly in hilly and sloped landscapes. Heavy rainfall, coupled with improper land use, results in runoff that carries away soil particles, creating gullies and reducing the land's ability to retain moisture. Effective methods to control water-induced erosion include:

a. Contour Farming

Definition: Contour farming involves plowing and planting crops along the natural elevation contours of a slope rather than in straight rows.
Benefits:

- Reduces the speed of surface water runoff.
- Enhances water infiltration, preventing excessive loss of topsoil.
- Increases moisture retention, improving crop growth in rainfed areas.
- Minimizes soil disturbance, promoting healthier root systems and microbial activity.

b. Terracing

Definition: Terracing transforms steep slopes into a series of leveled platforms resembling steps, which slow down water movement and reduce soil loss.
Benefits:

- Helps retain water, making it available for crops.
- Reduces the impact of heavy rainfall, preventing the formation of deep gullies.
- Controls nutrient loss by decreasing soil displacement.
- Supports agricultural activities in hilly regions where traditional farming would be difficult.

c. Check Dams & Bunds

Definition: Check dams are small, man-made barriers built across gullies and streams to control water flow, while bunds (raised earthen or stone embankments) help prevent runoff and retain soil.
Benefits:

- Slows down runoff, allowing water to infiltrate the soil rather than washing away nutrients.
- Reduces the velocity of water flow, preventing further deepening of gullies.
- Enhances groundwater recharge, supporting sustainable water availability.
- Helps restore degraded landscapes by stabilizing soil and preventing excessive loss of fertile land.

2. Reducing Wind Erosion

Wind erosion is a serious problem in **semi-arid and arid regions**, where high temperatures, low moisture levels, and sparse vegetation make soils more vulnerable to displacement by wind. The fine soil particles blown away by strong winds **deplete soil fertility, increase desertification, and contribute to airborne dust pollution**. Several strategies can help mitigate wind erosion:

a. Windbreaks & Shelterbelts

Definition: Windbreaks and shelterbelts are rows of trees, shrubs, or other vegetation planted around fields to act as barriers against wind.

Benefits:

- Reduce wind velocity, preventing soil particle displacement.
- Improve microclimate conditions by reducing temperature fluctuations.
- Increase biodiversity by providing habitat for birds and beneficial insects.
- Prevent loss of soil moisture by lowering evaporation rates.

b. Cover Crops & Mulching

Definition: Cover crops are plants grown primarily to **protect the soil from erosion**, while mulching involves covering the soil surface with organic or inorganic materials.

Benefits:

- Protects soil from direct exposure to wind, reducing dust storms.
- Enhances organic matter content, improving soil structure.
- Prevents evaporation, helping retain soil moisture.
- Suppresses weed growth and improves soil biodiversity.

Soil erosion remains a **significant threat to sustainable agriculture and environmental health**, but with the adoption of effective soil conservation techniques, its negative impacts can be minimized. Implementing **erosion control measures such as contour farming, terracing, windbreaks, and mulching** not only protects the soil from degradation but also improves water conservation, enhances biodiversity, and sustains agricultural productivity.

To achieve **long-term soil conservation**, a **combination of traditional and modern techniques, supported by government policies, farmer**

education, and community participation, is essential. By prioritizing soil protection, we can ensure sustainable agriculture for future generations while preserving natural resources.

Soil Structure Improvement

Healthy soil structure plays a crucial role in **water infiltration, root penetration, nutrient availability, and erosion resistance**. Well-structured soil improves plant growth by facilitating proper aeration, maintaining moisture levels, and supporting beneficial microbial activity. However, factors such as continuous cropping, excessive tillage, and soil compaction can degrade soil structure over time. To counteract these effects, farmers and land managers can adopt various **soil improvement techniques** that enhance soil aggregation, organic matter content, and overall stability.

1. Adding Organic Matter

Incorporating **organic materials** into the soil is one of the most effective ways to improve soil structure. Organic matter **binds soil particles together**, forming stable aggregates that enhance porosity, water-holding capacity, and microbial diversity.

a. Compost, Manure, and Green Manure

- **Compost:** Decomposed organic waste enriches soil with humus, improving moisture retention and aeration.
- **Animal Manure:** Supplies essential nutrients, enhances microbial activity, and promotes aggregate formation.
- **Green Manure:** Cover crops such as legumes and clover are plowed into the soil to improve nitrogen content and organic matter.

b. Benefits of Organic Matter Addition

- Increases soil **biological activity**, leading to better nutrient cycling.
- Enhances **soil aggregation**, reducing compaction and improving drainage.
- Improves **water infiltration and retention**, preventing surface runoff.
- Supports the growth of beneficial **microorganisms** that contribute to soil fertility.

2. Practicing Conservation Tillage

Traditional tillage methods **break down soil aggregates**, increasing susceptibility to erosion and compaction. Conservation tillage practices aim to **minimize soil disturbance**, preserving soil structure and organic matter content.

a. Minimum Tillage

- Reduces **plowing and soil inversion**, preventing loss of topsoil.
- Maintains **natural soil pores**, improving water movement and aeration.
- Preserves **soil organisms** such as earthworms, which enhance soil structure.

b. No-Till Farming

- Leaves **crop residues** on the soil surface, reducing erosion and moisture loss.
- Enhances **carbon sequestration**, promoting long-term soil fertility.
- Prevents **soil crusting**, allowing roots to penetrate more easily.

c. Benefits of Conservation Tillage

- Improves **soil organic matter retention**, enhancing microbial diversity.
- Prevents **soil erosion** by maintaining ground cover.
- Reduces **fuel and labor costs**, making farming more sustainable.

3. Using Soil Amendments

Soil amendments improve **soil texture, pH balance, and water-holding capacity**, ensuring optimal conditions for plant growth.

a. Lime and Gypsum

- **Lime** (calcium carbonate) neutralizes **acidic soils**, improving nutrient availability.
- **Gypsum** (calcium sulfate) helps **break up compacted clay soils**, enhancing drainage.

b. Biochar

- A **carbon-rich material** derived from organic waste, biochar enhances **soil carbon content**.
- Improves **water retention**, making soil more resilient to drought.

- Increases **cation exchange capacity (CEC)**, improving nutrient availability.

c. Benefits of Soil Amendments

- Enhances **soil texture**, preventing excessive compaction.
- Regulates **soil pH**, optimizing conditions for plant growth.
- Increases **nutrient retention**, reducing fertilizer dependency.

Improving soil structure is fundamental to **sustainable agriculture** and **long-term land productivity**. By incorporating **organic matter, adopting conservation tillage, and using soil amendments**, farmers can enhance soil health, reduce erosion risks, and promote efficient water use. A well-structured soil not only supports higher crop yields but also strengthens **ecosystem resilience** against climate variability.

Soil Moisture Conservation

Water availability is one of the most critical factors influencing soil health, crop productivity, and overall agricultural sustainability. Insufficient moisture can lead to poor plant growth, reduced nutrient uptake, and increased soil erosion, while excessive evaporation can deplete water reserves. To combat these challenges, various soil moisture conservation techniques have been developed to reduce evaporation, enhance water infiltration, and optimize soil water-holding capacity.

1. **Mulching: Reducing Evaporation and Enhancing Soil Moisture**

Mulching involves covering the soil surface with **organic or synthetic materials** to **reduce water loss, moderate soil temperature, and suppress weed growth.**

a. **Organic Mulches**

- **Examples:** Straw, dry leaves, wood chips, crop residues, and grass clippings.
- **Benefits:**

  - Enhances **water retention** by reducing direct exposure to sunlight.
  - Adds **organic matter** to the soil as it decomposes, improving fertility.
  - Supports **microbial activity**, which enhances soil structure.

b. **Synthetic Mulches**

- **Examples:** Plastic film, polyethylene sheets, and landscape fabric.
- **Benefits:**

  - Effectively prevents **moisture evaporation** in arid and semi-arid regions.
  - Controls **weed growth**, reducing competition for water.
  - Provides **long-term soil protection**, especially in high-value crops.

2. Cover Crops: Preserving Soil Moisture and Improving Fertility

Cover cropping is an effective strategy where **temporary crops** are grown primarily to **protect and enrich the soil** rather than for harvest.

a. Leguminous Cover Crops

- **Examples:** Clover, alfalfa, cowpea, and vetch.
- **Benefits:**

  - Fix atmospheric **nitrogen** into the soil, reducing fertilizer dependency.
  - Reduces **moisture loss** by providing **continuous soil cover**.
  - Improves **soil organic matter** and microbial biodiversity.

b. Non-Leguminous Cover Crops

- **Examples:** Rye, oats, and mustard.
- **Benefits:**

  - Prevents **soil erosion** by anchoring topsoil with strong root systems.
  - Enhances **water infiltration** and soil aeration.
  - Suppresses **weed growth**, reducing competition for soil moisture.

3. Deep Plowing & Subsoiling: Enhancing Water Infiltration

Soil compaction **restricts root growth and limits water movement**, leading to poor crop development. Deep plowing and subsoiling are techniques designed to **break up compacted soil layers**, improving water penetration and retention.

a. Deep Plowing

- Involves turning the soil to a depth of **30-50 cm** using heavy-duty plows.

- Helps **loosen compacted soil layers**, allowing roots to access deeper moisture reserves.
- Improves **water percolation**, preventing waterlogging in clayey soils.

b. Subsoiling

- Uses a **subsoiler or chisel plow** to break up **hardpan layers** (densely compacted subsoil) without disturbing the topsoil.
- Enhances **root penetration**, allowing crops to access **deeper groundwater sources**.
- Reduces **surface runoff**, increasing moisture absorption by soil profiles.

4. Furrow & Ridge Cultivation: Optimizing Soil Drainage and Water Retention

Furrow and ridge cultivation is a **soil management practice** that modifies field topography to improve water distribution and retention.

a. Furrow Irrigation

- **Definition:** Furrows (shallow trenches) are dug between crop rows to guide water flow and promote uniform infiltration.
- **Benefits:**

  - Prevents **excessive runoff**, ensuring efficient water use.
  - Facilitates **deep water penetration**, reducing evaporation losses.
  - Ideal for **row crops** such as maize, cotton, and sugarcane.

b. Ridge Farming

- **Definition:** Crops are planted on raised ridges, with furrows acting as water channels.
- **Benefits:**

  - Prevents **waterlogging** in heavy clay soils.
  - Enhances **aeration** and promotes **stronger root growth**.
  - Improves **drainage** while maintaining moisture at the root zone.

Soil moisture conservation is essential for improving crop productivity, maintaining soil health, and ensuring resilience against drought conditions.

Techniques such as mulching, cover cropping, deep plowing, and furrow-ridge cultivation help retain moisture, improve soil structure, and reduce water loss. By integrating these strategies, farmers can enhance water-use efficiency, sustain crop yields, and promote long-term agricultural sustainability in rainfed and semi-arid regions.

Enhancing Biological Activity in Soil

Soil microorganisms are fundamental to maintaining **soil fertility, structure, and overall ecosystem stability**. These microscopic organisms—including **bacteria, fungi, actinomycetes, and protozoa**—decompose organic matter, fix atmospheric nitrogen, and improve soil aggregation. Enhancing soil biological activity not only boosts **nutrient availability** but also strengthens **plant resilience against environmental stresses**. Various agricultural practices can **stimulate microbial diversity** and support a healthy soil ecosystem.

1. Crop Rotation & Intercropping: Promoting Microbial Diversity

a. Crop Rotation

- Crop rotation involves alternating **different plant species** on the same field across multiple growing seasons.
- **Benefits:**

  - Prevents **soil nutrient depletion** by balancing nutrient demands.
  - Disrupts **pest and disease cycles**, reducing reliance on chemical inputs.
  - Enhances **soil microbial diversity**, encouraging beneficial bacteria and fungi.
  - **Example:** Rotating nitrogen-fixing legumes (e.g., soybean, lentils) with cereals (e.g., wheat, maize) improves **soil nitrogen levels**.

b. Intercropping

- Intercropping involves growing **two or more crops together** in the same field to **maximize resource utilization**.
- **Benefits:**

  - Increases **root exudates**, which feed microbial populations.
  - Improves **nutrient cycling**, reducing the need for synthetic fertilizers.

- ◦ Supports **mutualistic interactions**, such as nitrogen-fixing bacteria in legume-based intercropping systems.
- ◦ **Example:** Maize intercropped with cowpea enhances **soil nitrogen availability** and suppresses weeds naturally.

2. Mycorrhizal Fungi Inoculation: Boosting Nutrient Absorption
a. Role of Mycorrhizal Fungi

- Mycorrhizal fungi form **symbiotic associations** with plant roots, extending their root network and enhancing nutrient uptake.
- These fungi improve access to **phosphorus, nitrogen, and micronutrients** from the soil.

b. Benefits of Mycorrhizal Fungi Inoculation

- Increases **root surface area**, allowing plants to absorb more water and nutrients.
- Enhances **drought tolerance**, as fungal hyphae retain soil moisture.
- Reduces dependency on **chemical fertilizers**, promoting sustainable soil fertility.
- Protects plants from **soil-borne pathogens** by enhancing root immunity.

c. Practical Applications

- **Seed or root inoculation** with mycorrhizal spores during planting.
- Application of **biofertilizers containing arbuscular mycorrhizal (AM) fungi** in degraded soils.
- **Example:** Inoculating wheat or maize fields with **Glomus spp.** improves phosphorus uptake and yield in nutrient-poor soils.

3. Vermiculture & Earthworm Management: Enhancing Soil Aeration and Organic Matter Decomposition
a. Role of Earthworms in Soil Health

- Earthworms are natural soil engineers that **break down organic matter, aerate soil, and enhance microbial activity.**
- Their movement creates **soil pores**, improving **water infiltration and root penetration.**

b. Benefits of Vermiculture & Earthworm Management

- Increases **soil organic carbon**, enhancing microbial populations.
- Improves **nutrient cycling** by converting organic waste into humus-rich **vermicompost**.
- Enhances **soil structure**, reducing compaction and improving aeration.
- **Example:** Earthworm species like **Eisenia fetida** (red wiggler) and **Lumbricus rubellus** are widely used in vermiculture for organic farming.

c. Practical Strategies

- Introducing **vermicomposting systems** to convert organic farm waste into nutrient-rich compost.
- Encouraging **natural earthworm populations** by minimizing pesticide use and maintaining adequate soil moisture.
- Adding **organic residues** like crop stubble and farmyard manure to attract earthworms.

Enhancing soil biological activity is a key strategy for improving soil fertility, structure, and resilience. By adopting crop rotation, intercropping, mycorrhizal fungi inoculation, and vermiculture, farmers can increase microbial diversity, improve nutrient cycling, and boost soil aeration. These practices not only reduce dependency on chemical inputs but also promote long-term agricultural sustainability and productivity.

Sustainable Land Use Management

Proper land management is fundamental to maintaining soil health, preventing over-exploitation, and ensuring long-term agricultural productivity. Degraded soils lead to reduced crop yields, increased erosion, and loss of biodiversity. Implementing sustainable land management strategies enhances soil stability, preserves organic matter, and mitigates environmental degradation.

1. Agroforestry: Enhancing Soil Stability and Biodiversity

Agroforestry is a **sustainable land-use system** that integrates **trees, shrubs, and crops** in the same area to improve soil structure and **increase resilience against climate variability.**

a. Benefits of Agroforestry

- **Reduces Soil Erosion**: Tree roots stabilize the soil, preventing wind and water erosion.
- **Improves Soil Fertility**: Leguminous trees like **Gliricidia and Acacia** fix atmospheric nitrogen, enriching the soil.
- **Enhances Water Retention**: Tree canopies **reduce surface runoff** and increase water infiltration.
- **Supports Biodiversity**: Provides habitat for beneficial organisms such as **pollinators and pest predators.**

b. Agroforestry Techniques

- **Alley Cropping**: Planting crops between rows of trees to provide shade and reduce soil degradation.
- **Silvopasture**: Integrating trees and livestock grazing to improve forage availability and reduce land degradation.
- **Windbreaks & Shelterbelts**: Planting tree rows along field boundaries to reduce wind erosion.

c. Example

In semi-arid regions of India, integrating **Prosopis cineraria (Khejri tree) with millet cultivation** has improved soil organic matter and enhanced drought resilience.

2. Grazing Management: Preventing Overgrazing and Maintaining Grass Cover

Uncontrolled grazing **depletes soil nutrients, compacts the land, and increases erosion.** Sustainable grazing management is essential to **preserve pasturelands and improve soil structure.**

a. Rotational Grazing

- Involves **systematic movement of livestock** between pastures to allow grass regeneration.
- Prevents soil compaction, maintains **ground cover**, and improves organic matter cycling.

b. Deferred Grazing

- Allowing pastures to **rest and recover** during critical growth periods.
- Encourages deep-rooted grass species, improving **soil water retention.**

c. Controlled Stocking Rates

- Adjusting the number of animals per unit area to **match the carrying capacity** of the land.
- Prevents depletion of vegetation, reducing the risk of **desertification**.

d. Example

In **Rajasthan, India,** rotational grazing in **community pastures** has helped restore **grasslands and reduce soil erosion**, enhancing fodder availability for livestock.

3. Afforestation & Reforestation: Restoring Degraded Lands

a. Afforestation

- Planting trees in **previously barren or non-forested areas** to enhance soil fertility and prevent erosion.
- Helps **sequester carbon**, mitigating climate change effects.

b. Reforestation

- Restoring **previously deforested lands** to rebuild soil health.
- Improves **water cycle regulation** by reducing evaporation losses.

c. Role in Soil Conservation

- **Tree roots anchor the soil**, reducing landslides and sediment loss.
- **Leaf litter decomposition** adds organic matter, increasing microbial activity and soil fertility.
- **Canopy coverage reduces soil temperature extremes**, maintaining moisture levels.

d. Example

China's **Loess Plateau Reforestation Project** successfully reduced soil erosion by **over 60%** and restored agricultural productivity.

Implementing sustainable land management practices such as agroforestry, controlled grazing, and afforestation is essential for preventing soil degradation and ensuring agricultural sustainability. These strategies help maintain soil productivity, reduce dependency on chemical inputs, and protect natural ecosystems from further deterioration. By adopting these approaches, farmers can enhance resilience to climate change, improve food security, and ensure long-term environmental stability.

5.2 Soil Conservation Techniques

Soil conservation techniques are essential for preventing soil degradation, enhancing fertility, and ensuring long-term agricultural sustainability. These methods focus on reducing soil erosion, improving water retention, and maintaining soil structure to support productive farming systems. Research papers have extensively documented various effective techniques to prevent soil degradation and enhance soil health. Soil conservation is critical in sustaining food production and maintaining ecological balance. Degraded soils lead to reduced agricultural productivity, loss of biodiversity, and increased vulnerability to climate change. Without proper conservation practices, soil erosion can strip away topsoil, deplete essential nutrients, and disrupt the natural water cycle. Consequently, effective soil conservation techniques not only preserve soil quality but also enhance crop resilience and long-term agricultural sustainability.

Erosion control measures play a crucial role in preserving soil stability and fertility. Contour farming, which involves plowing along natural contours, helps reduce water runoff and soil displacement, while terracing creates step-like structures on slopes to minimize rapid water movement and soil loss. Windbreaks and shelterbelts, consisting of strategically planted rows of trees or shrubs, effectively reduce wind velocity, preventing soil erosion. Additionally, check dams and bunds serve as small barriers designed to slow down surface runoff and encourage water infiltration, further mitigating soil degradation.

Water retention and moisture conservation techniques are equally vital for maintaining soil health. Mulching, using organic or synthetic materials, reduces evaporation and helps retain soil moisture. Cover crops, particularly legumes, not only prevent moisture loss but also enhance soil fertility by fixing atmospheric nitrogen. Deep plowing and subsoiling break compacted soil layers, allowing better water infiltration and root penetration, while furrow and ridge cultivation improves drainage and optimizes soil moisture retention for crops.

Improving soil structure enhances root penetration, microbial activity, and resistance to erosion. Adding organic matter such as compost, manure, and green manure boosts soil aggregation and fertility. Conservation tillage, including minimum or no-till farming, reduces soil disturbance and maintains its natural structure while preserving organic matter. The application of soil amendments like lime, gypsum, and biochar improves soil texture, balances pH, and enhances water-holding capacity, contributing to overall soil health.

Enhancing soil biological activity is fundamental to sustaining soil fertility. Crop rotation and intercropping diversify microbial communities, improving nutrient cycling and soil structure. Mycorrhizal fungi inoculation strengthens plant-root interactions, facilitating better nutrient uptake, while vermiculture and earthworm management promote soil aeration and organic matter decomposition, further improving soil productivity.

Sustainable land management ensures that soil resources are not over-exploited. Agroforestry, which integrates trees and crops, enhances soil stability, increases biodiversity, and reduces land degradation. Grazing management practices, such as rotational grazing, help prevent overgrazing and maintain grass cover, ensuring long-term soil health. Additionally, afforestation and reforestation efforts restore degraded lands, improve soil structure, and increase carbon sequestration, contributing to environmental sustainability.

By adopting these soil conservation techniques, farmers can improve soil health, increase agricultural productivity, and mitigate the adverse effects of climate change. Research-based strategies ensure that these methods remain effective in varying climatic and soil conditions, ultimately contributing to global food security and environmental sustainability.

1. Contour Farming: Reducing Water Runoff and Soil Loss

a. Concept Contour farming is an agricultural technique that involves plowing and planting crops along the natural contour lines of a slope rather than following a straight up-and-down pattern. This practice is designed to slow the movement of water across the field, reducing runoff velocity and allowing more time for water infiltration. By following the land's natural shape, contour farming helps distribute water more evenly across the field, preventing soil displacement and enhancing moisture retention. This method is particularly useful in sloped and hilly terrains, where conventional plowing can lead to severe soil erosion and nutrient loss.

b. Benefits Contour farming provides multiple advantages for soil conservation and agricultural productivity. One of its primary benefits is the reduction of surface runoff, which helps control erosion and soil loss by 30–50% in sloped areas. The technique improves moisture retention in the soil, ensuring better water availability for crops and reducing dependency on irrigation. This enhanced soil moisture promotes plant growth and improves crop resilience during dry periods. Additionally, contour farming helps in reducing the risk of gully formation, which can degrade agricultural land and lower its productivity over time. It also enhances soil structure by minimizing the displacement of fertile topsoil, which is essential for sustaining high crop yields.

c. Example In hilly regions of India, contour farming has been widely adopted to mitigate soil erosion and improve agricultural productivity. Studies indicate that farmers using this method have observed a 15–25% increase in crop yields due to improved soil retention and moisture conservation (Perennia, 2018). Similar success has been reported in other parts of the world, such as in the Andes and African highlands, where contour farming has significantly improved soil fertility and water management in sloped agricultural lands. These results highlight the effectiveness of contour farming as a sustainable soil conservation technique for enhancing food security and environmental resilience.

2. Terracing: Controlling Erosion on Sloped Lands

a. Concept Terracing is a soil conservation technique that involves constructing step-like structures on steep slopes to create flat surfaces for cultivation. These terraces act as barriers that slow down water runoff, reducing its velocity and preventing soil erosion. By breaking the natural slope into smaller, level sections, terracing helps retain water, enhances soil stability, and allows for more effective agricultural practices in hilly and mountainous regions. This technique has been widely implemented in regions prone to heavy rainfall and soil erosion, making it a crucial method for sustainable land management.

b. Benefits Terracing offers numerous advantages, particularly in preventing soil degradation and improving agricultural productivity. It significantly reduces soil erosion, with studies indicating a reduction of up to 80%, especially in high-rainfall areas where runoff is a major concern. By slowing down water movement, terracing promotes better water infiltration, increasing soil moisture content and aiding in groundwater recharge. This enhanced water retention benefits crops by ensuring a more consistent water supply, reducing dependency on artificial irrigation. Additionally, terracing enables cultivation on steep terrains that would otherwise be unsuitable for farming, transforming previously unproductive land into arable fields. The practice also minimizes landslide risks by stabilizing slopes and preventing mass soil movement, further contributing to land conservation.

c. Example Terracing has been successfully implemented in various parts of the world to combat soil erosion and improve agricultural productivity. In China's Loess Plateau, large-scale terracing initiatives have played a key role in restoring degraded lands, increasing crop yields, and enhancing water conservation (Perennia, 2018). Similar projects in the Andean regions of South America and the highlands of Ethiopia have demonstrated the long-term benefits of terracing in preserving soil fertility, reducing erosion, and improving farmers' livelihoods. These examples highlight the effectiveness of terracing as a sustainable agricultural practice for soil and water conservation in challenging landscapes.

3. Bunding: Preventing Soil and Water Runoff
a. Concept

- Bunding involves **constructing earthen embankments** along field edges to control **water flow and prevent erosion.**

b. Types of Bunds

- **Contour Bunds**: Built along slopes to reduce runoff.
- **Graded Bunds**: Designed with slight gradients to direct excess water to **safe drainage outlets.**
- **Stone Bunds**: Made with rocks to prevent soil loss in **semi-arid regions**.

c. Benefits

- Increases **rainwater infiltration**, reducing soil moisture loss.
- Prevents **nutrient depletion**, preserving soil fertility.
- Helps in **flood control** by slowing runoff.

d. Example
In **semi-arid regions of Africa**, bunding has increased **crop yields by 25–40%** by improving soil moisture retention (Perennia, 2018).

4. Vegetation Cover: Natural Protection Against Erosion
a. Concept Bunding is a soil and water conservation technique that involves constructing earthen embankments along field edges to control water flow, minimize runoff, and prevent soil erosion. These embankments

act as barriers, slowing down water movement and allowing for greater infiltration, which helps retain soil moisture and sustain crop growth. Bunding is widely practiced in regions prone to erratic rainfall and soil degradation, making it an effective measure for improving agricultural sustainability.

b. Types of Bunds • Contour Bunds: Constructed along the natural contour lines of sloped fields, contour bunds help reduce surface runoff and prevent soil loss by slowing water movement. • Graded Bunds: Designed with a slight gradient, graded bunds channel excess water toward safe drainage outlets, reducing waterlogging and directing runoff in a controlled manner. • Stone Bunds: Built using rocks and stones, these bunds are particularly useful in semi-arid and arid regions where soil erosion and moisture loss are significant concerns. They provide structural stability and long-term protection against soil degradation.

c. Benefits Bunding offers several advantages in improving soil conservation and water management. One of the primary benefits is increased rainwater infiltration, which enhances soil moisture retention and supports crop growth during dry periods. By reducing surface runoff, bunding also prevents nutrient depletion, ensuring that essential minerals remain within the root zone for plant uptake. Additionally, bunds contribute to flood control by slowing down water movement and reducing the impact of heavy rainfall events, thereby protecting agricultural fields from erosion and water damage.

d. Example Bunding has been successfully implemented in various regions worldwide to improve agricultural productivity and soil conservation. In the semi-arid regions of Africa, the adoption of bunding techniques has led to a 25–40% increase in crop yields by enhancing soil moisture retention and reducing erosion (Perennia, 2018). Similar successes have been observed in parts of India, where contour and graded bunding have played a crucial role in sustaining rainfed agriculture by preventing soil degradation and optimizing water use.

5. Conservation Tillage: Enhancing Soil Structure

a. Concept Vegetation cover is a crucial soil conservation technique that involves maintaining plant cover, such as grass, shrubs, or crops, to shield the soil from erosion and degradation. This method plays a significant role in stabilizing soil, reducing both water and wind erosion, and improving soil organic matter content. By protecting the soil surface from direct exposure to rainfall and strong winds, vegetation cover helps maintain soil structure, prevent nutrient loss, and enhance long-term agricultural sustainability.

b. Benefits Implementing vegetation cover provides multiple benefits for soil health and water conservation. One of the key advantages is the reduction of surface runoff, as plant roots and foliage slow down water movement, allowing for better infiltration and minimizing soil loss. Additionally, vegetation cover is highly effective in preventing wind erosion, particularly in dryland farming regions where strong winds can rapidly deplete topsoil. The presence of plant matter also enhances soil organic content, promoting microbial activity and improving soil fertility, which supports healthier crop growth and higher agricultural productivity.

c. Techniques Several techniques are used to establish and maintain effective vegetation cover: • Cover Crops: Leguminous plants such as clover and alfalfa are commonly used as cover crops. These plants not only prevent erosion but also fix atmospheric nitrogen, enriching soil fertility and reducing the need for synthetic fertilizers. • Mulching: Applying organic materials like straw, leaves, or crop residues to the soil surface helps retain moisture, reduce evaporation, suppress weed growth, and enhance soil structure. • Live Fences: Growing shrubs, grasses, or trees as windbreaks can effectively reduce wind velocity, preventing soil displacement in open fields and improving microclimatic conditions for crops.

d. Example The effectiveness of vegetation cover in improving soil health and preventing erosion has been demonstrated in various agricultural regions worldwide. In Brazil's Cerrado region, the introduction of cover crops has led to a 35% increase in soil organic matter, significantly improving soil fertility and productivity (ScienceDirect, 2015). Similar practices in other parts of the world, such as conservation agriculture in Sub-Saharan Africa and agroforestry systems in Southeast Asia, have shown remarkable benefits in sustaining soil health and enhancing agricultural resilience.

6. Agroforestry: Integrating Trees into Agriculture

a. Concept Agroforestry is a sustainable land management practice that integrates trees and shrubs into farming systems to enhance soil conservation and improve overall agricultural productivity. By combining woody perennials with crops and livestock, agroforestry creates a diversified and resilient farming system that provides multiple environmental and economic benefits. This approach is widely recognized for its role in soil erosion control, nutrient cycling, and biodiversity enhancement, making it a key strategy for sustainable agriculture and climate resilience.

b. Benefits Agroforestry offers several advantages in improving soil conservation and farm productivity: • Improves soil stability by reducing runoff and controlling wind and water erosion. The root systems of trees and shrubs help bind soil particles, preventing topsoil loss and maintaining soil structure. • Enhances carbon sequestration, contributing to climate change mitigation by capturing and storing atmospheric carbon in biomass and soil organic matter. • Supports biodiversity by creating habitats for beneficial insects, birds, and microorganisms, promoting ecological balance within agricultural landscapes. • Provides additional income opportunities for farmers through the production of timber, fruits, fodder, medicinal plants, and other valuable products, diversifying farm revenue streams.

c. Example Agroforestry has been successfully implemented in various regions to improve soil health and agricultural productivity. In sub-Saharan Africa, agroforestry practices, such as intercropping nitrogen-fixing trees with staple crops, have led to a 20–50% increase in crop yields while enhancing soil fertility and water retention (SAGENS, 2024). Similar initiatives in South Asia and Latin America have demonstrated long-term benefits in restoring degraded lands, reducing the need for chemical fertilizers, and improving smallholder farmers' livelihoods.

7. Grazing Management: Sustainable Land Use

a. Concept Rotational grazing is a livestock management strategy that involves systematically moving animals between different grazing areas to prevent overgrazing and maintain healthy pasture conditions. By allowing grasslands time to recover between grazing periods, this practice ensures sustained forage availability, maintains soil integrity, and prevents land degradation. Additionally, rotational grazing minimizes soil compaction, which enhances water infiltration and reduces erosion, making it an effective technique for sustainable livestock farming.

b. Benefits Rotational grazing offers several advantages in soil and pasture management: • Enhances forage production by allowing vegetation to regenerate, leading to improved pasture quality and increased soil organic matter. • Promotes better soil moisture retention by reducing surface runoff and allowing deeper root growth, which helps in drought resilience. • Reduces the risks of desertification in arid and semi-arid regions by maintaining vegetative cover and preventing land degradation. • Improves biodiversity in grazing lands by supporting a variety of plant species, which enhances habitat for beneficial insects and wildlife.

c. Example The effectiveness of rotational grazing has been demonstrated in various parts of the world. In Australia, grazing management strategies have significantly reduced soil degradation, improved pasture productivity, and enhanced ecosystem resilience. Studies have shown that properly managed rotational grazing systems can increase grassland biomass, improve soil health, and support long-term agricultural sustainability (SAGENS, 2024).

Conclusion

Implementing soil conservation techniques such as contour farming, terracing, bunding, conservation tillage, agroforestry, and grazing management is crucial for maintaining soil health, improving water retention, and ensuring agricultural sustainability. These methods contribute to enhanced soil structure, increased organic matter content, and better water infiltration, ultimately leading to higher agricultural productivity. Additionally, they help mitigate the adverse effects of climate change by reducing soil erosion, sequestering carbon, and maintaining ecosystem stability.

By adopting these practices, farmers can optimize soil use while preserving natural resources for future generations. Sustainable land management through soil conservation not only reduces environmental degradation but also supports long-term food security and rural livelihoods. Policymakers, researchers, and agricultural stakeholders must work together to promote these techniques and integrate them into modern farming systems to ensure resilient and sustainable agriculture.

5.3 Water Conservation Techniques

Water conservation techniques are essential for ensuring efficient water use in agriculture, improving soil moisture retention, and mitigating the impacts of drought. These strategies help optimize available water resources, enhance crop productivity, and promote sustainable farming practices. Given the growing concerns over water scarcity and climate variability, adopting effective water conservation measures is crucial for long-term agricultural resilience and food security.

a. Rainwater Harvesting

Rainwater harvesting is a crucial water conservation technique that involves collecting and storing rainwater for agricultural, domestic, and industrial use. This method plays a vital role in improving water availability, especially in arid and semi-arid regions where water scarcity is a significant challenge.

Concept

Rainwater harvesting is based on the principle of capturing precipitation before it is lost as runoff. The collected water is stored in various structures and can be used for irrigation, livestock watering, and even drinking purposes after proper treatment.

Techniques of Rainwater Harvesting

1. **Farm Ponds** – Small water reservoirs constructed in agricultural fields to capture and store runoff, ensuring water availability for crops during dry spells.
2. **Check Dams** – Low-height barriers built across seasonal streams to slow down water flow, promote infiltration, and prevent soil erosion.
3. **Percolation Pits** – Small pits or trenches dug in the field to allow rainwater to percolate into the groundwater table, improving water recharge.
4. **Rooftop Rainwater Harvesting** – Collection of rainwater from rooftops of houses, schools, and industrial buildings through a system of pipes and storage tanks for later use.
5. **Contour Trenches** – Shallow ditches dug along the contour lines of a slope to capture and store rainwater, preventing erosion and increasing soil moisture.

Benefits of Rainwater Harvesting

- **Enhances groundwater recharge**, replenishing aquifers and ensuring a sustainable water supply.
- **Reduces dependency on external water sources**, making agriculture more self-sufficient.
- **Minimizes surface runoff and soil erosion**, preserving soil fertility and reducing land degradation.
- **Provides supplementary irrigation**, helping farmers cope with irregular rainfall and prolonged dry spells.
- **Improves water security in drought-prone regions**, ensuring a reliable water source for various needs.

Example

In India's Rajasthan region, check dams and farm ponds have significantly improved groundwater levels, leading to a 30–50% increase in agricultural productivity (IWMI, 2023). Similarly, in African drylands, rooftop rainwater harvesting has helped communities meet their drinking and irrigation needs, reducing water stress and enhancing food security.

Rainwater harvesting is an essential component of sustainable water management, helping mitigate the effects of climate change while ensuring long-term agricultural resilience.

b. Drip Irrigation

Micro-irrigation is an advanced water conservation technique that ensures efficient water delivery directly to plant roots, reducing wastage and optimizing resource utilization. This method is particularly beneficial in arid and semi-arid regions where water scarcity is a major constraint to agricultural productivity.

Concept

Micro-irrigation involves the precise application of water in small quantities at frequent intervals, targeting the root zone of plants rather than the entire field. By delivering water exactly where it is needed, this system minimizes losses due to evaporation, runoff, and deep percolation.

Types of Micro-Irrigation Systems

1. **Drip Irrigation** – A network of pipes and emitters delivers water drop by drop directly to the root zone, ensuring optimal moisture levels.
2. **Sprinkler Irrigation** – Mimics natural rainfall by dispersing water through nozzles at controlled pressure, covering larger areas efficiently.
3. **Subsurface Irrigation** – Buried pipes or tubes deliver water underground, reducing surface evaporation and enhancing root uptake.
4. **Micro-Sprinklers and Foggers** – Used for high-value crops and greenhouses to maintain humidity and prevent excessive soil drying.

Benefits of Micro-Irrigation

- **Improves water-use efficiency by 30–60%** compared to traditional flood irrigation.
- **Reduces evaporation and water loss**, ensuring maximum utilization of available water.
- **Enhances crop yields** by maintaining optimal soil moisture and preventing water stress.

- **Minimizes soil erosion and nutrient leaching**, promoting better soil health.
- **Saves labor and energy costs**, as automated systems require less manual intervention.
- **Ideal for high-value crops** like fruits, vegetables, spices, and medicinal plants, where precise water control is essential.

Example

In Israel, the adoption of drip irrigation has led to a **50% increase in water savings** and a **30% rise in agricultural productivity** (FAO, 2023). Similarly, in India's Maharashtra region, sugarcane farmers using drip irrigation have reduced water consumption by **40% while doubling their yields**.

Micro-irrigation is a game-changer for sustainable agriculture, enabling farmers to produce more with less water while mitigating the impacts of climate change and water scarcity.

c. Mulching

Mulching is a widely used soil and water conservation technique that involves covering the soil surface with organic or synthetic materials to reduce evaporation, retain moisture, and improve soil health. This method plays a crucial role in enhancing crop growth, preventing erosion, and promoting sustainable agriculture.

Concept

Mulching acts as a protective layer over the soil, reducing direct exposure to sunlight, minimizing water loss, and regulating soil temperature. Organic mulches decompose over time, enriching the soil with essential nutrients and improving its structure.

Types of Mulching

1. **Organic Mulches** – Derived from natural materials such as straw, leaves, grass clippings, bark, compost, and crop residues. These materials gradually break down, enhancing soil fertility and microbial activity.
2. **Synthetic Mulches** – Made from plastic films, polyethylene sheets, or geotextiles. These are commonly used in commercial farming to control weeds and optimize water retention.
3. **Living Mulches** – Low-growing cover crops (e.g., clover, vetch) that provide ground cover while enriching the soil with nitrogen.

Benefits of Mulching

- **Reduces evaporation**, helping soil retain up to **25% more moisture** for plant growth.
- **Minimizes soil erosion** by reducing the impact of raindrops and wind on exposed soil.
- **Suppresses weed growth**, decreasing competition for water and nutrients.
- **Enhances soil structure** by increasing organic matter and microbial activity.
- **Regulates soil temperature**, preventing heat stress and frost damage in plants.
- **Improves water infiltration** and reduces surface runoff, ensuring better utilization of available water.

Example

Research in India's semi-arid regions has shown that applying straw mulch can **increase crop yields by 20–30%** while reducing soil moisture loss by **25%** (ICAR, 2023). Similarly, vegetable growers in China using plastic mulch have **boosted water-use efficiency by 40%** while maintaining higher yields (FAO, 2022).

By incorporating mulching into agricultural practices, farmers can significantly improve water conservation, soil health, and overall crop productivity, making it a vital strategy for climate-resilient farming.

d. Conservation Tillage

Concept

Conservation tillage refers to a set of soil management practices that minimize soil disturbance to maintain moisture, preserve organic matter, and enhance soil structure. Unlike conventional tillage, which involves frequent plowing and turning of soil, conservation tillage techniques help reduce erosion, improve water retention, and support sustainable farming systems.

Types of Conservation Tillage

1. **Zero Tillage (No-Till Farming)** – Seeds are directly planted into undisturbed soil with minimal soil disruption. This technique maintains soil structure, reduces compaction, and enhances microbial activity.

2. **Reduced Tillage (Minimum Tillage)** – Limits the intensity and frequency of plowing while leaving crop residues on the field to protect the soil surface.
3. **Strip Tillage** – Involves tilling only narrow strips of soil where seeds are planted, leaving the rest of the field covered with residues.
4. **Mulch Tillage** – Retains crop residues on the soil surface while using specialized equipment to prepare the seedbed with minimal disturbance.

Benefits of Conservation Tillage

- **Improves soil moisture retention**, reducing evaporation and conserving up to **20% more water** compared to conventional tillage.
- **Enhances water infiltration**, allowing rainwater to seep into the soil instead of running off.
- **Reduces soil erosion**, especially in sloped and semi-arid regions.
- **Preserves soil organic matter**, supporting microbial diversity and soil fertility.
- **Reduces fuel and labor costs**, making farming more economically sustainable.
- **Increases carbon sequestration**, helping mitigate climate change effects.

Example

Studies in North America and Europe have shown that conservation tillage can **increase soil water retention by 15–25%** while improving crop yields (FAO, 2022). In India's dryland regions, zero tillage in wheat farming has **boosted productivity by 10–15%** while reducing irrigation needs (ICAR, 2023).

By adopting conservation tillage, farmers can achieve long-term sustainability by enhancing soil resilience, improving water efficiency, and reducing environmental degradation.

e. Agroforestry for Water Management

Concept

Agroforestry is a sustainable land-use system that integrates trees, shrubs, and crops within agricultural landscapes to enhance water conservation, soil health, and overall farm productivity. By combining deep-rooted perennials with seasonal crops, agroforestry improves water availability, minimizes evaporation losses, and enhances soil moisture retention.

How Agroforestry Enhances Water Conservation

1. **Reduces Evaporation** – Tree canopies provide shade, lowering soil surface temperatures and decreasing water loss due to evaporation.
2. **Increases Water Infiltration** – The root systems of trees and shrubs improve soil porosity, allowing rainwater to seep into deeper soil layers rather than running off.
3. **Prevents Runoff and Erosion** – Tree roots stabilize the soil, reducing surface water runoff and preventing erosion in sloped or fragile landscapes.
4. **Enhances Groundwater Recharge** – Deep-rooted species help channel excess water into underground aquifers, improving long-term water availability.
5. **Supports Ecosystem Resilience** – Agroforestry systems contribute to biodiversity, supporting pollinators, beneficial microorganisms, and resilient cropping environments.

Benefits of Agroforestry in Water Conservation

- **Increases soil moisture retention**, reducing irrigation needs in drought-prone areas.
- **Mitigates the effects of climate variability**, ensuring stable agricultural productivity.
- **Improves nutrient cycling**, enhancing soil fertility and organic matter content.
- **Provides additional income sources**, such as timber, fruits, fodder, and medicinal plants.

Example

Research in sub-Saharan Africa has shown that **agroforestry-based farming increases soil moisture levels by 20–40%** compared to conventional monocropping systems (FAO, 2023). In India's semi-arid regions, agroforestry practices, such as integrating leguminous trees with cereal crops, have **boosted soil water retention by up to 30%**, improving overall crop resilience during droughts (ICAR, 2024).

By incorporating agroforestry into agricultural landscapes, farmers can enhance water conservation, improve ecosystem sustainability, and build resilience against climate change.

f. Cover Cropping

Concept

Cover cropping is a sustainable farming practice that involves planting specific crops, such as legumes, grasses, or cereals, to protect the soil and improve water retention. These crops are grown primarily to cover the soil rather than for direct harvest, helping to enhance soil structure, minimize erosion, and increase water infiltration.

How Cover Crops Enhance Water Conservation

1. **Reduce Surface Runoff** – The dense root systems of cover crops hold the soil in place, reducing water runoff and allowing more rainfall to infiltrate the ground.
2. **Improve Soil Moisture Retention** – Organic matter from decaying cover crops enhances soil structure, increasing its water-holding capacity.
3. **Enhance Groundwater Recharge** – By improving infiltration, cover crops facilitate better groundwater recharge, especially in dry regions.
4. **Prevent Soil Erosion** – The protective vegetative cover shields the soil from wind and water erosion, preserving topsoil and nutrients.
5. **Improve Soil Health** – Leguminous cover crops, such as clover and alfalfa, fix nitrogen in the soil, improving fertility while enhancing moisture availability.

Benefits of Cover Crops in Water Conservation

- **Retain up to 30% more soil moisture,** reducing irrigation needs.
- **Prevent nutrient leaching,** ensuring long-term soil fertility.
- **Increase microbial activity,** enhancing soil organic matter decomposition and water absorption.
- **Improve resilience to drought and extreme weather conditions.**

Example

Studies conducted in the **Midwestern United States** have shown that fields planted with cover crops experience **20–40% higher soil moisture retention** compared to bare soil fields (USDA, 2023). In **Brazil's Cerrado region,** farmers using leguminous cover crops have **increased soil organic matter by 35%,** leading to improved water availability and crop productivity (ScienceDirect, 2025).

By integrating cover crops into farming systems, agricultural landscapes become more resilient to drought, improving both water conservation and long-term soil health.

g. Contour Farming and Terracing

Concept

Contour farming and terracing are soil and water conservation techniques that involve modifying the landscape to slow down water runoff, enhance infiltration, and prevent soil erosion. These methods are particularly beneficial in sloped and hilly terrains, where uncontrolled water movement can lead to severe land degradation.

1. **Contour Farming** – Involves plowing and planting along the natural contours of the land, forming ridges that slow down surface runoff and allow more water to infiltrate the soil.
2. **Terracing** – Involves constructing step-like, leveled platforms across slopes to reduce slope steepness and prevent rapid water flow. Each terrace acts as a barrier that retains water and minimizes soil displacement.

How Contour Farming and Terracing Enhance Water Conservation

- **Reduce Surface Runoff** – By following natural land contours, water movement is slowed, preventing soil erosion and water wastage.
- **Increase Water Infiltration** – Slowing down runoff gives water more time to seep into the soil, replenishing groundwater and improving soil moisture retention.
- **Prevent Soil Degradation** – These techniques reduce the risk of gully formation and topsoil loss, maintaining soil productivity.
- **Improve Crop Growth** – Enhanced water availability supports better root development, leading to improved crop yields.

Benefits

- Contour farming can **reduce water runoff by up to 50%**, improving soil moisture levels.
- Terracing has been shown to **increase water retention in sloped areas by 30–60%**, reducing irrigation dependency.

- Helps in **flood control** by directing excess water safely to drainage channels.
- Increases **groundwater recharge**, benefiting both agriculture and drinking water supplies.

Example

In **China's Loess Plateau**, large-scale terracing has restored degraded lands, **increasing crop yields by up to 40%** and reducing soil erosion significantly (FAO, 2024). Similarly, in **the Western Ghats of India**, contour farming has improved soil retention, leading to a **15–25% increase in crop productivity** (Perennia, 2018).

By adopting contour farming and terracing, farmers can significantly enhance water conservation, ensuring sustainable land use and improved agricultural resilience.

Conclusion

Water is a fundamental resource for agriculture, directly influencing crop productivity, soil health, and ecosystem sustainability. However, due to climate change, erratic rainfall patterns, and increasing water demand, the availability of freshwater for irrigation is becoming more limited. Water conservation techniques are essential strategies for ensuring sustainable agricultural production, optimizing available water resources, and reducing the adverse impacts of drought and water scarcity. These techniques focus on improving soil moisture retention, minimizing water wastage, and enhancing groundwater recharge to ensure long-term agricultural resilience.

CHAPTER SIX

WATER HARVESTING TECHNIQUES

Water scarcity is one of the most significant challenges facing global agriculture, particularly in arid and semi-arid regions. Climate change, population growth, and increased water demand have put immense pressure on freshwater resources. According to the **United Nations World Water Development Report (2022)**, nearly **2.3 billion people** live in water-stressed countries, and **over 70% of freshwater withdrawals worldwide** are used for agriculture. Efficient water harvesting techniques play a crucial role in mitigating these challenges by capturing, storing, and utilizing rainwater effectively to enhance agricultural productivity, improve groundwater recharge, and ensure water security.

Agriculture depends heavily on rainfall and irrigation, but **only about 20–30% of global precipitation** effectively contributes to crop production, while the rest is lost through runoff, evaporation, or deep percolation. In regions with erratic rainfall patterns, farmers often struggle with prolonged dry spells, leading to reduced crop yields and food insecurity. **India, for example, receives an annual average rainfall of approximately 1,170 mm, but nearly 50% of it is lost as runoff** (Ministry of Jal Shakti, Government of India, 2023). Similarly, in Africa, where nearly **40% of the continent is classified as arid or semi-arid,** water harvesting techniques are vital for sustainable agricultural development.

Water harvesting techniques refer to methods designed to **collect, store, and manage rainwater for productive use** in agriculture, domestic consumption, and groundwater recharge. These techniques have been used for centuries in various parts of the world, with traditional practices evolving into modern, more efficient systems.

Water harvesting can be categorized into three primary types:

1. **In-situ Water Harvesting** – Techniques that focus on **storing water in the soil** where it falls, improving soil moisture for crops. Examples include contour farming, mulching, and conservation tillage.
2. **Surface Water Harvesting** – Capturing and storing runoff water in **ponds, reservoirs, and tanks** for future use. This includes farm ponds, check dams, and rooftop water harvesting.
3. **Subsurface Water Harvesting** – Enhancing **groundwater recharge** through percolation pits, recharge wells, and subsurface dams.

Water harvesting techniques have shown **significant improvements in water conservation and agricultural productivity** across different regions. Some key statistics include:

- **Rainwater harvesting systems can increase water availability by 35–50% in water-scarce regions** (FAO, 2021).
- **In India, watershed management programs incorporating rainwater harvesting have increased crop yields by 20–50%** (ICAR, 2022).
- **Micro-catchment water harvesting techniques in Africa have improved soil moisture retention, increasing crop yields by 30–60%** (World Bank, 2023).
- **Farm ponds in the United States have contributed to 40% more efficient water use in dryland farming systems** (USDA, 2022).

Benefits of Water Harvesting Techniques

1. **Drought Mitigation:** Ensures water availability during dry periods, reducing dependency on erratic rainfall.
2. **Improved Groundwater Recharge:** Helps replenish aquifers, preventing depletion and ensuring long-term water sustainability.
3. **Soil Conservation:** Reduces soil erosion and nutrient loss by controlling surface runoff.
4. **Enhanced Agricultural Productivity:** Provides supplementary irrigation, leading to **30–50% higher crop yields** in rainfed agriculture.
5. **Climate Resilience:** Helps farmers adapt to **changing rainfall patterns and climate variability** by securing water resources.

Water harvesting techniques are essential for ensuring sustainable water management in agriculture, particularly in regions facing water scarcity. By adopting traditional and modern water harvesting methods, communities can enhance water availability, improve agricultural productivity, and build resilience against climate change. Governments, research institutions, and farmers must collaborate to promote the widespread adoption of these techniques, ensuring **food security and water sustainability for future generations.**

6.1 *Importance of Water Harvesting in Rainfed Agriculture*

Rainfed agriculture is one of the most widespread farming systems globally, playing a crucial role in food security and rural livelihoods. It covers approximately **80% of the world's cultivated land** and contributes nearly **60% of global food production** (FAO, 2023). This sector is especially significant in **developing regions such as Africa, Asia, and Latin America**, where smallholder farmers depend heavily on seasonal rainfall for their crops. Rainfed agriculture supports the livelihoods of over **2.5 billion people**, providing employment, food, and economic stability to rural communities.

Despite its importance, rainfed agriculture is highly **vulnerable to climate variability and water scarcity. Erratic rainfall, prolonged dry spells, and extreme weather events** significantly impact crop productivity, leading to food insecurity and economic instability. Studies show that **rainfall variability can reduce yields by up to 50% in drought-prone areas**, making rainfed systems increasingly unreliable (ICRISAT, 2023). **For example, in India, irregular monsoons have caused a decline in rainfed crop yields by 20–30% in recent years** (ICAR, 2023). Similarly, **in Sub-Saharan Africa, where 95% of agriculture is rainfed, droughts and rainfall fluctuations have led to major food shortages affecting millions** (CGIAR, 2023).

The impacts of climate change are exacerbating these challenges, with rising temperatures, shifting precipitation patterns, and increased frequency of droughts putting further pressure on rainfed farming systems. **Global temperature rise is expected to decrease crop productivity by 10–25% in rainfed regions by 2050 if no adaptive measures are taken** (IPCC, 2023).

To mitigate these risks and ensure sustainable agricultural production, **water harvesting techniques have emerged as essential strategies**. These methods help **capture, store, and efficiently utilize rainwater**, reducing dependency on unpredictable rainfall. Water harvesting improves **soil moisture retention, minimizes runoff losses, and supports supplementary irrigation**, ultimately enhancing agricultural productivity and resilience. **Research has shown that effective water harvesting can increase crop yields by 30–50% in rainfed regions** (World Bank, 2023). Additionally, these techniques contribute to **groundwater recharge, improved soil fertility, and long-term sustainability of farming systems.**

By integrating water harvesting strategies with improved land management practices, farmers can **adapt to climate variability, reduce crop failures, and enhance food security**. Governments, research institutions, and international organizations are increasingly promoting water conservation initiatives to support rainfed agriculture, recognizing its **critical role in feeding a growing global population amid changing climatic conditions.**

The Need for Water Harvesting in Rainfed Farming

Many rainfed regions receive **adequate annual rainfall** for crop cultivation; however, only **10–30% of this water is effectively utilized by crops**, while the remaining portion is lost due to **runoff, deep percolation, or evaporation** (ICAR, 2023). This inefficient water use leads to **frequent crop failures, food insecurity, and land degradation**, particularly in drought-prone areas where rainfall distribution is erratic. The consequences of this inefficiency are severe, contributing to **soil erosion, declining groundwater levels, and reduced agricultural productivity**, which ultimately threaten **rural livelihoods and food security.**

For instance, in **India, nearly 68% of total cultivated land is rainfed**, making it the backbone of the country's **agriculture and food production systems**. This sector contributes approximately **44% of India's total food production**, supplying essential crops such as **pulses, oilseeds, and coarse cereals** (Ministry of Agriculture, 2023). However, **erratic monsoon patterns, delayed rainfall onset, and extended dry spells** have resulted in **yield losses of 20–30%** in major rainfed crops. Similarly, in **Sub-Saharan Africa, 95% of agricultural land relies solely on rainfall**, leaving over **200 million smallholder farmers vulnerable to water scarcity, droughts, and declining soil moisture levels** (CGIAR, 2023). These conditions contribute to **chronic food shortages, economic instability, and environmental**

degradation in the region.

To **mitigate the challenges of water scarcity** and improve agricultural resilience, **water harvesting techniques** have become an essential strategy in rainfed farming. These techniques are designed to **capture, store, and efficiently utilize rainwater** for multiple purposes, including **crop irrigation, livestock watering, and groundwater recharge**. By reducing **runoff losses and improving soil moisture retention**, water harvesting systems enhance **water availability during dry periods**, ensuring **better crop yields, improved soil health, and sustainable water management**. Research indicates that **effective water harvesting techniques can improve rainwater utilization rates by 30–50%**, leading to significant **increases in agricultural productivity** (World Bank, 2023).

Integrating water harvesting practices with **conservation agriculture, agroforestry, and soil moisture management** can further **enhance the efficiency of rainfed farming systems**. Governments, NGOs, and research institutions worldwide are promoting **innovative water conservation technologies** to **strengthen rainfed agriculture**, recognizing its **critical role in feeding a growing global population under changing climate conditions**. By adopting these strategies, farmers can **reduce dependency on erratic rainfall patterns, stabilize crop production, and enhance food security for future generations**.

Key Benefits of Water Harvesting in Rainfed Agriculture

1. Enhancing Soil Moisture for Crop Growth

Rainwater harvesting techniques play a crucial role in **retaining soil moisture**, reducing **water runoff**, and enhancing **crop resilience to dry spells**. Methods such as **mulching, contour bunding, and conservation tillage** have been widely adopted to **improve water infiltration and slow down evaporation losses**, ensuring that crops have access to adequate moisture for a longer duration. These techniques are particularly beneficial in **semi-arid and arid regions**, where rainfall is erratic and soil water retention is a key factor in sustaining agricultural productivity.

Studies conducted by **ICRISAT (2022)** indicate that **soil moisture conservation through rainwater harvesting** can **increase available soil water by 20–40%**, directly influencing crop performance. The improved water availability can lead to a **30–50% increase in crop yields**, making rainwater harvesting a **cost-effective and sustainable strategy for climate-resilient agriculture**. Additionally, **mulching with organic materials** such as straw or crop residues has been shown to **reduce soil evaporation rates** by 25%, further enhancing soil moisture levels.

The success of rainwater harvesting is evident in large-scale implementations, such as in **the Loess Plateau of China**, where **terracing has increased soil moisture by 18% and improved wheat yields by 35%** (World Bank, 2023). Similar interventions in **India's semi-arid tropics** have demonstrated **enhanced groundwater recharge and improved productivity in rainfed cropping systems**. By integrating **rainwater harvesting with soil conservation measures**, farmers can **increase agricultural sustainability**, reduce dependency on external irrigation, and mitigate the adverse effects of droughts and water scarcity.

2. Reducing Dependence on Erratic Rainfall

Water harvesting structures are **critical for storing excess rainwater** and providing **supplementary irrigation** during dry spells. By capturing runoff and directing it to **storage ponds, tanks, or underground reservoirs**, these structures help reduce dependence on erratic rainfall and enable **more consistent crop production. Smallholder farmers in water-scarce regions** benefit significantly from these systems, as they help **stabilize yields and extend cropping seasons**.

In **Maharashtra, India**, the widespread adoption of **farm ponds** has **extended the cropping season by 25–40 days**, allowing farmers to cultivate an **additional short-season crop**, such as vegetables or pulses, even after the monsoon season (ICAR, 2023). These ponds **enhance groundwater recharge**, ensuring **a reliable water source for irrigation** during critical crop growth stages. Similarly, in **Sudan, micro-catchment techniques**, which involve **small-scale water collection systems such as half-moon bunds and infiltration pits**, have **increased sorghum yields by 50%**, even in **low-rainfall years** (FAO, 2023).

The implementation of **check dams and percolation tanks** in **semi-arid regions of India** has also demonstrated **long-term benefits**, including a **15–30% increase in groundwater levels** and improved water availability for **livestock and domestic use**. These systems not only **improve agricultural productivity** but also contribute to **climate resilience and water security** in drought-prone areas.

3. Preventing Soil Erosion and Land Degradation

One of the key benefits of water harvesting techniques is their ability to **reduce surface runoff and prevent soil erosion**, ensuring that rainwater is effectively **absorbed and retained in the soil** rather than lost as runoff. Techniques such as **terracing, check dams, and vegetative cover** slow down water movement, allowing for **greater infiltration and improved soil moisture retention**. These methods are especially critical in **hilly and semi-arid regions**, where **soil erosion poses a major threat to agricultural productivity**.

In **Ethiopia's Tigray region**, the integration of **soil conservation measures** with **water harvesting techniques** has successfully **reduced soil erosion by 50%** and **boosted land productivity by 35%** (World Bank, 2022). This has been achieved through the widespread adoption of **stone bunds, terraces, and check dams**, which **trap sediment and allow water to percolate** into the soil. Farmers in the region have reported **higher crop yields and improved soil fertility** due to the **reduced loss of topsoil**.

Similarly, in **Kenya**, the use of **bunding and agroforestry** has significantly **reduced soil loss from farmlands by 45%**, leading to **better nutrient retention and improved soil structure** (CGIAR, 2023). The planting of **trees and perennial grasses** alongside bunds has further helped **stabilize soil, reduce wind erosion, and increase organic matter content**.

By implementing these **nature-based solutions**, farming communities can **preserve soil fertility, enhance water infiltration, and mitigate the impacts of climate variability**, ultimately ensuring **sustainable agricultural productivity** in rainfed areas.

4. Improving Groundwater Recharge

Rainwater harvesting plays a crucial role in **recharging groundwater levels**, ensuring the availability of **water for both irrigation and drinking purposes** in water-scarce regions. Structures such as **percolation tanks, recharge wells, and check dams** allow rainwater to **infiltrate the soil and replenish underground aquifers**, reducing dependence on rapidly depleting groundwater reserves.

In **Rajasthan, India**, community-led **watershed management programs** have successfully **raised groundwater levels by 1–2 meters annually**, enabling farmers to **expand agricultural activities and improve crop yields** (Central Groundwater Board, 2023). The widespread implementation of **check dams and percolation ponds** has helped **store monsoon rainfall**, ensuring water availability even during **prolonged dry spells**.

Similarly, in **semi-arid regions of Brazil**, the construction of **recharge pits and infiltration trenches** has led to the **restoration of groundwater tables**, making an additional **15,000 hectares of farmland cultivable** (ScienceDirect, 2023). These water conservation efforts have provided **long-term water security** for farmers, enabling **diversification of crops** and increased **agricultural resilience** against climate variability.

By adopting **effective groundwater recharge strategies,** rainfed farming communities can **reduce water scarcity risks, enhance irrigation potential, and ensure sustainable agricultural productivity** even in **drought-prone regions.**

5. Increasing Agricultural Productivity and Farmer Income

Water harvesting techniques play a crucial role in **stabilizing crop yields,** reducing the risk of **crop failure,** and ensuring **food security** in rainfed agricultural systems. By **capturing and efficiently utilizing rainfall,** these techniques help mitigate **seasonal drought stress,** allowing farmers to sustain **higher productivity levels** even in **low-rainfall years.**

In **Burkina Faso,** the implementation of **stone bunding** has led to a **40–60% increase in millet and sorghum yields,** providing a **reliable food supply** for thousands of smallholder farmers (IFPRI, 2023). This technique **slows down runoff, enhances soil moisture retention, and reduces soil erosion,** creating more favorable conditions for crop growth.

Similarly, in **Ethiopia's Rift Valley,** smallholder farmers adopting **water harvesting techniques—such as micro-catchments and farm ponds—**have experienced a **50% rise in farm income** due to **higher crop yields and reduced irrigation costs** (CGIAR, 2023). By securing **greater water availability,** these practices enable **more consistent agricultural output,** reducing farmers' vulnerability to **climate variability and erratic rainfall patterns.**

With **increasing climate uncertainties,** water harvesting remains a **sustainable and cost-effective solution** for **enhancing food production, improving rural livelihoods, and ensuring long-term agricultural resilience** in rainfed regions.

Economic and Social Impact of Water Harvesting

Beyond its **agricultural and environmental advantages,** water harvesting contributes significantly to **economic stability and social well-being.** By ensuring **efficient water use,** these techniques reduce farmers' dependency on **expensive irrigation systems,** improve **drought resilience,** and generate **employment opportunities** in rural communities.

One of the key benefits is **cost savings for farmers.** By enhancing **soil moisture retention,** water harvesting reduces the need for **costly irrigation methods,** helping farmers save **20–30% on irrigation expenses annually** (ICAR, 2023). This financial relief allows smallholder farmers to **invest in better seeds, fertilizers, and farm equipment,** ultimately boosting productivity and profitability.

Additionally, **drought resilience** is significantly improved through water harvesting techniques. In **drought-prone regions**, studies show that **crop failure rates can be reduced by up to 50%**, ensuring **food security** for vulnerable populations (FAO, 2023). By stabilizing water availability, these practices help sustain **consistent crop production**, preventing food shortages and reducing reliance on **government aid and food imports.**

Moreover, large-scale **water conservation projects** create employment opportunities, fostering **economic growth** in rural areas. In **India**, the **Mahatma Gandhi National Rural Employment Guarantee Act (MGNREGA) watershed programs** have provided **jobs for over 2 million people**, supporting **local economies** while improving **water infrastructure** (Ministry of Rural Development, 2023). Similar initiatives in **Africa and Latin America** have enabled **community-led watershed development**, empowering **farmers with skills and resources** to manage water effectively.

By integrating **water harvesting into agricultural planning**, governments and organizations can promote **sustainable farming, economic resilience, and social development**, ensuring **long-term benefits** for both farmers and rural communities.

Conclusion

Water harvesting is a **critical strategy** for enhancing the **sustainability and productivity** of **rainfed agriculture**, particularly in regions vulnerable to **erratic rainfall and water scarcity**. With **80% of global cultivated land** dependent on **rainfed systems** (FAO, 2023), adopting **efficient water conservation techniques** is essential for ensuring **stable crop production** and **food security.**

Techniques such as **farm ponds, check dams, terracing, mulching, and agroforestry** have demonstrated **significant benefits** in improving **soil moisture retention, reducing soil erosion, and securing water sources** for agriculture. Research findings indicate that **integrating water harvesting into farming systems** can lead to **30–50% increases in crop yields**, enhance **groundwater recharge**, and **strengthen climate resilience** (ICRISAT, 2023). In addition to **agricultural benefits**, water conservation techniques also contribute to **economic stability** by reducing **irrigation costs**, creating **rural employment opportunities**, and enhancing **community resilience against climate change-induced water shortages.**

To maximize the **impact of water harvesting**, investment in **water conservation infrastructure** and **farmer training programs** is crucial.

Governments, research institutions, and agricultural organizations must work collaboratively to promote **scalable and locally adapted water harvesting solutions**. By prioritizing **sustainable water management**, the global agricultural sector can move towards a **more resilient, productive, and food-secure future**.

6.2 Types of Water Harvesting Systems

Water harvesting systems are categorized based on their method of collection, storage, and utilization. These systems play a vital role in enhancing water availability for agriculture, groundwater recharge, and domestic use, particularly in rainfed regions where water scarcity is a major challenge. Efficient water harvesting not only ensures a stable water supply but also mitigates the impacts of erratic rainfall, reduces soil erosion, and improves soil moisture retention. Studies indicate that effective water harvesting techniques can enhance water availability by **30–50%**, leading to increased agricultural productivity and resilience against climate change (FAO, 2023). By adopting suitable water harvesting methods, communities can optimize water resources, ensure food security, and promote sustainable livelihoods in water-stressed areas. The major types of water harvesting systems include:

1. In-Situ Water Harvesting

In-situ water harvesting is a crucial technique for optimizing rainwater use in agriculture by capturing and storing moisture directly in the soil. These methods help **reduce runoff, prevent soil erosion, and enhance water infiltration**, ensuring that crops receive adequate moisture during dry periods.

Key Techniques of In-situ Water Harvesting:

1. **Mulching**

   - Involves covering the soil surface with organic materials (such as crop residues, straw, or leaves) or synthetic covers.
   - **Benefits:** Reduces evaporation, regulates soil temperature, suppresses weeds, and improves microbial activity.
   - **Impact:** Studies have shown that mulching can **retain 25% more soil moisture,** leading to increased crop productivity (ICAR, 2023).

2. Contour Bunding

- Involves the construction of small earthen ridges along the natural contour lines of sloping land.
- **Benefits**: Slows down runoff, enhances infiltration, and prevents topsoil loss.
- **Impact**: Research in **semi-arid India** shows that contour bunding has increased soil moisture by **25–40%**, resulting in improved crop yields (ICRISAT, 2023).

3. Conservation Tillage

- Includes reduced tillage, zero tillage, and strip tillage techniques that minimize soil disturbance.
- **Benefits**: Preserves soil structure, enhances water infiltration, reduces erosion, and maintains organic matter.
- **Impact**: Conservation tillage has been found to **increase soil water availability by up to 20%**, improving resilience to drought conditions (FAO, 2023).

These in-situ water harvesting techniques are **cost-effective and easy to implement**, making them particularly valuable for smallholder farmers in water-scarce regions. By integrating these methods into agricultural practices, farmers can **improve water-use efficiency, enhance soil fertility, and ensure long-term sustainability** of their farming systems.

2. Surface Water Harvesting

Ex-situ water harvesting involves **capturing and storing rainwater in man-made structures** such as ponds, tanks, and reservoirs. These systems help **supplement irrigation, recharge groundwater, and mitigate drought effects**, ensuring water availability during dry periods.

Key Types of Ex-situ Water Harvesting Systems:

1. Farm Ponds

- Small, excavated depressions designed to store rainwater for later use in irrigation.
- **Benefits**: Provides a reliable water source during dry spells, enhances crop diversification, and improves farm productivity.

- ◦ **Impact**: In **Maharashtra, India**, farm ponds have **extended the cropping season by 25–40 days**, allowing farmers to cultivate an additional short-season crop (ICAR, 2023).

2. Check Dams

- ◦ Small barriers built across seasonal streams and rivers to slow down water flow and capture runoff.
- ◦ **Benefits**: Enhances groundwater recharge, reduces soil erosion, and maintains stream flow during dry periods.
- ◦ **Impact**: Check dams in **Rajasthan, India**, have increased groundwater levels by **1–2 meters annually**, supporting agricultural expansion (Central Groundwater Board, 2023).

3. Percolation Tanks

- ◦ Large storage structures designed to **hold runoff water and allow slow percolation into the ground**, replenishing aquifers.
- ◦ **Benefits**: Supports well irrigation, increases groundwater availability, and prevents seasonal water shortages.
- ◦ **Impact**: In **semi-arid regions of Brazil**, percolation tanks have **restored groundwater levels, making 15,000 hectares of farmland cultivable again** (ScienceDirect, 2023).

Conclusion

Ex-situ water harvesting systems **play a crucial role in securing water availability** for farmers in rainfed regions. By **capturing excess rainwater, reducing runoff, and improving groundwater recharge**, these techniques enhance agricultural sustainability, **increase resilience to drought, and boost overall farm productivity**.

3. Groundwater Recharge Systems

Groundwater recharge systems focus on **replenishing underground water reserves** by **facilitating the infiltration of rainwater into aquifers**. These methods are essential for maintaining **long-term water security, supporting irrigation, and preventing groundwater depletion**.

Key Types of Groundwater Recharge Systems:

1. Recharge Wells

- Deep wells constructed to **collect rainwater and channel it into underground aquifers** for long-term storage.
- **Benefits**: Improves groundwater availability, supports well irrigation, and prevents over-extraction.
- **Impact**: In **Rajasthan, India**, recharge wells have helped **increase groundwater levels by 1–2 meters annually**, benefiting thousands of farmers (Central Groundwater Board, 2023).

2. Injection Wells

- Artificial recharge structures that **directly pump rainwater into underground reservoirs** using borewells.
- **Benefits**: Enhances aquifer recharge in urban and peri-urban areas, preventing land subsidence and water shortages.
- **Impact**: In **California, USA**, injection wells have helped **restore depleted aquifers**, securing water for agricultural and industrial use (USGS, 2023).

3. Sand Dams

- Low concrete or stone barriers built across seasonal riverbeds that **trap sand and store water beneath the surface.**
- **Benefits**: Reduces evaporation, enhances water availability during dry periods, and supports rural water supply.
- **Impact**: In **Kenya**, sand dams have **increased water storage capacity for over 1 million people**, ensuring water access for farming and household use (CGIAR, 2023).

Conclusion

Groundwater recharge systems **help mitigate water scarcity, restore aquifers, and support sustainable water management**. These techniques are particularly beneficial in **arid and semi-arid regions** where rainfall is seasonal and groundwater depletion is a major concern. By implementing **effective recharge strategies, communities can enhance water security and build resilience against climate change.**

4. Rooftop Rainwater Harvesting (RRWH)

Rooftop rainwater harvesting is a method of **collecting and storing rainwater from building rooftops**, directing it into **storage tanks or**

recharge pits for later use. This technique is particularly effective in **urban and semi-urban areas**, where water demand is high, and groundwater levels are depleting.

Key Types of Rooftop Rainwater Harvesting Systems:

1. **Household Rainwater Storage**

    - **Tanks collect rainwater** from rooftops for domestic use, drinking water (after filtration), and irrigation.
    - **Benefits**: Reduces dependence on municipal water supply, provides a clean water source, and supports home gardening.
    - **Impact**: In **Bangladesh**, rooftop rainwater harvesting has provided safe drinking water to over **1 million people in water-scarce coastal regions** (UNDP, 2023).

2. **Urban Rainwater Harvesting**

    - Large-scale collection of rooftop rainwater for **green spaces, parks, and community irrigation** in cities.
    - **Benefits**: Reduces urban flooding, conserves freshwater, and enhances city greenery.
    - **Impact**: In **Singapore**, urban rainwater harvesting contributes **30% of the city's total water supply**, supporting sustainable water management (PUB, 2023).

3. **Recharge Pits**

    - Excess rooftop rainwater is **channeled into underground recharge pits** to replenish groundwater levels.
    - **Benefits**: Helps mitigate urban water shortages, prevents surface runoff, and improves groundwater availability.
    - **Impact**: In **Chennai, India**, government-mandated rooftop rainwater harvesting has **increased groundwater levels by 50%**, significantly reducing urban water scarcity (World Bank, 2023).

Conclusion

Rooftop rainwater harvesting is a **cost-effective, environmentally friendly** solution for **water conservation, urban flood control, and** groundwater recharge. By **integrating these systems** into **residential, commercial, and public buildings**, cities can **enhance water security and build climate resilience** while **reducing reliance on external water sources**.

5. Micro-Catchment Systems

Micro-catchment water harvesting systems are **small-scale structures** designed to **collect and store rainwater** in localized areas, particularly in **dryland and arid regions**. These systems maximize water use efficiency by **reducing runoff and enhancing soil moisture retention**, ensuring better crop growth and productivity.

Key Types of Micro-Catchment Water Harvesting Systems:

1. **Semi-Circular Bunds**

   - **Crescent-shaped ridges** that trap rainwater around individual plants or trees.
   - **Benefits:** Improves water retention for tree plantations and reduces soil erosion.
   - **Impact:** Used extensively in **Niger** for tree planting, increasing survival rates of seedlings by **75% in arid zones** (FAO, 2023).

2. **Zai Pits**

   - **Small, manually dug pits** that capture rainwater and organic matter, creating a **nutrient-rich environment** for crops.
   - **Benefits:** Enhances moisture availability, particularly for drought-resistant crops like millet and sorghum.
   - **Impact:** In **Burkina Faso**, farmers using Zai pits have seen **millet and sorghum yields increase by 40–60%**, significantly improving food security (IFPRI, 2023).

3. **Trapezoidal Bunds**

   - **Earthen bunds shaped like a trapezoid,** designed to **capture and retain runoff** in small farm plots.
   - **Benefits:** Reduces soil erosion, conserves rainwater, and improves water availability for crops.

- ○ **Impact**: In **Kenya**, trapezoidal bunds have increased **crop survival rates by 50%,** making farming more sustainable in **semi-arid regions** (CGIAR, 2023).

Water harvesting systems play a crucial role in optimizing water resources, particularly in rainfed agricultural regions where rainfall is often erratic and insufficient. By adopting effective water harvesting techniques, farmers can mitigate the risks associated with seasonal water shortages, enhance soil moisture retention, and improve overall crop productivity. These practices help ensure a steady water supply for agricultural activities, reducing dependence on unreliable rainfall patterns and external irrigation sources.

Efficient water harvesting significantly improves agricultural productivity by enabling better moisture availability for crops. Studies indicate that implementing water conservation measures such as farm ponds, check dams, and in-situ moisture conservation can increase crop yields by 30–50% (ICRISAT, 2023). In addition, these techniques help prevent soil degradation by reducing water runoff and erosion, further enhancing the sustainability of farmlands. By integrating multiple water harvesting methods, farmers can optimize their water use and sustain agricultural production even during dry spells.

Water harvesting also enhances resilience to climate variability by reducing the impact of droughts and erratic rainfall patterns. Techniques like mulching, bunding, and groundwater recharge help retain rainwater for extended periods, ensuring crops have sufficient moisture even during prolonged dry conditions. As climate change continues to intensify water scarcity challenges, implementing effective water harvesting strategies becomes even more critical in securing long-term agricultural sustainability.

The selection of appropriate water harvesting systems depends on various factors, including climatic conditions, soil type, and local water demand. While in-situ techniques like conservation tillage and contour bunding are suitable for retaining soil moisture, surface water harvesting structures such as check dams and farm ponds provide essential storage for supplementary irrigation. Groundwater recharge methods like percolation tanks and recharge wells further ensure long-term water security by replenishing underground aquifers.

In conclusion, investing in water harvesting infrastructure, farmer education, and supportive policies is essential for securing water resources and enhancing food security in rainfed agricultural systems. By adopting region-specific water harvesting techniques, communities can strengthen their resilience to climate variability, reduce their reliance on unpredictable rainfall, and achieve sustainable agricultural growth. Implementing a combination of in-situ, surface, groundwater recharge, rooftop, and micro-catchment systems will help farmers maximize water efficiency, ensuring long-term water security for both agricultural and domestic needs.

6.3. *Traditional and Modern Methods of Water Harvesting*

Traditional water harvesting methods have been developed based on local knowledge and experience, ensuring sustainable water use in different regions. These methods are often simple, cost-effective, and environmentally friendly. For instance, **Johads** in India are small earthen embankments built to capture and store rainwater, improving groundwater recharge in arid and semi-arid regions. Similarly, **Zai pits** in West Africa are small, dug-out pits that collect rainwater and improve soil moisture for crops, significantly increasing yields. Another example is the **Ahar-Pyne** system in Bihar, India, which diverts excess monsoon water into storage channels for use during dry periods. Traditional techniques such as **Kunds** in the Thar Desert and **Foggara** in North Africa have allowed communities to survive in water-scarce environments for centuries by effectively collecting and storing rainwater.

Modern water harvesting methods integrate advanced engineering and technology to optimize water collection and storage. These include **micro-irrigation systems** like drip and sprinkler irrigation, which deliver water directly to plant roots, reducing evaporation and improving water-use efficiency by up to 60%. **Check dams** and **percolation tanks** are constructed to capture surface runoff and enhance groundwater recharge. **Rooftop rainwater harvesting** has gained popularity in urban and rural settings, allowing buildings to collect and store rainwater for household and irrigation use. Additionally, **recharge wells** and **injection wells** pump harvested rainwater directly into underground aquifers, ensuring long-term groundwater availability. Advanced methods such as **desalination and wastewater recycling** are now being used in water-scarce regions to provide an additional supply of fresh water.

Both traditional and modern water harvesting methods play a crucial role in sustainable water management. Traditional techniques, deeply rooted in indigenous knowledge, continue to be effective in rural and drought-prone regions, requiring minimal investment and maintenance. In contrast, modern techniques utilize technology to maximize efficiency and scalability but often require higher initial investment and technical expertise. A combined approach that integrates traditional wisdom with modern advancements can offer the most efficient and sustainable solutions for long-term water security, ensuring resilience against climate change and water scarcity challenges.

Traditional Water Harvesting Methods

Traditional and modern water harvesting methods play a crucial role in ensuring sustainable water management by optimizing water collection, storage, and distribution for agricultural, domestic, and industrial use. Traditional methods have been developed based on local knowledge and experience, ensuring cost-effective and environmentally friendly water conservation solutions. These methods have sustained communities for centuries, particularly in arid and semi-arid regions.

Traditional techniques include **Johads** (small earthen embankments in India) that capture rainwater to recharge groundwater, **Zing** (glacier water harvesting systems in Ladakh) that channel meltwater into storage ponds, and **Ahar-Pyne** (an ancient floodwater harvesting system in Bihar) that diverts monsoon water into storage channels for dry season use. Other notable traditional methods include **Zai Pits** in West Africa, which improve soil moisture retention; **Foggara** in North Africa, underground tunnels for water transportation; and **Kunds** in the Thar Desert, circular underground tanks that store rainwater for drinking and irrigation. These traditional approaches remain effective in mitigating water scarcity, particularly in drought-prone regions.

Modern water harvesting methods integrate advanced engineering and technology to enhance efficiency and ensure long-term water availability. **Check dams** are constructed across seasonal streams to slow runoff, increasing percolation and groundwater recharge. **Percolation tanks** allow water to seep into the ground, replenishing aquifers, while **rooftop rainwater harvesting** collects rainwater from rooftops and directs it into storage tanks or recharge wells. **Recharge wells and injection wells** further enhance groundwater replenishment by directly channeling harvested rainwater into underground aquifers.

In addition to these storage techniques, modern irrigation methods such as **drip and sprinkler irrigation** significantly improve water-use efficiency, reducing wastage by 30–60% compared to conventional irrigation. **Micro-catchment systems** are designed to capture and store rainwater in small depressions, improving water availability in dryland farming systems. Furthermore, advanced technologies like **desalination and wastewater recycling** help convert seawater into freshwater and repurpose wastewater for irrigation and industrial use in water-scarce regions.

By integrating both traditional wisdom and modern innovations, water harvesting can be optimized to ensure sustainable water management. Implementing a combination of these approaches helps address water scarcity challenges, enhance agricultural productivity, and build climate-resilient farming systems, ensuring water security for present and future generations.

Top of Form

Bottom of Form

Modern Water Harvesting Methods

Modern water harvesting methods integrate advanced engineering, technology, and improved management practices to optimize water collection, storage, and utilization. These techniques enhance water efficiency, reduce wastage, and ensure long-term water availability, particularly in regions facing water scarcity due to climate change and population growth.

Micro-Irrigation Systems such as drip and sprinkler irrigation deliver water directly to plant roots, significantly reducing evaporation and improving water-use efficiency by up to 60%. These systems help conserve water while enhancing crop yields, making them ideal for arid and semi-arid regions.

Percolation Tanks are large artificial reservoirs designed to enhance groundwater recharge by allowing rainwater to slowly percolate into underground aquifers. These tanks play a crucial role in replenishing groundwater levels, supporting both agriculture and drinking water supplies in dry regions.

Check Dams are small concrete or stone barriers built across seasonal streams to capture runoff, slow down water flow, and increase groundwater recharge. These structures prevent soil erosion and help maintain water availability for agriculture and livestock.

Roof Rainwater Harvesting is a widely adopted method in both urban and rural areas, where rainwater from rooftops is collected and stored in tanks for domestic use or directed into recharge pits to replenish groundwater. This technique reduces dependency on external water sources and improves water security.

Recharge Wells and Injection Wells are deep wells used to directly inject harvested rainwater into underground aquifers, improving groundwater availability. These structures are essential in regions experiencing rapid groundwater depletion due to over-extraction for agriculture and industry.

Desalination and Water Recycling are advanced technologies used in water-scarce regions to convert seawater into freshwater and treat wastewater for reuse. Desalination plants provide an alternative source of freshwater, while wastewater recycling ensures efficient water utilization in agriculture and industrial applications.

By implementing a combination of these modern water harvesting methods, communities can enhance water security, improve agricultural sustainability, and mitigate the effects of drought and climate change.

Conclusion

Both traditional and modern water harvesting methods play a crucial role in ensuring sustainable water management by conserving, storing, and efficiently utilizing rainwater. Traditional techniques, deeply rooted in indigenous knowledge, have been practiced for centuries and remain effective in rural and drought-prone regions. Methods such as **Johads** in India, **Zing irrigation** in Ladakh, **Ahar-Pyne** systems in Bihar, **Zai pits** in West Africa, and **Foggara** systems in North Africa demonstrate how communities have historically adapted to water scarcity using locally available resources and simple, cost-effective structures. These methods are environmentally friendly, promote groundwater recharge, and ensure long-term water availability for agriculture and domestic use.

In contrast, modern water harvesting methods incorporate advanced technology and engineering solutions to enhance water conservation and agricultural productivity. Techniques like **drip and sprinkler irrigation** improve water-use efficiency, while **percolation tanks, check dams, and recharge wells** facilitate groundwater replenishment. **Rooftop rainwater harvesting** has been widely implemented in urban and rural areas to store and utilize rainwater efficiently. Furthermore, **desalination and wastewater recycling** provide innovative solutions to address water scarcity in highly water-stressed regions.

A combined approach that integrates traditional wisdom with modern advancements can offer the most efficient and sustainable solutions for long-term water security. By leveraging the strengths of both systems, communities can enhance water availability, improve agricultural resilience, and mitigate the impacts of climate change. Governments, policymakers, and farmers must work together to promote these integrated water management strategies, ensuring the sustainability of water resources for future generations.

Bottom of Form

Recent Innovations in Water Harvesting Technology

With increasing water scarcity due to climate change and population growth, innovative water harvesting technologies are emerging to optimize water conservation, storage, and utilization. These advancements integrate modern science with sustainable practices to enhance efficiency in agriculture, urban water management, and environmental conservation.

1. Fog Harvesting Technology

Fog harvesting involves collecting water droplets from fog using specialized mesh nets. This technique is particularly useful in arid and coastal regions where fog is frequent but rainfall is limited.

? **Example:** The **FogNet Project** in Chile and Peru has successfully captured fog water, providing potable water to local communities.

2. Atmospheric Water Generators (AWGs)

AWGs extract moisture from the air and convert it into liquid water using condensation techniques. These systems can operate in humid regions and are powered by solar energy, making them sustainable.

? **Example:** The **WaterSeer device** can generate up to 37 liters of potable water per day using wind and solar energy.

3. Smart Rainwater Harvesting Systems

These systems use IoT (Internet of Things) and AI-driven sensors to monitor rainfall, water levels, and soil moisture in real-time. They optimize rainwater collection, distribution, and usage.

? **Example:RainMachine** is an AI-based irrigation controller that uses weather forecasts to optimize rainwater usage in farming.

4. 3D-Printed Water Harvesting Structures

3D printing is being used to design advanced water collection structures with optimized shapes for better rain capture and infiltration.

? **Example:** Scientists at MIT have developed **3D-printed fog-harvesting**

structures with improved water collection efficiency.

5. Underground Rainwater Storage Systems

Unlike traditional open ponds, underground storage prevents evaporation and contamination. Advanced underground reservoirs help store and distribute rainwater efficiently.

? **Example:Modular underground water tanks** in Singapore are used to store and supply rainwater for irrigation and domestic use.

6. Desalination and Solar-Powered Water Purification

Innovations in desalination technology, such as **solar desalination and nanofiltration membranes,** have improved freshwater availability in coastal and arid regions.

? **Example:Graphene-based desalination membranes** have increased water filtration efficiency while reducing energy consumption.

7. Micro-Catchment Water Harvesting

Modern micro-catchment techniques involve landscape modifications to maximize rainwater infiltration and minimize runoff. These include precision-designed **semi-circular bunds and bio-swales** for dryland farming.

? **Example:** In **Kenya**, micro-catchments have increased soil moisture by up to 40%, improving crop yields in drylands.

8. Hydrogel-Based Water Retention Technology

Hydrogels are superabsorbent polymers that can retain water and release it slowly to crops. These are used in rainfed agriculture to enhance soil moisture retention.

? **Example:Biodegradable hydrogels** are being tested in India and Brazil to improve crop yields in drought-prone areas.

These recent innovations in water harvesting technology demonstrate how advanced scientific solutions are addressing global water challenges. Widespread adoption of these techniques can improve water security, agricultural productivity, and climate resilience.

CHAPTER SEVEN

EFFICIENT WATER UTILIZATION TECHNIQUES

Water is a fundamental resource for agriculture, industry, and daily human activities. However, increasing water scarcity due to population growth, climate change, and inefficient water management poses a significant challenge to global water security. According to the **United Nations (2023)**, nearly **2.3 billion people** live in water-stressed regions, and by 2050, global water demand is expected to increase by **55%**. In agriculture alone, irrigation accounts for nearly **70% of freshwater withdrawals**, yet much of this water is lost due to inefficient practices such as surface runoff, evaporation, and poor irrigation methods.

Efficient water utilization techniques aim to maximize water productivity while minimizing wastage, ensuring that available water resources are used sustainably. These techniques include **precision irrigation, rainwater harvesting, soil moisture conservation, wastewater recycling**, and **smart water management systems** powered by **IoT and AI**. Advanced methods such as **desalination and water purification** further provide alternative water sources, particularly in arid and water-scarce regions.

By implementing **modern water conservation technologies** alongside **traditional knowledge-based practices**, communities can improve agricultural productivity, enhance groundwater recharge, and build resilience against climate variability. The adoption of efficient water utilization techniques is not just an environmental necessity but also an economic and social imperative to ensure long-term food security and sustainable development worldwide.

7.1 Soil Management Practices for Water Conservation

Soil plays a fundamental role in water conservation, serving as a natural reservoir that regulates water retention, infiltration, and availability for plant growth. Healthy soils with good structure and organic matter content enhance moisture storage, reducing the need for frequent irrigation and ensuring long-term agricultural sustainability. However, soil degradation—caused by erosion, excessive tillage, deforestation, and unsustainable farming practices—has significantly reduced soil water-holding capacity in many regions. According to the **Food and Agriculture Organization (FAO, 2023)**, nearly **33% of the world's agricultural land** is affected by soil degradation, leading to increased surface runoff, reduced infiltration, and heightened vulnerability to droughts.

In water-scarce areas, effective soil management practices such as conservation tillage, mulching, agroforestry, and cover cropping have been proven to improve soil moisture retention and reduce water loss. Studies indicate that implementing these techniques can enhance water-use efficiency by **20–40%**, ensuring crops receive adequate moisture even during dry spells. Additionally, soil organic matter plays a crucial role in water retention, with research showing that a **1% increase in soil organic carbon can boost soil water-holding capacity by up to 20,000 gallons per acre** (NRCS, 2023). By adopting soil conservation strategies, farmers can minimize dependency on external water sources, improve crop resilience to erratic rainfall patterns, and mitigate the adverse impacts of climate change on agriculture.

Investing in soil health not only benefits water conservation but also enhances soil fertility, promotes biodiversity, and supports long-term agricultural productivity. Governments and agricultural organizations worldwide are increasingly advocating for soil conservation measures as a cost-effective strategy to address water scarcity challenges. By integrating traditional knowledge with modern innovations, sustainable soil management can contribute to global food security while preserving water resources for future generations.

Key Soil Management Practices for Water Conservation

1. Mulching

Mulching is an effective soil management practice that involves applying a protective layer of organic or synthetic materials over the soil surface to reduce evaporation and enhance moisture retention. Organic mulches, such as **straw, leaves, crop residues, and compost**, decompose over time, improving soil structure and fertility. Synthetic mulches, like **plastic films**, are commonly used in commercial agriculture to conserve water and suppress weeds.

One of the key benefits of mulching is its ability to **regulate soil temperature**, keeping it cooler during hot weather and warmer during cold conditions. This creates a more favorable environment for root growth and microbial activity, which in turn enhances nutrient cycling and soil health. Additionally, mulching acts as a **barrier against weed growth**, reducing competition for water and nutrients. This is particularly beneficial in rainfed farming systems, where moisture conservation is critical for crop productivity.

Scientific studies have shown that mulching can significantly **increase soil moisture by 25–30%**, reducing the need for frequent irrigation. According to research by **ICRISAT (2023)**, farmers practicing mulching have observed **higher crop yields**, particularly in drought-prone areas. For instance, in semi-arid regions of India, mulching has led to a **20–40% increase in maize and wheat yields** due to improved soil moisture retention.

In addition to its water-saving benefits, mulching also **prevents soil erosion** by protecting the soil from direct impact of raindrops and reducing surface runoff. Over time, organic mulches enrich the soil with essential nutrients, fostering better root development and overall plant health. Given its multiple advantages, mulching is widely recommended as a simple yet highly effective technique for improving water efficiency and ensuring sustainable agricultural production.

2.Conservation Tillage

Conservation tillage is a sustainable soil management practice that minimizes soil disturbance to maintain its natural structure, enhance water retention, and reduce erosion. Techniques such as **zero-tillage, minimum tillage, and strip tillage** help preserve organic matter, improve soil health, and sustain moisture levels, making them particularly beneficial in **dryland farming systems** where water scarcity is a major challenge.

One of the primary benefits of conservation tillage is its ability to **enhance water infiltration and reduce surface runoff**. By avoiding excessive plowing, the soil retains its natural porosity, allowing rainwater to penetrate deeper and be stored in the root zone rather than being lost as runoff. Studies indicate that conservation tillage can **conserve up to 20% more water** compared to conventional tillage, making it an effective strategy for improving water efficiency in agriculture.

Additionally, conservation tillage helps in **preventing soil erosion** by maintaining a protective layer of crop residues on the surface. These residues act as a barrier against wind and water erosion, reducing the loss of topsoil and essential nutrients. This is particularly important in regions prone to **desertification and land degradation**, where soil conservation is critical for sustaining agricultural productivity.

Moreover, by preserving soil structure and organic matter, conservation tillage **enhances microbial activity and improves soil fertility**. Organic matter plays a key role in **water-holding capacity**, allowing crops to withstand dry spells and reducing dependency on irrigation. Research conducted by **ICRISAT (2023)** has shown that in semi-arid regions, farmers practicing zero-tillage have reported **higher crop yields and improved drought resilience** compared to conventional plowing methods.

Given its multiple benefits, conservation tillage is widely adopted in **rainfed and dryland agriculture** as a cost-effective and eco-friendly method to sustain soil moisture levels, reduce labor costs, and promote long-term agricultural sustainability.

3. Cover Cropping

Cover cropping is an effective soil management practice that involves **growing specific crops, such as legumes, grasses, or green manures**, to protect and improve soil health. These crops serve as a natural barrier against erosion, **reduce surface runoff**, and **enhance water retention**, making them an essential strategy for sustainable water management in agriculture.

One of the key benefits of cover crops is their ability to **improve soil structure and organic matter content**. As they grow, their root systems **bind soil particles together**, reducing compaction and increasing soil porosity. This facilitates better **water infiltration** and absorption, ensuring that rainwater is effectively stored in the soil rather than lost as runoff.

Studies by **FAO (2023)** indicate that cover cropping can **increase soil organic matter**, leading to **higher water-holding capacity** and improved drought resistance.

Cover crops also play a vital role in **enhancing soil fertility**, particularly when leguminous plants such as **clover, alfalfa, and vetch** are used. These plants **fix atmospheric nitrogen** through symbiotic relationships with soil bacteria, enriching the soil with essential nutrients and reducing the need for chemical fertilizers. This not only lowers production costs but also promotes **long-term soil health and sustainability**.

Furthermore, cover crops act as a **protective mulch** when left on the soil surface after termination. They suppress weed growth, **reduce evaporation**, and **moderate soil temperature**, creating a favorable microclimate for crop growth. In addition, they help in **carbon sequestration**, mitigating the effects of climate change while supporting soil biodiversity.

Research has shown that cover cropping can **reduce soil erosion by up to 50% and increase water retention capacity by 30%** in rainfed agricultural systems. This makes it particularly beneficial for **semi-arid and drought-prone regions**, where efficient water management is critical for sustaining crop yields. By integrating cover crops into crop rotation systems, farmers can **conserve water, enhance soil fertility, and improve agricultural resilience** against climate variability.

4. Contour Farming and Terracing

Contour farming and terracing are **effective land management techniques** designed to conserve water, reduce soil erosion, and enhance infiltration. These methods involve **aligning farming activities with the natural topography** of the land to slow down water movement, allowing more moisture to penetrate the soil. They are particularly beneficial in **hilly and sloped terrains**, where uncontrolled runoff can lead to significant soil degradation.

In **contour farming**, crops are planted along the natural contours of the land, creating **small ridges and furrows** that act as barriers to slow down water flow. This prevents **rapid runoff**, allowing water to seep gradually into the soil, improving **moisture retention** and reducing the risk of soil erosion. By reducing **surface runoff by up to 30–50%**, contour farming helps in **groundwater recharge** and ensures better water availability for crops, especially in rainfed agricultural systems **(World Bank, 2023)**.

Terracing takes this concept a step further by **constructing stepped levels along slopes**, effectively creating flat areas that hold water and prevent soil displacement. Each terrace acts as a **mini reservoir**, capturing rainwater and allowing it to infiltrate the soil rather than washing away valuable topsoil. Terracing has been shown to **increase soil moisture by 20–40%**, leading to higher crop yields and improved farm productivity in steep landscapes. For example, in the **Loess Plateau of China**, terracing has resulted in an **18% increase in soil moisture levels and a 35% improvement in wheat yields (World Bank, 2023)**.

In addition to preventing soil erosion, contour farming and terracing also support **sustainable land use** by maintaining soil fertility, reducing the need for artificial irrigation, and **enhancing ecosystem stability**. These methods are particularly valuable in **climate-vulnerable regions**, where erratic rainfall patterns threaten agricultural productivity. By implementing contour farming and terracing, farmers can **optimize water use efficiency**, protect their land from degradation, and improve long-term sustainability in food production.

5. Organic Matter Addition

ncorporating **organic matter** into the soil is a highly effective strategy for **improving water retention, enhancing soil structure, and increasing nutrient availability**. Organic amendments such as **compost, farmyard manure, and biochar** help in **building soil health**, making agricultural systems more resilient to drought and water scarcity.

Soils with **higher organic matter content** have **better water-holding capacity** because organic materials act like sponges, absorbing and retaining moisture for extended periods. **Compost and farmyard manure** improve soil **porosity and aggregation**, reducing **compaction and enhancing infiltration rates**. This ensures that rainfall or irrigation water penetrates deeply into the soil, **minimizing runoff and evaporation losses**. According to studies, **soils rich in organic matter can hold 20–30% more water** than degraded soils, making them more drought-resistant and productive.

Biochar, a carbon-rich material produced from biomass pyrolysis, has gained attention as a **sustainable soil amendment** due to its ability to enhance **soil moisture retention and nutrient availability**. It improves soil aeration, reduces leaching losses, and provides a stable environment for beneficial microbial activity. Research has shown that **biochar application**

can increase **soil water retention by 15–25%**, particularly in sandy and degraded soils, making it a valuable tool for water conservation in arid and semi-arid regions.

Additionally, organic matter contributes to **carbon sequestration,** helping mitigate **climate change impacts** while promoting **soil biodiversity and long-term soil fertility.** By integrating organic matter into farming systems, farmers can **improve crop resilience, reduce dependency on synthetic inputs, and ensure sustainable water management**, leading to **higher yields and improved agricultural productivity.**

6. Agroforestry

Agroforestry, the practice of integrating **trees, shrubs, and crops** into farming systems, plays a crucial role in **enhancing soil stability, reducing water loss, and improving overall ecosystem resilience**. This approach not only contributes to **soil moisture conservation** but also aids in **reducing soil erosion, improving groundwater recharge, and enhancing biodiversity.**

The deep root systems of trees and shrubs help **increase water infiltration rates**, reducing **surface runoff and soil erosion**. By allowing rainwater to penetrate deeper into the soil, agroforestry contributes to **groundwater recharge**, ensuring long-term water availability for crops. The presence of vegetation also **shields the soil from direct sunlight**, reducing **evaporation losses** and maintaining **cooler soil temperatures**, which further helps in **retaining moisture.**

Research indicates that **agroforestry systems can improve soil moisture levels by 15–35% in semi-arid regions** (CGIAR, 2023). This is particularly beneficial in drought-prone areas, where water availability is a limiting factor for crop production. For instance, **alley cropping**, where trees are planted in rows with crops grown in between, has been shown to **enhance soil fertility, increase organic matter content, and improve overall water-use efficiency.**

Additionally, trees in agroforestry systems contribute to **carbon sequestration, microclimate regulation, and biodiversity conservation**, making them a **sustainable solution for climate-resilient agriculture**. Incorporating **leguminous trees** (e.g., Gliricidia, Sesbania) further improves soil fertility by **fixing atmospheric nitrogen**, reducing the need for chemical fertilizers and enhancing overall productivity.

By adopting agroforestry, farmers can **reduce dependence on external irrigation, improve soil structure,** and **ensure long-term water conservation,** leading to **higher crop yields, economic benefits, and environmental sustainability.**

Conclusion

Soil management is a fundamental component of sustainable water conservation strategies, playing a critical role in maintaining agricultural productivity, improving water-use efficiency, and mitigating the adverse effects of climate change. By implementing practices such as **mulching, conservation tillage, cover cropping, contour farming, organic amendments, and agroforestry,** farmers can significantly **enhance soil moisture retention, reduce surface runoff, prevent erosion, and improve soil structure.** These methods not only help in **storing rainwater more effectively** but also contribute to **groundwater recharge and the restoration of degraded lands.**

Moreover, integrating **traditional soil conservation methods with modern innovations** ensures long-term sustainability, making agricultural systems more **resilient to erratic rainfall patterns and prolonged droughts.** Healthy soils rich in **organic matter** act as **carbon sinks, reducing greenhouse gas emissions** while simultaneously **supporting biodiversity and improving soil fertility.** Additionally, sustainable soil management promotes **nutrient cycling, enhances microbial activity, and increases soil aeration,** leading to **higher crop yields and improved food security.**

In the face of **increasing climate uncertainties,** adopting soil conservation strategies is essential for securing water resources, ensuring ecosystem stability, and safeguarding livelihoods, particularly in **water-scarce and drought-prone regions.** A holistic approach that combines **scientific advancements with indigenous knowledge** can help farmers **adapt to changing environmental conditions, optimize resource utilization, and promote sustainable agricultural development** on a global scale.

7.2 Crop Management Practices for Efficient Water Use

With the growing challenges of water scarcity worldwide, implementing efficient crop management strategies has become crucial for optimizing water use, sustaining agricultural productivity, and ensuring long-term food security. The increasing demand for agricultural products, coupled with climate change and erratic rainfall patterns, has intensified pressure on water resources, making it essential for farmers to adopt practices that maximize water efficiency. Efficient crop management plays a significant role in reducing water loss, improving soil moisture retention, and ensuring stable crop yields, even in regions facing prolonged dry spells.

To address these challenges, researchers and agricultural experts have developed various innovative techniques aimed at enhancing water-use efficiency while maintaining or even increasing productivity. These include the adoption of drought-resistant crop varieties, optimized planting techniques that align with rainfall patterns, the use of mulching to reduce evaporation, and intercropping systems that improve soil health and moisture conservation. Additionally, precision irrigation methods such as drip and sprinkler irrigation help deliver water directly to plant roots, minimizing wastage and improving water-use efficiency. Soil amendments, including organic matter and biochar, further enhance the soil's capacity to retain moisture, making crops more resilient to drought conditions.

By integrating these research-backed strategies into farming systems, farmers can significantly reduce their reliance on excessive irrigation while improving overall crop performance. These practices not only help in conserving water but also contribute to climate-resilient and sustainable agricultural systems. As global water availability continues to decline, adopting such approaches will be essential in mitigating the impacts of water scarcity, securing food production, and promoting environmental sustainability.

1. Selecting Drought-Resistant and Water-Efficient Crops

Selecting crop varieties with low water requirements and high drought tolerance is a crucial strategy for improving water-use efficiency in agriculture, particularly in regions facing frequent water shortages. Advances in crop breeding programs have led to the development of high-yielding varieties of staple crops such as maize, wheat, rice, and sorghum that can thrive with up to 40% less water compared to conventional varieties. These improved crops ensure stable productivity even under water-limited conditions, reducing dependence on irrigation and making agriculture more resilient to climate variability.

Short-duration crops and deep-rooted plant species are particularly advantageous in rainfed agricultural systems. Short-duration varieties complete their life cycle in a shorter period, reducing the overall water demand, while deep-rooted crops can access moisture from deeper soil layers, enabling them to survive extended dry spells. This makes them highly suitable for regions with erratic rainfall patterns.

Studies have demonstrated that integrating drought-resistant crop varieties into farming systems can lead to significant improvements in yield stability. In areas with limited water availability, these resilient crops have been shown to boost yields by as much as 35%, providing food security and economic benefits for farmers. By adopting these climate-smart crop choices, agricultural systems can become more sustainable, reducing vulnerability to drought and optimizing water resources for long-term productivity.

2. Optimized Sowing and Planting Techniques

Implementing effective planting strategies plays a critical role in conserving soil moisture and minimizing water loss in agricultural systems. One of the most important approaches is adjusting planting schedules to align with local rainfall patterns. By timing crop establishment to coincide with periods of higher soil moisture availability, farmers can reduce their reliance on supplemental irrigation and optimize water use for plant growth. This practice is particularly beneficial in rainfed farming, where unpredictable rainfall can significantly impact yields.

Innovative planting techniques such as raised-bed planting and paired-row sowing further enhance water-use efficiency by improving root access to moisture. Raised-bed planting involves growing crops on slightly elevated soil beds, which facilitates better drainage, reduces waterlogging, and improves root aeration. Paired-row sowing, on the other hand, optimizes space utilization and increases root-zone moisture availability, enabling plants to access stored soil water more efficiently. Research indicates that these methods can reduce irrigation water requirements by up to 30%, making them valuable tools for sustainable crop production in water-scarce regions.

By adopting strategic planting methods, farmers can improve water retention in the soil, enhance root development, and ensure more efficient use of available water resources, ultimately leading to higher productivity and resilience to climate variability.

3. Mulching for Soil Moisture Conservation

Mulching is a widely adopted soil management practice that plays a crucial role in conserving moisture, regulating soil temperature, and suppressing weed growth. By applying organic materials such as straw, leaves, and crop residues to the soil surface, farmers can significantly reduce evaporation and enhance soil water retention. This is particularly beneficial in arid and semi-arid regions, where water availability is a major constraint to crop production.

Research indicates that mulching can improve soil moisture levels by 25–30%, providing plants with a more stable water supply, especially during dry spells. Organic mulch not only conserves water but also enriches the soil with organic matter as it decomposes, promoting microbial activity and improving soil structure. Additionally, using crop residues as mulch has been shown to reduce evaporation losses by up to 40%, further contributing to overall water conservation efforts.

By integrating mulching into crop management practices, farmers can enhance soil health, increase water-use efficiency, and sustain higher crop yields while reducing dependence on irrigation. This makes mulching a vital strategy for improving agricultural sustainability in water-limited environments.

4. Efficient Water Management in Rice Cultivation

Alternate Wetting and Drying (AWD) is an effective water-saving technique in rice cultivation that involves intermittent irrigation, allowing the soil to dry between watering cycles before re-irrigation. This method optimizes water use by reducing excessive flooding, which is traditionally practiced in paddy fields.

Studies have shown that AWD can decrease water consumption by approximately 30% without negatively impacting rice yields. By controlling water application, farmers can improve root development, enhance nutrient uptake, and reduce unnecessary water loss through seepage and evaporation. Additionally, AWD has significant environmental benefits, as it lowers methane emissions from rice fields. Continuous flooding in conventional rice farming creates anaerobic conditions that promote methane production, whereas periodic drying disrupts these conditions, reducing greenhouse gas emissions.

As a climate-smart agricultural practice, AWD not only conserves water but also contributes to sustainable rice production by improving water-use efficiency and reducing the environmental footprint of rice farming. Widespread adoption of AWD can help address water scarcity while ensuring food security and climate resilience in rice-growing regions.

5. Intercropping and Crop Rotation for Better Water Utilization

Intercropping and crop rotation are effective agronomic strategies that optimize water use, enhance soil fertility, and improve overall crop resilience to water stress. By growing multiple crops together or alternating crops in a given field, farmers can maximize resource utilization while minimizing soil degradation and water loss.

Legume-based intercropping systems, such as maize-pigeon pea or sorghum-cowpea combinations, have demonstrated significant improvements in water-use efficiency—up to 35% in some cases. Legumes contribute to nitrogen fixation, reducing the need for synthetic fertilizers while enhancing soil organic matter and moisture retention. Additionally, diversified root structures in intercropped systems promote efficient water uptake, leading to reduced evaporation and improved soil health.

Crop rotation also plays a crucial role in sustainable water management. Alternating deep-rooted and shallow-rooted crops prevents excessive depletion of soil moisture, allowing for better water retention over time. Rotational cropping can disrupt pest cycles, reduce disease incidence, and enhance soil structure, further contributing to sustainable agricultural productivity.

By integrating intercropping and crop rotation into farming systems, producers can optimize limited water resources, improve yield stability, and enhance climate resilience, making these practices essential for long-term food security.

6. Precision Irrigation and Deficit Irrigation Strategies

Optimizing irrigation techniques is crucial for enhancing water efficiency in agriculture while maintaining crop productivity. Traditional irrigation methods, such as flood irrigation, often lead to excessive water loss through evaporation, runoff, and deep percolation. In contrast, modern irrigation strategies focus on delivering water more precisely to where it is needed, reducing wastage and improving soil moisture availability.

Deficit irrigation is one such approach that involves applying water at critical growth stages while limiting it at less sensitive phases. Research has shown that this method can reduce total water use by up to 40% without significantly affecting crop yields. This strategy is particularly effective for drought-tolerant crops, which can adapt to temporary water stress without major productivity losses.

Drip and sprinkler irrigation systems further enhance water-use efficiency by delivering water directly to plant roots in controlled amounts. Drip irrigation, in particular, reduces evaporation and deep percolation losses, increasing efficiency by up to 60% compared to traditional methods. Additionally, sprinkler systems distribute water more uniformly across the field, ensuring optimal moisture levels for plant growth.

By integrating these advanced irrigation techniques, farmers can significantly conserve water resources while sustaining agricultural productivity, making these methods essential for adapting to increasing water scarcity and climate change challenges.

7. Soil Amendments for Improved Water Retention

Enhancing soil properties through organic and inorganic amendments is a crucial strategy for improving water retention and ensuring sustainable crop production, especially in water-scarce regions. Organic amendments such as compost, farmyard manure, and crop residues contribute to the formation of stable soil aggregates, which enhance soil porosity and water-holding capacity. These materials also improve microbial activity, further supporting soil health and nutrient availability.

Biochar, a carbon-rich material derived from biomass pyrolysis, has gained significant attention for its ability to enhance soil moisture retention. Studies suggest that biochar application can increase soil water-holding capacity by up to 18%, reducing the frequency and intensity of drought stress on crops. Additionally, biochar improves soil aeration and nutrient retention, leading to better root development and overall plant resilience.

Inorganic amendments, such as gypsum and zeolites, also play a role in improving soil structure and water retention. Gypsum, for instance, helps break up compacted soils, enhancing infiltration and reducing surface runoff. Zeolites, due to their porous nature, act as reservoirs that gradually release stored water to plant roots, optimizing water availability.

By integrating these soil amendments into agricultural practices, farmers can significantly enhance the soil's ability to retain moisture, reduce dependency on frequent irrigation, and increase crop resilience against drought. This approach not only conserves water but also supports long-term soil health and productivity.

Effective crop management plays a vital role in sustainable water conservation and agricultural resilience, particularly in the face of increasing water scarcity. By incorporating strategies such as selecting drought-resistant crop varieties, optimizing planting schedules to align with rainfall patterns, and using mulching techniques, farmers can significantly enhance soil moisture retention and reduce water loss. Additionally, intercropping and crop rotation improve soil health, enhance moisture absorption, and reduce overall water consumption, making agricultural systems more sustainable.

Precision irrigation techniques, such as drip and sprinkler irrigation, further optimize water use by delivering moisture directly to plant roots, minimizing evaporation and runoff. Methods like deficit irrigation and Alternate Wetting and Drying (AWD) in rice cultivation have proven effective in reducing water use while maintaining crop productivity. Moreover, enhancing soil properties through organic and inorganic amendments, such as compost, manure, and biochar, improves soil structure and increases its capacity to retain water, further strengthening crop resilience to drought.

By integrating traditional water-saving practices with modern innovations, farmers can minimize their reliance on excessive irrigation while sustaining high yields. These approaches not only contribute to long-term food security but also support climate adaptation efforts, ensuring that agricultural systems remain productive and sustainable in an era of changing environmental conditions. Adopting a combination of these techniques will be key to achieving water security and long-term agricultural sustainability worldwide.

Selecting Drought-Tolerant Crops and Crop Diversification Strategies for Water Conservation

Water scarcity is an increasing challenge for agriculture worldwide, driven by factors such as climate change, population growth, and competing demands for limited water resources. In response, adopting sustainable crop management strategies has become essential to optimize water use and maintain agricultural productivity. Among the most effective approaches to mitigating water shortages are selecting drought-tolerant crops and implementing crop diversification strategies. These methods help conserve water, improve soil health, and stabilize yields even under unpredictable rainfall conditions.

Drought-tolerant crops are specially bred or naturally adapted to survive with minimal water, making them ideal for regions experiencing frequent dry spells. By incorporating these crops into farming systems, producers can maintain stable harvests despite reduced water availability. Many improved drought-resistant varieties of staple crops such as maize, wheat, sorghum, and millet have been developed through advanced breeding techniques, offering high yields while using up to 40% less water. Additionally, deep-rooted crops can access moisture from lower soil layers, enhancing resilience to prolonged drought periods.

Crop diversification strategies, including intercropping, crop rotation, and agroforestry, further contribute to sustainable water use. Intercropping, where multiple crop species are grown together, enhances soil moisture retention and nutrient availability while reducing competition for water resources. Similarly, crop rotation breaks pest and disease cycles while improving soil structure and water infiltration. Integrating trees and shrubs into farming systems through agroforestry also helps conserve water by reducing evaporation and enhancing groundwater recharge.

By adopting drought-tolerant crops and diversification strategies, farmers can reduce their reliance on intensive irrigation, making agricultural systems more resilient to climate variability. These techniques not only promote sustainable food production but also contribute to long-term water conservation efforts, ensuring food security for future generations. A comprehensive approach that combines traditional and modern methods of crop management will be crucial for maintaining agricultural sustainability in an era of increasing water scarcity.

Drought-Tolerant Crop Selection

Drought-tolerant crops exhibit specialized physiological and morphological adaptations that enable them to survive and thrive under water-limited conditions. These adaptations include deep root systems that allow plants to access moisture from lower soil layers, efficient stomatal regulation to minimize water loss, reduced transpiration rates, and enhanced water-use efficiency. Some crops also possess waxy leaf coatings or smaller leaf surfaces to reduce evaporation.

Selecting and cultivating drought-tolerant crops is a crucial strategy for improving agricultural resilience in regions prone to water scarcity. These crops, such as sorghum, millet, pigeon pea, and drought-resistant varieties of maize and wheat, are specifically bred or naturally adapted to perform well with minimal water input. Their ability to maintain growth and yield despite limited rainfall ensures stable food production, reducing dependence on irrigation and safeguarding farmers against unpredictable climatic conditions.

Furthermore, breeding programs and biotechnological advancements have played a significant role in developing high-yielding drought-resistant varieties. These improved cultivars integrate traits such as early maturation, osmotic adjustment, and enhanced root architecture, making them better suited for dryland farming systems. By incorporating drought-tolerant crops into agricultural practices, farmers can optimize water use, maintain soil health, and ensure sustainable food production in the face of growing climate challenges.

Characteristics of Drought-Tolerant Crops

Drought-tolerant crops exhibit unique physiological and structural traits that enable them to survive and produce yields under water-limited conditions. These adaptations enhance their ability to access, utilize, and conserve water efficiently, making them well-suited for cultivation in arid and semi-arid regions.

- **Deep Root Systems**: Many drought-resistant crops, such as sorghum and pearl millet, develop extensive and deep root networks that allow them to extract moisture from lower soil layers. This characteristic helps maintain plant hydration during prolonged dry periods, ensuring continued growth and productivity.
- **Efficient Water-Use Mechanisms**: Certain crops utilize specialized photosynthetic pathways, such as crassulacean acid metabolism (CAM) and C4 photosynthesis, which enhance water-use efficiency. C4 crops like maize and sugarcane have specialized leaf anatomy that minimizes water loss while maximizing carbon fixation, making them more resilient to heat and drought stress. CAM plants, including some succulents, open their stomata at night to reduce water loss through evaporation.
- **Reduced Transpiration**: Many drought-tolerant crops exhibit structural modifications to minimize water loss. Features such as smaller leaf surfaces, waxy coatings, and trichomes (hair-like structures) reduce transpiration by limiting direct exposure to sunlight and dry air. For instance, pearl millet and cowpea have thickened cuticles that reduce water loss and improve drought resistance.
- **High Osmotic Adjustment Ability**: Under drought stress, some plants maintain cell turgor and metabolic activity by accumulating osmolytes such as proline, soluble sugars, and glycine betaine. These compounds help retain cellular water, stabilize proteins, and protect cell membranes, ensuring continued growth even under severe moisture deficits.

By incorporating these drought-tolerant crops into agricultural systems, farmers can enhance resilience against erratic rainfall, improve soil moisture utilization, and ensure food security in water-scarce environments.

Key Drought-Tolerant Crops for Dryland Farming

Drought-tolerant crops play a vital role in ensuring food security in water-scarce regions. These crops have evolved physiological and structural adaptations that enable them to withstand prolonged dry spells while maintaining productivity. By incorporating these resilient varieties into farming systems, agricultural communities can reduce their reliance on irrigation and improve yield stability.

1. **Sorghum (*Sorghum bicolor*)** – A widely grown cereal crop in arid and semi-arid regions, sorghum is highly resistant to drought due to its deep root system, waxy leaves, and efficient water-use mechanisms. It can survive under extreme water stress and is a primary source of food, fodder, and biofuel.

2. **Pearl Millet (*Pennisetum glaucum*)** – Known for its exceptional drought tolerance, pearl millet thrives in hot and dry climates with minimal rainfall. Its ability to grow in poor soils makes it an important staple in dryland agriculture, providing both grain for human consumption and fodder for livestock.

3. **Pigeon Pea (*Cajanus cajan*)** – A hardy leguminous crop that not only survives prolonged dry periods but also improves soil fertility by fixing atmospheric nitrogen. Its deep-rooting ability enables it to access water from deeper soil layers, making it an excellent choice for rainfed farming systems.

4. **Chickpea (*Cicer arietinum*)** – This legume requires significantly less water than other pulses and is well-suited for semi-arid regions. It is an essential protein source and contributes to soil health by enhancing organic matter and microbial activity.

5. **Drought-Resistant Wheat and Maize** – Advances in crop breeding have led to the development of genetically improved wheat and maize varieties with enhanced water-use efficiency and resistance to heat and drought stress. These varieties ensure stable yields even under fluctuating rainfall conditions, supporting food production in regions facing climate variability.

Adopting drought-resistant crop varieties can increase yield stability by up to 35% in regions experiencing frequent water shortages. As climate change continues to intensify drought risks, integrating these resilient crops into agricultural systems will be crucial for maintaining food production and ensuring sustainable farming practices.

Crop Diversification Strategies

Crop diversification involves growing a variety of crops in a given area to enhance agricultural sustainability, improve soil health, and optimize water use. Diversification minimizes the risk of crop failure due to drought and reduces the pressure on water resources. Crop diversification is a crucial agricultural strategy that involves cultivating multiple crop species in a given area to enhance sustainability, improve soil health, and optimize water use. By integrating different crops with varying water needs and growth cycles, farmers can reduce dependency on a single crop, lower the risk of crop failure due to drought, and make more efficient use of available water resources.

Crop diversification plays a critical role in enhancing agricultural sustainability, improving soil health, and optimizing water use. By implementing various diversification strategies, farmers can make better use of available water resources while reducing the risks associated with drought and climate variability. Below are some of the most effective crop diversification strategies:

1. Crop Rotation

Crop rotation involves alternating different crops in successive planting seasons to improve soil health, enhance nutrient cycling, and optimize water use. By rotating deep-rooted and shallow-rooted crops, soil moisture levels are maintained more effectively, reducing the depletion of groundwater reserves. For example, rotating cereals like wheat with legumes such as chickpeas improves soil fertility while reducing water loss.

2. Intercropping

Intercropping is the practice of growing two or more crops simultaneously on the same plot. This strategy increases biodiversity, improves land productivity, and reduces soil evaporation by providing ground cover. Common intercropping systems include maize-pigeon pea and sorghum-cowpea, which enhance water-use efficiency by utilizing soil moisture at different depths.

3. Agroforestry Systems

Agroforestry integrates trees and shrubs with agricultural crops to improve soil moisture retention, reduce wind erosion, and promote groundwater recharge. Trees act as natural barriers against excessive evaporation while improving soil structure through organic matter deposition. Drought-resistant species such as Acacia and Moringa are commonly incorporated into dryland farming systems to enhance water conservation.

4. Relay Cropping

Relay cropping involves planting a second crop before the first one is fully harvested. This method maximizes land and water use efficiency by ensuring continuous crop production without leaving the soil bare and exposed to moisture loss. For instance, planting legumes before a cereal crop is harvested allows both crops to utilize available soil moisture without overburdening water resources.

5. Polyculture

Polyculture is the practice of cultivating multiple crop species in the same area to increase ecosystem resilience and reduce dependence on a single water-intensive crop. By diversifying crops, farmers can optimize water usage across different plant species with varying water needs, reducing the overall water footprint of the farming system.

Adopting crop diversification strategies is essential for achieving sustainable water management in agriculture. By implementing crop rotation, intercropping, agroforestry, relay cropping, and polyculture, farmers can enhance water efficiency, improve soil fertility, and build resilience against drought and climate change. These strategies not only optimize resource utilization but also contribute to long-term food security and environmental sustainability.

Benefits of Crop Diversification for Water Conservation

Crop diversification offers multiple benefits beyond just improving agricultural productivity. By incorporating diverse cropping systems, farmers can significantly enhance soil moisture retention, nutrient cycling, and overall water-use efficiency. Below are the key benefits of crop diversification for water conservation and sustainable farming:

1. Improved Soil Moisture Retention

Crop diversification enhances soil moisture levels by incorporating different plant species with varying root structures and organic matter contributions. Deep-rooted crops help break compacted soil layers, allowing better water infiltration, while shallow-rooted plants create ground cover that reduces evaporation. Additionally, crop residues left in the field act as a natural mulch, slowing down water loss and improving overall soil water-holding capacity.

2. Enhanced Nutrient Cycling

Different crops extract and replenish soil nutrients in complementary ways, reducing nutrient depletion and enhancing soil fertility. Leguminous crops, for example, fix atmospheric nitrogen, enriching the soil for subsequent cereal crops. This process decreases reliance on synthetic fertilizers, lowering input costs and promoting sustainable soil health.

3. Reduction in Water Demand

Diversified cropping systems optimize water usage by reducing overall irrigation needs. By intercropping or rotating crops with different water requirements, farmers can balance soil moisture use, preventing excessive water depletion. Additionally, agroforestry and polyculture systems reduce water runoff and increase groundwater recharge, making better use of available water resources.

4. Increased Farm Resilience

A diverse cropping system enhances farm resilience by mitigating risks associated with drought, pests, and diseases. Different crop species respond differently to environmental stresses, ensuring that at least some portion of the harvest remains productive even in adverse conditions. This stability is crucial for food security, particularly in regions facing erratic rainfall and climate variability.

Integrating crop diversification into farming practices is a practical and sustainable approach to improving water conservation, enhancing soil health, and increasing agricultural resilience. By implementing strategies such as intercropping, crop rotation, and agroforestry, farmers can optimize water use, reduce dependency on irrigation, and create a more sustainable agricultural system.

The adoption of drought-tolerant crops and diversified cropping systems is crucial for addressing the challenges posed by water scarcity in agriculture. These approaches not only optimize water use but also contribute to long-term agricultural sustainability by improving soil moisture retention, enhancing nutrient cycling, and reducing dependence on irrigation.

Looking ahead, advancements in crop breeding, agroecological practices, and precision water management technologies will play a pivotal role in further improving agricultural resilience. The development of genetically improved drought-resistant crop varieties with enhanced water-use efficiency will provide farmers with more adaptable options for varying climatic conditions. Additionally, agroecological approaches such as integrated cropping systems, agroforestry, and conservation agriculture will help in maintaining soil health and improving water retention capacity.

Furthermore, precision water management strategies, including real-time soil moisture monitoring, smart irrigation systems, and alternative water sources like treated wastewater, will enable more efficient use of limited water resources. By integrating these innovations with traditional knowledge, farmers can build climate-smart agricultural systems that ensure productivity even under water-limited conditions.

Scaling up the implementation of drought-tolerant crops and crop diversification strategies can make a significant impact on global food security. With proper policy support, investment in agricultural research, and knowledge dissemination to farming communities, these approaches can contribute to sustainable water management and long-term resilience in regions facing increasing water stress.

7.3 Enhancing Water Use Efficiency (WUE) in Rainfed Agriculture

Water Use Efficiency (WUE) is a key determinant of sustainable agricultural productivity, particularly in rainfed systems where water availability fluctuates due to unpredictable rainfall patterns. It is defined as the ratio of crop yield or biomass to the total water used through transpiration, evaporation, and soil moisture loss. Enhancing WUE is crucial for maximizing crop production while minimizing water wastage, making it an essential strategy in regions facing water scarcity and climate variability.

Efforts to improve WUE involve adopting water-saving technologies, optimizing soil moisture conservation practices, selecting drought-resistant crop varieties, and implementing precision irrigation techniques. By increasing WUE, farmers can produce more food with limited water resources, thereby ensuring food security and resilience against drought conditions. Sustainable water management practices that enhance WUE not only support long-term agricultural sustainability but also contribute to ecosystem conservation by reducing pressure on groundwater and surface water sources.

Concept of Water Use Efficiency (WUE)

Water Use Efficiency (WUE) is a fundamental metric for assessing the effectiveness of water utilization in crop production. It is expressed as the ratio of crop yield (or total biomass) to the amount of water used through transpiration, evaporation, and soil moisture loss. A higher WUE indicates that a crop is able to produce more yield with less water, which is particularly vital in rainfed and drought-prone regions.

Several factors influence WUE, including crop species and variety, soil texture and organic matter content, local climatic conditions, and farm management practices. Certain crops, such as drought-tolerant and deep-rooted species, naturally exhibit higher WUE due to their ability to access water from deeper soil layers and regulate transpiration more efficiently. Similarly, soil properties, such as water-holding capacity and infiltration rate, affect the extent to which plants can access and utilize stored moisture.

Enhancing WUE requires an integrated approach that focuses on reducing water losses, maximizing water uptake, and improving crop productivity per unit of water used. Strategies such as conservation tillage, mulching, efficient irrigation methods, cover cropping, and precision agriculture techniques play a crucial role in minimizing water wastage while ensuring optimal plant growth. By improving WUE, farmers can sustain crop yields even in water-limited environments, reduce dependency on irrigation, and contribute to long-term agricultural resilience.

Methods for Maximizing WUE in Rainfed Conditions

1. **Soil Moisture Conservation Techniques**

Efficient soil moisture conservation is essential for enhancing Water Use Efficiency (WUE) in rainfed agricultural systems. By reducing evaporation, improving infiltration, and retaining soil moisture for longer periods, these techniques help optimize water availability for crops.

- **Mulching:** The application of organic materials (such as straw, crop residues, and leaves) or synthetic materials (such as plastic films) on the soil surface significantly reduces evaporation and improves moisture retention. Mulching also regulates soil temperature, suppresses weeds, and enhances soil microbial activity. Studies indicate that mulching can improve soil moisture levels by 20–30%, thereby boosting WUE and crop yields, particularly in water-scarce regions.

- **Conservation Tillage:** Practices like reduced tillage or no-till farming help maintain soil structure, reduce soil compaction, and enhance water infiltration. By minimizing disturbance, conservation tillage allows organic matter to accumulate, which improves soil porosity and moisture-holding capacity. These practices are especially beneficial in dryland agriculture, where they can reduce water loss and improve soil health.
- **Cover Cropping:** Growing cover crops such as legumes, grasses, or green manures between main cropping seasons protects the soil from direct exposure to sunlight, wind, and water erosion. Cover crops reduce surface evaporation, improve organic matter content, and increase soil water storage capacity. Additionally, leguminous cover crops contribute to nitrogen fixation, enhancing soil fertility while maintaining adequate moisture levels for subsequent crops.

Integrating these soil moisture conservation techniques into farming systems helps optimize water use, sustain crop productivity, and improve resilience to climatic variability.

2. Optimizing Crop Selection and Management

Selecting the right crops and employing efficient management practices are crucial for maximizing **Water Use Efficiency (WUE)** in rainfed agriculture. By choosing drought-resistant varieties, adjusting planting schedules, and utilizing short-duration crops, farmers can significantly enhance crop productivity while minimizing water consumption.

- **Drought-Tolerant Crops:** Certain crops, such as **sorghum, pearl millet, pigeon pea, and cowpea**, possess physiological adaptations that allow them to survive and yield well under water-limited conditions. These crops have deep root systems, efficient water uptake mechanisms, and reduced transpiration rates, making them ideal for dryland farming. Research indicates that drought-tolerant crops can maintain stable yields with up to **40% less water** compared to conventional varieties.
- **Short-Duration Varieties:** Crops with shorter growth cycles require less water throughout their lifecycle, making them well-suited for rainfed conditions. Short-duration varieties of **rice, wheat, and legumes** can complete their growth before peak dry periods, thereby avoiding severe water stress. These varieties also allow for better crop rotation and diversification, which can further enhance soil moisture retention and

nutrient cycling.

- **Proper Planting Time:** Aligning sowing dates with seasonal rainfall patterns ensures that crops receive adequate soil moisture during critical growth stages. Early planting at the onset of monsoon rains, for instance, can **maximize water absorption and reduce the need for supplementary irrigation**. In some cases, staggered or delayed planting may help crops avoid dry spells, ensuring optimal growth and yield stability.

By integrating **drought-tolerant crops, short-duration varieties, and strategic planting schedules**, farmers can optimize water use, enhance resilience to climate variability, and sustain agricultural productivity in water-limited regions.

3. Efficient Water Management Practices

Implementing **efficient water management strategies** is essential for improving **Water Use Efficiency (WUE)** in rainfed and irrigated agricultural systems. By adopting innovative techniques such as **Alternate Wetting and Drying (AWD), deficit irrigation, and rainwater harvesting**, farmers can optimize water use while maintaining crop yields.

- **Alternate Wetting and Drying (AWD):** This water-saving technique is widely used in **rice cultivation** to **reduce irrigation water use by up to 30%** without compromising yield. AWD involves **intermittently allowing the soil to dry between irrigation cycles**, rather than continuously flooding the field. This approach not only conserves water but also reduces methane emissions, making it a **climate-smart** practice for sustainable rice production.
- **Deficit Irrigation:** This method involves applying **water only during critical growth stages** of crops, such as flowering and grain filling, while **withholding irrigation during less-sensitive stages**. Deficit irrigation has been shown to **reduce overall water use by 20–40%** while maintaining crop yields, making it particularly beneficial for regions experiencing water shortages. Crops like **wheat, maize, and cotton** respond well to this strategy, ensuring efficient water utilization without significant yield loss.
- **Rainwater Harvesting:** Capturing and storing rainwater through **farm ponds, check dams, and percolation tanks** provides a valuable source of supplementary irrigation during dry spells. These small-scale storage

structures **reduce dependence on groundwater**, improve soil moisture retention, and help **stabilize agricultural productivity in rainfed regions**. Studies indicate that integrating rainwater harvesting with efficient irrigation can **enhance crop yields by 15–25%** in water-scarce areas.

By adopting **AWD, deficit irrigation, and rainwater harvesting**, farmers can significantly **improve WUE, reduce water wastage, and build resilience against climate variability**, ensuring **sustainable and productive agricultural systems**.

4. Agroforestry and Crop Diversification

Agroforestry and crop diversification are **effective strategies** for enhancing **Water Use Efficiency (WUE)** by improving soil moisture retention, reducing water loss, and optimizing land productivity. These approaches contribute to **climate resilience** and **sustainable agriculture** by integrating multiple plant species that complement each other's water and nutrient needs.

- **Intercropping Systems:** Growing compatible crops together, such as **maize and legumes (e.g., pigeon pea or cowpea)**, improves WUE by **enhancing soil moisture retention and reducing evaporation**. Legumes **fix atmospheric nitrogen**, enriching soil fertility and reducing the need for chemical fertilizers. Studies indicate that intercropping can **increase WUE by up to 35%** compared to monocropping systems, while also reducing the risk of crop failure in drought-prone regions.
- **Agroforestry Practices:** Integrating trees and shrubs into farming systems offers multiple benefits for water conservation. Tree roots **enhance soil infiltration, reduce surface runoff**, and **promote groundwater recharge**, making more water available for crops. Additionally, trees provide **shade**, which lowers soil temperature and **reduces evaporation losses**. Agroforestry systems, such as **alley cropping and windbreaks**, have been shown to **increase soil moisture by 15–35%**, particularly in **semi-arid** and **drought-prone** areas.

By **combining intercropping with agroforestry**, farmers can **diversify income sources, enhance WUE, and improve long-term agricultural sustainability**, ensuring **better adaptation to water scarcity and climate variability**.

5. Precision Agriculture and Smart Technologies

The integration of **precision agriculture** and **smart technologies** is revolutionizing water management by **enhancing Water Use Efficiency (WUE)** through **real-time monitoring, data-driven decision-making, and advanced crop breeding**. These innovations enable farmers to **optimize water usage, minimize losses, and increase agricultural sustainability**, particularly in **water-scarce regions**.

- **Soil Moisture Sensors:** These devices provide **real-time data** on soil moisture levels, allowing farmers to **schedule irrigation precisely** based on crop water needs. By preventing **over-irrigation and under-irrigation**, soil moisture sensors can **reduce water waste by up to 30%**, ensuring that crops receive adequate moisture while conserving resources.
- **Drought-Resilient Crop Breeding:** Advances in **genetic engineering, marker-assisted selection, and traditional breeding** have led to the development of **high-WUE crop varieties** that require less water while maintaining **optimal yields**. Genetically modified and selectively bred crops, such as **drought-tolerant maize, wheat, and rice**, have shown **yield stability increases of up to 35% in arid and semi-arid regions**.
- **Remote Sensing and GIS Applications:**Satellite **imagery, drones, and Geographic Information Systems (GIS)** allow for large-scale assessment of **soil moisture, vegetation health, and crop stress**. These technologies help farmers **detect early signs of drought stress**, optimize irrigation planning, and implement **site-specific water management strategies**, leading to **improved crop performance with minimal water input**.

By adopting **precision agriculture and smart technologies**, farmers can **significantly improve WUE**, reduce water consumption, and build **climate-resilient agricultural systems** that ensure **sustainable food production** in the face of growing water scarcity.

By integrating **soil moisture conservation techniques, efficient water management practices, crop diversification, and precision agriculture technologies**, farmers can **maximize Water Use Efficiency (WUE) in rainfed agriculture**. These methods help **reduce water loss, improve soil moisture retention, and enhance crop resilience** to drought conditions, ensuring **higher productivity with minimal water inputs**.

A **balanced approach** that combines **traditional soil conservation techniques**, such as **mulching, conservation tillage, and agroforestry**, with **modern innovations**, like **remote sensing, soil moisture sensors, and drought-resilient crop breeding**, will be essential for **sustaining food production in water-scarce regions**. This **integrated strategy** not only enhances **agricultural sustainability** but also contributes to **long-term water resource management and food security** in the face of **climate change and increasing water scarcity.**

CHAPTER EIGHT

MANAGEMENT OF CROPS IN RAINFED AREAS

Rainfed agriculture plays a crucial role in global food production, supporting millions of farmers and providing a significant portion of the world's staple crops. However, its dependence on natural rainfall makes it highly vulnerable to unpredictable weather patterns, prolonged dry spells, and shifting climate conditions. Ensuring productivity in these regions requires strategic approaches that optimize water use, enhance soil moisture retention, and build resilience against environmental stressors.

One of the most effective ways to improve crop yields in rainfed areas is by integrating soil and water conservation techniques with smart farming practices. Methods such as growing drought-resistant crops, adjusting planting schedules, adopting conservation tillage, and using water-efficient irrigation systems help maximize water availability and reduce the risks associated with erratic rainfall.

Additionally, sustainable agricultural techniques like cover cropping, intercropping, mulching, and agroforestry contribute to better soil health and moisture retention. Modern technologies, including remote sensing, soil moisture sensors, and data-driven decision-making tools, further enhance water and crop management by providing real-time insights.

A well-balanced approach that combines traditional wisdom with modern innovations is key to long-term sustainability in rainfed farming. By adopting adaptive and water-efficient farming practices, farmers can increase productivity, reduce dependency on unpredictable rainfall, and contribute to global food security despite ongoing climate challenges.

8.1 Selecting Suitable Crops for Rainfed Farming

Choosing the right crops for rainfed farming is crucial for achieving optimal yields while minimizing reliance on external irrigation sources. Rainfed agriculture, which constitutes nearly 80% of the world's cultivated land, plays a significant role in global food production, particularly in regions with limited access to reliable irrigation. However, the dependence on natural rainfall makes crop productivity highly vulnerable to seasonal variations, climate change, and prolonged dry spells. To mitigate these challenges, it is essential to select crops that can adapt to fluctuating moisture levels, maintain growth under water stress, and sustain productivity with minimal water input.

According to research by the Food and Agriculture Organization (FAO), approximately **60% of staple food production in developing countries comes from rainfed farming systems**. However, water scarcity and erratic rainfall patterns can reduce crop yields by **up to 50% in drought-prone regions**. To combat these challenges, selecting drought-resilient crops with high water-use efficiency (WUE) has proven to be an effective strategy. Studies indicate that incorporating drought-tolerant crop varieties in rainfed farming can enhance yield stability by **20–35%** compared to conventional varieties under water-deficit conditions.

Furthermore, research from the International Crops Research Institute for the Semi-Arid Tropics (ICRISAT) highlights that rainfed crop selection should prioritize **deep-rooted species, crops with short growth cycles, and plants with physiological mechanisms for moisture conservation**. For instance, crops like **sorghum and pearl millet** exhibit superior drought resistance due to their ability to extract water from deeper soil layers and regulate transpiration efficiently. Similarly, pulses like **chickpea and pigeon pea** improve soil health through nitrogen fixation while thriving with minimal water input, making them ideal choices for rainfed systems.

By selecting suitable crops and adopting adaptive management practices, farmers can enhance the resilience of rainfed agriculture, reduce the risk of crop failure, and contribute to long-term food security. Investing in climate-resilient crop varieties and sustainable farming practices will be crucial in ensuring agricultural productivity in the face of increasing water scarcity and climate uncertainties.

Key Characteristics of Suitable Crops for Rainfed Farming

Selecting crops with specific traits that enable them to survive and produce stable yields under rainfed conditions is essential for sustainable agriculture. Given the challenges posed by erratic rainfall and limited water availability, farmers must prioritize crop varieties that are well-adapted to such conditions. Below are the key characteristics of crops best suited for rainfed farming:

1. **Drought Tolerance**

   Crops with deep and extensive root systems can access moisture from deeper soil layers, allowing them to withstand prolonged dry periods. These crops also exhibit physiological adaptations such as **stomatal regulation, reduced transpiration, and osmotic adjustment**, which enhance their ability to conserve water. Studies have shown that **sorghum, pearl millet, and pigeon pea** can maintain productivity even when rainfall is 30–50% below normal levels, making them ideal choices for water-scarce regions.

2. **Short Growth Cycle**

   Fast-maturing crops require less water over their lifecycle and can take advantage of short or unpredictable rainy seasons. Short-duration varieties of **legumes, cereals, and oilseeds** have been developed to complete their life cycle before severe moisture deficits occur. For instance, early-maturing **chickpea and groundnut varieties** have been found to yield **25–30% more grain** in rainfed systems compared to long-duration varieties under the same conditions.

3. **High Water-Use Efficiency (WUE)**

   Some crops have adapted to **use available water more efficiently**, minimizing losses through evaporation and transpiration while maintaining high productivity. Crops with **C4 photosynthesis, such as maize and sorghum**, have been shown to use water **40% more efficiently** than C3 crops under similar conditions. Moreover, integrating **drought-tolerant wheat and rice varieties** can increase grain yield per unit of water used, thereby improving overall water productivity.

4. **Soil Adaptability**

   Rainfed farming is often practiced in marginal soils with low fertility and organic matter content. Crops that can tolerate **poor soil conditions, salinity, or nutrient deficiencies** are more suitable for such environments. For example, **pigeon pea, cowpea, and millets** can grow in sandy, acidic, or degraded soils while also **contributing to soil fertility through nitrogen fixation**. Research indicates that incorporating these crops in rotation or intercropping systems can improve **soil structure and water retention capacity**, reducing dependency on chemical inputs.

By selecting crops with these adaptive traits, farmers can improve agricultural productivity, enhance resilience to climatic variations, and optimize water use efficiency in rainfed farming systems. Combining crop selection with sustainable land management practices will further support food security and environmental conservation in water-limited regions.

Best Crop Choices for Rainfed Agriculture

1. **Cereals:**

Cereal crops play a crucial role in rainfed agriculture due to their adaptability to water-limited conditions and their significance as staple foods. Selecting the right cereal varieties can help ensure stable yields even in unpredictable rainfall patterns. Below are some of the most suitable cereals for rainfed farming:

- **Sorghum (Sorghum bicolor)**
  Sorghum is one of the most drought-resistant cereals, thanks to its **deep root system and high water-use efficiency**. It can survive prolonged dry spells by **entering a temporary dormancy phase during water stress and resuming growth once moisture is available**. Studies have shown that sorghum can maintain yield stability even with **40–50% less water** compared to other cereals, making it a preferred choice for semi-arid and arid regions.
- **Pearl Millet (Pennisetum glaucum)**
  Pearl millet thrives in **poor, sandy, and saline soils** where other cereals struggle to grow. It has a **high tolerance for extreme temperatures and minimal water availability**, making it one of the best crops for regions with erratic rainfall. Research indicates that pearl millet requires **30–40% less water than maize** while maintaining **consistent grain and fodder production**, making it a resilient option for rainfed farming systems.

- **Maize (Drought-Tolerant Varieties)**
  Traditional maize varieties are highly sensitive to drought, but **improved drought-tolerant hybrids** have been developed to withstand dry conditions. These varieties have **shorter growth cycles, deeper roots, and better osmotic adjustment mechanisms**, allowing them to produce stable yields under rainfed conditions. Studies show that drought-tolerant maize varieties can **reduce yield losses by up to 25–30%** in regions experiencing frequent dry spells, making them a valuable option for rainfed agriculture.

By incorporating these cereals into rainfed cropping systems, farmers can improve food security, enhance resilience to water stress, and maximize productivity with limited water resources.

1. **Pulses and Legumes:**

Legumes are highly beneficial for rainfed agriculture due to their **drought tolerance, soil-enriching properties, and ability to improve water-use efficiency**. They are an essential component of sustainable dryland farming systems, providing **protein-rich food and fodder** while enhancing soil fertility through nitrogen fixation. Below are some of the most suitable legumes for rainfed farming:

- **Pigeon Pea (Cajanus cajan)**
  Pigeon pea is a deep-rooted legume that can **access moisture from lower soil layers**, making it highly resilient to prolonged dry spells. Its ability to withstand **low and irregular rainfall (as little as 600 mm annually)** makes it a staple crop in semi-arid regions. Additionally, pigeon pea improves soil structure and **fixes atmospheric nitrogen**, reducing the need for synthetic fertilizers. Research indicates that intercropping pigeon pea with cereals like sorghum or millet **enhances soil moisture retention and boosts overall system productivity**.
- **Chickpea (Cicer arietinum)**
  Chickpea is well-suited for **dryland farming** as it requires **30–40% less water** than other legumes. Its **short growth cycle and deep-rooting system** allow it to efficiently extract soil moisture and tolerate drought conditions. Studies have shown that chickpea can **maintain yield stability even under rainfall deficits of up to 50%**, making it an ideal

choice for rainfed farming. Furthermore, it contributes to **soil fertility restoration** by fixing nitrogen, benefiting subsequent crops in rotation-based systems.

- **Cowpea (Vigna unguiculata)**
Cowpea is highly adaptable to **hot and arid climates**, thriving in areas with **as little as 300–500 mm of annual rainfall**. Its fast growth and deep root system enable it to **withstand dry conditions while preventing soil erosion**. Cowpea is also known for its ability to **improve soil fertility by fixing atmospheric nitrogen**, making it an excellent rotational crop in rainfed systems. Research suggests that incorporating cowpea into cropping systems can **increase overall land productivity by 20–30%** through improved soil health and water conservation.

By incorporating these drought-tolerant legumes into rainfed farming systems, farmers can **enhance food security, improve soil fertility, and increase resilience against climate variability.**

3. Oilseeds:

Oilseed crops play a crucial role in **rainfed agriculture**, offering both **economic benefits and resilience to drought**. These crops are well-suited for **low-rainfall regions**, requiring minimal irrigation while contributing to soil health and farm profitability.

- **Groundnut (Arachis hypogaea)**
Groundnut is a **low-water-requiring crop** that performs exceptionally well in **sandy and well-drained soils**. It has a **short growing cycle (90–120 days)** and can tolerate **moderate drought conditions**. Research indicates that groundnut cultivation in rainfed systems can **enhance soil organic matter and improve water infiltration**, making it a suitable crop for drylands. Additionally, as a legume, groundnut **fixes nitrogen**, reducing fertilizer dependence and improving soil fertility. Studies show that improved groundnut varieties with **drought resistance can increase yields by up to 30% in semi-arid regions.**
- **Sesame (Sesamum indicum)**
Sesame is a highly **drought-tolerant oilseed crop** that thrives in **hot, dry environments with minimal rainfall (300–600 mm annually)**. It has an extensive root system that allows it to **extract moisture from**

deep soil layers, making it resilient in water-scarce conditions. Research has shown that **sesame can maintain stable yields even under severe moisture stress**, making it an **ideal cash crop for smallholder farmers in rainfed regions**. Additionally, sesame enhances **soil conservation** by reducing erosion and improving organic matter content.

By integrating these **drought-resilient oilseeds** into rainfed cropping systems, farmers can **diversify their income sources, enhance soil health, and improve water-use efficiency**, ensuring **sustainable agricultural productivity in dryland regions**.

4. **Root and Tuber Crops:**

Root and tuber crops are highly **suitable for rainfed agriculture** due to their **drought resilience, deep-rooting systems, and ability to grow in marginal soils**. These crops serve as an **important food security option** in regions with **erratic rainfall and prolonged dry spells**.

- **Cassava (Manihot esculenta)**
  Cassava is one of the **most drought-resistant crops**, capable of **surviving long dry periods** due to its **deep root system and ability to store carbohydrates in its tubers**. It can grow in **poor soils** with minimal inputs and remains productive **even when rainfall is as low as 500 mm annually**. Studies indicate that cassava can yield well in **semi-arid regions**, making it a **reliable staple crop** in rainfed farming systems. Additionally, its **flexible harvesting window** allows farmers to leave the tubers in the ground until needed, reducing post-harvest losses.

- **Sweet Potato (Ipomoea batatas)**
  Sweet potato is an **adaptable and fast-growing crop** that thrives in **low-fertility and sandy soils** with minimal rainfall. It has a **short growth cycle (90–150 days)**, allowing farmers to **harvest multiple times in a year**, even in rainfed conditions. Research has shown that drought-tolerant varieties of sweet potato can **withstand moisture stress and continue producing yields when other crops fail**. Additionally, sweet potato plays a crucial role in **nutritional security** due to its high content of **vitamin A, fiber, and carbohydrates**, making it a valuable crop for resource-poor farmers.

By incorporating **cassava and sweet potato** into rainfed farming systems, **farmers can improve food security, stabilize yields, and enhance soil resilience** against **climate variability.**

5. **Agroforestry and Perennial Crops:**

Agroforestry plays a crucial role in **enhancing soil moisture retention, reducing erosion, and improving land productivity** in rainfed regions. Perennial crops, particularly drought-resistant trees, provide **long-term economic and environmental benefits**, making them valuable additions to sustainable rainfed farming systems.

*   **Moringa (Moringa oleifera)**
    Moringa, often referred to as the "**miracle tree**," is highly **drought-tolerant** and thrives in **semi-arid and arid regions** with minimal water. It grows rapidly, reaching maturity within a year, and produces **nutrient-rich leaves, seeds, and pods** that serve as food, medicine, and livestock feed. Research shows that moringa **can survive with as little as 400 mm of annual rainfall**, making it an ideal crop for water-scarce areas. Additionally, it improves soil fertility through **leaf litter decomposition**, contributing to sustainable land management in rainfed systems.
*   **Acacia (Acacia spp.) and Prosopis (Prosopis spp.)**
    These drought-resistant trees are widely used for **land restoration, soil stabilization, and fodder production** in degraded and arid lands. Acacia species, such as **Acacia nilotica and Acacia senegal**, fix atmospheric nitrogen, **improving soil fertility** and supporting the growth of intercropped food crops. Prosopis species, particularly **Prosopis juliflora**, are resilient to extreme drought and provide **valuable fuelwood, charcoal, and livestock fodder**. Studies indicate that integrating these trees into rainfed farming systems **reduces soil erosion by 30–50% and enhances groundwater recharge**, making them vital for climate-resilient agriculture.

By incorporating **Moringa, Acacia, and Prosopis** into rainfed farming, **farmers can enhance food security, restore degraded lands, and diversify income sources** while promoting **long-term sustainability in water-scarce regions.**

8.2 Integrated Crop Management (ICM) for Rainfed Agriculture

Integrated Crop Management (ICM) is a **comprehensive and adaptive approach** that integrates various **agronomic, ecological, and technological** practices to optimize crop productivity while ensuring environmental sustainability. In rainfed agriculture, where **water availability is unpredictable and climate variability is high**, implementing ICM is crucial to **maintaining stable yields, improving soil fertility, and enhancing crop resilience**. By adopting a holistic management system that includes **efficient pest control, balanced nutrient management, and effective weed suppression**, farmers can **maximize resource efficiency, reduce crop losses, and improve long-term sustainability**.

Importance of ICM in Rainfed Agriculture

Rainfed farming accounts for approximately **60% of global cropland** and supports over **80% of smallholder farmers in developing countries** (FAO, 2023). However, **low and erratic rainfall, nutrient depletion, and high pest infestations** often lead to **reduced yields** and increased risks of crop failure. Research indicates that **integrated crop management strategies can increase productivity by 20–40% in rainfed systems** (ICRISAT, 2022). By implementing ICM, farmers can **enhance water-use efficiency, maintain soil health, and reduce external input dependence**, making their farming systems more resilient to climate change.

1. Pest Management in Rainfed Areas

Pest infestations pose a significant threat to crop yields in rainfed systems, where crops are already vulnerable due to **irregular water availability and fluctuating environmental conditions**. In the absence of irrigation support, **pest outbreaks can further exacerbate yield losses**, making pest management a critical component of **sustainable rainfed farming**. Unlike irrigated systems, where pests can be controlled with chemical interventions, rainfed agriculture requires a more **integrated and resource-efficient approach** to pest control.

Effective Pest Management Strategies

1. **Biological Control**
   Utilizing natural predators and beneficial organisms helps control pest populations while **maintaining ecological balance**.

- Predatory insects such as **ladybugs, spiders, and parasitoid wasps** prey on harmful insect pests, reducing infestation levels naturally.
- Research from **ICRISAT (2022)** found that releasing **Trichogramma parasitoids** in sorghum fields reduced stem borer populations by **40%**, leading to yield increases of up to **25%**.
- The introduction of **entomopathogenic fungi** like *Beauveria bassiana* has been effective in controlling whiteflies and aphids, reducing their populations by **30–50%**.

2. **Resistant Crop Varieties**
   Developing and cultivating **pest-resistant crop varieties** helps reduce losses and minimizes the need for chemical pesticides.

   - **Sorghum varieties resistant to shoot fly and stem borers** have demonstrated **20–30% higher yields** in rainfed areas (ICAR, 2023).
   - **Blast-resistant finger millet varieties** have shown a **35% reduction in disease incidence**, enhancing grain production.
   - **Pigeon pea and cowpea varieties bred for pod borer resistance** have significantly reduced crop damage in semi-arid regions.

3. **Cultural Practices**
   Agronomic practices play a crucial role in disrupting **pest life cycles and reducing their survival rates.**

   - **Crop rotation:** Alternating **legumes with cereals** helps break pest breeding cycles, reducing infestations by **25–40%** (FAO, 2023).
   - **Intercropping:** Mixing crops like **maize and pigeon pea or sorghum and cowpea** confuses insect pests and enhances biodiversity, lowering pest incidence.
   - **Timely sowing:** Adjusting planting dates to **avoid peak pest emergence periods** can reduce damage; for example, early sowing of **groundnut and chickpea** minimizes infestation by leaf miners and pod borers.

4. **Botanical Pesticides**
   Plant-based pesticides provide **eco-friendly and cost-effective** alternatives to synthetic chemicals.

- **Neem-based formulations** (*Azadirachta indica*) have been shown to reduce aphid and whitefly populations by **50%**, improving crop health.
- **Garlic and chili extracts** serve as natural repellents against sucking pests like thrips and mites.
- **Datura (Datura stramonium) and marigold extracts** have demonstrated **significant suppression of soil-borne pests and nematodes** in rainfed vegetable systems.

By integrating these pest management strategies, farmers in rainfed areas can **reduce crop losses, enhance productivity, and promote sustainable farming practices** without over-reliance on chemical pesticides.

2. Nutrient Management in Rainfed Agriculture

Soil fertility is often a major constraint in **rainfed farming systems**, primarily due to **nutrient leaching, organic matter depletion, and limited access to synthetic fertilizers**. Unlike irrigated agriculture, where nutrient availability can be managed through **regular fertilizer applications**, rainfed systems must rely on **sustainable nutrient management strategies** to maintain soil health and ensure long-term productivity.

Sustainable Nutrient Management Strategies

1. **Integrated Nutrient Management (INM)**
   A balanced approach that **combines organic and inorganic sources of nutrients** helps improve soil health while maintaining crop productivity.

   - The use of **farmyard manure, compost, and green manure** enhances soil organic matter and microbial activity, leading to improved **nutrient availability**.
   - **Biofertilizers such as Azotobacter, Rhizobium, and phosphorus-solubilizing bacteria** contribute to better **nutrient cycling** and **higher crop yields** in low-input systems.
   - Studies from **ICAR (2022)** indicate that INM practices in **sorghum-based rainfed systems** have improved **soil organic carbon levels by 18%** and enhanced **yield stability by 25%** over five years.

2. **Legume-Based Cropping Systems**
   Integrating **nitrogen-fixing legumes** into rainfed cropping systems helps

improve soil fertility naturally by enriching nitrogen levels.

- Crops like **pigeon pea, chickpea, cowpea, and green gram** host **Rhizobium bacteria**, which fix atmospheric nitrogen, reducing the need for synthetic fertilizers.
- Research in semi-arid regions has shown that **pigeon pea-based intercropping systems increase soil nitrogen content by 30–40 kg/ha**, significantly improving the subsequent cereal crop yields.
- **Rotating legumes with cereals** not only enhances soil fertility but also **improves water-use efficiency** by reducing evaporation losses.

3. **Microbial Inoculants for Nutrient Enhancement**
The use of **beneficial soil microbes** helps enhance **nutrient uptake and soil biological activity,** making nutrients more available to plants.

- **Rhizobium inoculation in legumes** can increase biological nitrogen fixation, reducing dependency on synthetic nitrogen fertilizers.
- **Mycorrhizal fungi improve phosphorus solubilization,** leading to enhanced root growth and water absorption.
- Trials conducted in **rainfed wheat systems** showed that applying **Azotobacter inoculants increased grain yield by 15%,** while mycorrhizal fungi boosted **phosphorus uptake by 25%.**

4. **Mulching and Conservation Tillage**
Retaining **crop residues and reducing tillage** can significantly improve soil moisture conservation, minimize **nutrient loss,** and **prevent erosion.**

- **Mulching with crop residues or organic matter** has been found to reduce **nutrient runoff by 40%** and increase soil moisture by **25% in dryland regions.**
- **Zero tillage and minimum tillage practices** maintain soil structure and prevent the **breakdown of organic matter,** leading to **higher soil fertility over time.**
- Research from **ICRISAT (2023)** suggests that conservation tillage in **rainfed maize systems improves nutrient-use efficiency by 35%** and enhances overall crop productivity.

By adopting these nutrient management strategies, farmers in rainfed regions can **improve soil fertility, enhance crop resilience, and sustain agricultural productivity despite erratic rainfall patterns.**

3. Weed Management in Rainfed Areas

Weeds are a **major constraint** in rainfed farming systems as they **compete with crops** for **limited water, nutrients, and sunlight.** Since **rainfed crops already face moisture stress,** unchecked weed growth can **significantly reduce yields.** Studies have shown that **weed competition can cause up to 50% yield losses in rainfed crops like sorghum, millet, and pulses,** making **integrated weed management (IWM)** crucial for sustainable crop production.

Effective Weed Management Strategies

1. **Cultural Control**

    ◦ The use of **cover crops and intercropping** can **suppress weed growth** by **reducing open soil spaces,** limiting weed establishment.
    ◦ **Legume cover crops** such as **cowpea and sunn hemp** not only **reduce weed biomass by 40%** but also contribute to **soil fertility improvement** through nitrogen fixation.
    ◦ Research in **semi-arid regions** found that **intercropping maize with pigeon pea reduces weed infestation by 35%,** leading to better crop growth.

2. **Manual and Mechanical Weeding**

    ◦ **Timely hand weeding, hoeing, and shallow tillage** are traditional but **effective** methods for controlling weeds, especially in **low-resource farming systems.**
    ◦ Studies indicate that **manual weeding at 20 and 40 days after sowing** in rainfed pearl millet fields **increased grain yield by 25%** compared to unweeded fields.
    ◦ **Mechanical weeding** using **weeders or cultivators** can improve efficiency, especially in **row crops like sorghum and maize.**

3. **Minimal and Targeted Herbicide Use**

- Judicious use of pre-emergence herbicides can control aggressive weeds while minimizing soil degradation.
- Research has shown that applying pre-emergence herbicides like pendimethalin in rainfed soybean fields reduced weed density by 60%, leading to higher yields.
- However, over-reliance on herbicides can lead to resistance development, so integrating herbicide use with other methods is recommended.

4. Allelopathic Crops for Natural Weed Suppression

- Certain crops naturally release biochemical compounds (allelochemicals) that inhibit weed germination and growth.
- Sorghum, sunflower, and mustard are known for their allelopathic properties and can be incorporated into cropping systems to reduce weed pressure.
- Studies indicate that sorghum residue incorporation in wheat fields reduced weed biomass by 30%, minimizing the need for herbicides.

By adopting integrated weed management approaches, farmers in rainfed regions can effectively control weeds, preserve soil moisture, and enhance crop productivity, ensuring sustainable and resilient farming systems.

Integrated Crop Management (ICM) is a holistic and adaptive approach that enhances productivity, resource efficiency, and sustainability in rainfed agriculture. Given the uncertainties of rainfall and soil moisture availability, rainfed farming systems require innovative and integrated solutions to optimize pest, nutrient, and weed management while preserving the natural ecosystem.

By implementing biological pest control, organic and inorganic nutrient management, and strategic weed suppression techniques, farmers can achieve:

- Higher and more stable crop yields, even under unpredictable rainfall conditions.
- Improved soil fertility and water retention, ensuring long-term sustainability.

- Reduced dependency on synthetic inputs, lowering costs and minimizing environmental impact.
- Increased climate resilience, enabling better adaptation to droughts and shifting weather patterns.

Research highlights that integrating multiple ICM strategies can improve water-use efficiency by up to 40%, enhance soil fertility by 25%, and increase overall yield stability in rainfed systems. By adopting scientifically proven, yet locally adaptable approaches, farmers can transform rainfed agriculture into a more self-sufficient and sustainable system, contributing to food security and climate resilience in water-limited regions.

8.3 Adaptive Crop Planning for Unpredictable Weather

Rainfed agriculture is a cornerstone of global food production, supporting nearly 80% of the world's croplands and sustaining millions of smallholder farmers, particularly in semi-arid and tropical regions. However, its heavy reliance on natural rainfall makes it highly vulnerable to unpredictable weather patterns, prolonged dry spells, erratic monsoons, and extreme climatic events such as droughts and floods. These challenges frequently lead to crop failures, reduced yields, and food insecurity, especially in regions where alternative water sources are limited.

In the face of increasing climate variability, contingent crop planning has emerged as a critical strategy for stabilizing production in rainfed areas. This approach involves real-time adjustments in crop selection, sowing schedules, and field management based on evolving weather conditions. By integrating drought-tolerant crops, diversified cropping systems, and climate-smart farming practices, farmers can enhance resilience, optimize water use, and mitigate the risks posed by aberrant weather. Leveraging weather forecasting, remote sensing, and decision-support technologies further strengthens adaptive capacity, ensuring sustainable food production even in unpredictable environments.

Effective crop planning for adverse weather is not only essential for protecting farmer livelihoods but also plays a pivotal role in enhancing global food security amid the increasing threats posed by climate change.

Key Strategies for Adaptive Crop Planning

1. Choosing Climate-Resilient Crops
1. Drought-Resistant Crops

Drought-prone regions require crops that can survive extended dry spells while maintaining productivity. **Deep-rooted and water-efficient crops** are well-suited for such conditions.

- **Sorghum (Sorghum bicolor):** Known for its deep root system and high water-use efficiency, sorghum thrives in arid and semi-arid areas.
- **Pearl Millet (Pennisetum glaucum):** Adapted to sandy and degraded soils, it performs well under minimal moisture availability.
- **Pigeon Pea (Cajanus cajan):** With its **deep taproot system**, pigeon pea can extract moisture from deeper soil layers, ensuring growth even during dry spells.
- **Chickpea (Cicer arietinum):** A leguminous crop that requires significantly less water than other pulses, making it ideal for semi-arid regions.

2. Flood-Tolerant Crops

In regions where **heavy rainfall and waterlogging** are common, selecting crops that can withstand excessive moisture is critical.

- **Submergence-Tolerant Rice Varieties (e.g., Swarna Sub1):** These varieties can **withstand complete submergence for up to two weeks**, making them suitable for flood-prone areas.
- **Barnyard Millet (Echinochloa spp.):** Known for its **fast growth and waterlogging resistance**, it provides food security in regions prone to erratic monsoons.
- **Green Gram (Vigna radiata):** A short-duration legume that tolerates temporary flooding, making it suitable for regions with unpredictable rain patterns.

3. Short-Duration Varieties

Expanding the cultivation of **short-duration crops** in regions with **shorter or delayed rainy seasons** ensures **efficient water use and stable food production**. These crops are particularly beneficial in rainfed areas where unpredictable rainfall patterns can threaten yield stability.

Advantages of Short-Duration Crops

- **Efficient Water Utilization:** Completing their growth cycle in a **limited water window**, these crops reduce reliance on extended rainfall.

- **Lower Risk of Crop Failure:** Their ability to **mature quickly** minimizes exposure to mid-season droughts or erratic weather.
- **Enhanced Food Security:** Rapid-growing crops ensure a **continuous food supply**, especially in marginal environments.
- **Income Stability:** Short-duration legumes and vegetables provide **quick returns** to farmers, improving economic resilience.

Key Short-Duration Crops for Rainfed Regions
1. Early-Maturing Cereal Crops

- **Improved Hybrid Maize (Zea mays):** Some maize hybrids complete their lifecycle **within 80–90 days**, reducing dependence on prolonged rainfall.
- **Foxtail Millet (Setaria italica):** A hardy cereal that matures in **75–90 days**, suitable for regions with erratic monsoons.
- **Barley (Hordeum vulgare):** Certain varieties mature in **90–100 days**, making it a viable alternative to wheat in dryland areas.

2. Short-Duration Pulses

- **Black Gram (Vigna mungo):** A fast-growing legume that **matures in 70–90 days**, well-suited for rainfed intercropping systems.
- **Cowpea (Vigna unguiculata):** A **drought-tolerant pulse** completing its lifecycle in **60–90 days**, offering food and fodder security.
- **Green Gram (Vigna radiata):** Also known as mung bean, this pulse crop matures within **50–70 days**, making it an excellent choice for erratic rainfall regions.

3. Quick-Growing Vegetables

- **Amaranthus (Amaranthus spp.):** A nutrient-dense leafy vegetable that **grows within 30–40 days**, ideal for low-rainfall regions.
- **Radish (Raphanus sativus):** A root vegetable that matures **within 30–50 days**, requiring minimal water for growth.
- **Spinach (Spinacia oleracea):** A leafy green vegetable that can be harvested in **35–45 days**, ensuring a **continuous supply of essential micronutrients.**

Enhancing Climate Resilience through Crop Integration

By integrating **drought-tolerant, flood-resistant, and short-duration crops**, farmers can:

✔ **Reduce climate-related yield losses** by diversifying cropping systems.

✔ **Enhance food security** by ensuring a stable harvest even in erratic weather conditions.

✔ **Optimize water usage** by cultivating crops that **match the available moisture supply**.

✔ **Increase adaptability** to climate variability through a **balanced crop portfolio**.

Promoting **short-duration crops** alongside **other adaptive farming strategies** can **strengthen the resilience of rainfed agriculture**, ensuring **sustainable food production** even under shifting climatic conditions.

4. Adjusting Sowing Time to Weather Patterns

Erratic monsoon patterns, particularly **late or inconsistent rainfall**, pose a significant challenge to rainfed farming systems. Implementing **flexible cropping strategies** can help farmers **minimize losses and optimize productivity** despite uncertain climatic conditions.

1. Delayed Monsoon Adjustments

Adjusting **sowing schedules** based on **real-time weather forecasts** and **seasonal rainfall predictions** ensures better crop establishment and reduces the risk of crop failure.

Key Approaches:

✔ **Shifting Sowing Dates:** Rescheduling planting times to match **actual rainfall onset** improves seed germination and crop growth.

✔ **Selecting Short-Duration Varieties:** Switching to **early-maturing crops** compensates for the shortened growing season.

✔ **Interim Soil Moisture Conservation:** Practicing **pre-sowing irrigation**, conservation tillage, or mulching to **preserve residual moisture** before sowing.

Example:

- In **semi-arid India**, shifting **sorghum and pearl millet planting by 10–15 days** in response to **delayed monsoons** has shown to **reduce yield losses by 20–30%**.

2. Split Sowing Technique

Instead of sowing all seeds at once, **dividing crop planting into multiple phases** helps **mitigate risks associated with erratic rainfall** and **ensures a more stable harvest.**

Benefits of Split Sowing:

✓ **Risk Diversification:** If the first sowing fails due to insufficient rainfall, the second or third sowing increases chances of **successful establishment.**

✓ **Better Utilization of Moisture:** Different sowing times allow crops to **capitalize on intermittent rainfall,** improving **water-use efficiency (WUE).**

✓ **Staggered Harvests:** Harvesting crops at different intervals ensures a **steady food and income supply** for farmers.

Example:

- In **Madhya Pradesh, India,** farmers practicing **split sowing in soybean fields** observed a **15–20% higher yield stability** under erratic monsoon conditions compared to conventional single-sowing methods.

Integrating These Strategies for Resilient Rainfed Farming

By **combining delayed monsoon adjustments with split sowing,** farmers can:

✓ **Improve crop survival rates** even in unpredictable rainfall patterns.

✓ **Maximize available soil moisture** for enhanced productivity.

✓ **Reduce overall production risks,** ensuring **greater food and income security.**

Adaptive strategies like **flexible sowing dates and staggered planting techniques** are crucial for building **climate-resilient rainfed farming systems,** helping farmers thrive despite **changing monsoon patterns.**

5. Diversified Cropping Systems to Reduce Risk

In rainfed farming systems, **crop diversification** plays a crucial role in **reducing risks associated with erratic rainfall** while improving **soil fertility, moisture retention, and yield stability.** Two effective strategies—**intercropping and mixed cropping**—help optimize resource use and enhance drought resilience.

1. Intercropping Maize with Legumes for Improved Drought Resilience

Intercropping involves **growing two or more crops together** in the same field, allowing for **better soil moisture conservation and resource utilization**.

Benefits of Maize-Legume Intercropping:

✓ **Enhanced Soil Moisture Retention:** Legumes provide **ground cover**, reducing **evaporation losses** and maintaining **soil moisture levels**.

✓ **Improved Soil Fertility:** Legumes **fix atmospheric nitrogen**, reducing the need for synthetic fertilizers and enriching the soil for subsequent crops.

✓ **Drought Resilience:** The **shading effect of legumes** minimizes soil drying, creating a **microclimate** that helps maize withstand moisture stress.

✓ **Yield Stability:** Combining maize with legumes ensures **better land productivity**, as legumes continue to produce even under **moderate drought stress**.

Example:

- Studies in **Sub-Saharan Africa** have shown that intercropping **maize with cowpea or pigeon pea** can **increase water-use efficiency (WUE) by up to 30%** while maintaining **higher maize yields during dry spells.**

2. Mixed Cropping Systems for Sustainable Rainfed Farming

Mixed cropping involves **growing two or more crops together without a defined row arrangement**, creating a **diverse cropping environment** that boosts resilience against **climate variability**.

Sorghum-Cowpea Mixed Cropping: A Proven Strategy

✓ **Better Soil Fertility Management:** Cowpea fixes **nitrogen**, improving soil productivity for sorghum.

✓ **Reduced Yield Fluctuations:** If drought affects sorghum, cowpea continues to **produce biomass and yield**, ensuring **economic stability**.

✓ **Weed and Pest Suppression:** Dense canopy formation **limits weed growth**, while diversified crops **reduce pest outbreaks**.

✓ **Efficient Use of Soil Moisture:** Different rooting depths allow **maximum utilization of available water**, preventing **moisture competition**.

Example:

- Research in **semi-arid India** found that **sorghum intercropped with cowpea** improved **yield stability by 25%** and maintained **higher soil organic matter content** compared to sorghum monoculture.

Conclusion: Strengthening Rainfed Farming with Diversified Cropping Systems

By incorporating **intercropping and mixed cropping** in rainfed agriculture, farmers can:

✓ **Enhance soil moisture retention**, improving **drought resilience.**

✓ **Increase nitrogen availability**, reducing dependence on external fertilizers.

✓ **Stabilize yields**, even in **low or variable rainfall years.**

✓ **Promote long-term soil health**, making agricultural lands **more productive and sustainable.**

Adopting **climate-smart cropping strategies** like maize-legume intercropping and sorghum-cowpea mixed cropping ensures **higher resource efficiency, greater resilience to drought,** and **sustainable food production in rainfed regions.**

6. Conservation Agriculture for Rainwater Management

In rainfed agriculture, **water availability is unpredictable**, making it essential to adopt **conservation techniques** that maximize soil moisture retention and improve water-use efficiency. Two effective strategies—**mulching with reduced tillage and water harvesting structures**—play a crucial role in ensuring **sustained crop growth during dry periods.**

1. Mulching and Reduced Tillage for Soil Moisture Conservation

Mulching and reduced tillage help **retain soil moisture**, reduce **evaporation losses**, and **enhance soil structure**, ensuring **better water availability** for crops.

Benefits of Mulching & Reduced Tillage:

✓ **Lower Evaporation Losses:** Mulching with organic materials (straw, leaves) **reduces soil moisture evaporation by up to 30%**, keeping the root zone hydrated.

✓ **Improved Soil Health:** Retaining crop residues **enhances soil organic matter**, boosting water retention capacity.

✓ **Enhanced Water Infiltration:Reduced tillage maintains soil structure,** preventing **runoff and allowing rainwater to penetrate deeper.**

✓ **Weed Suppression:** Mulching **reduces weed growth**, decreasing competition for moisture and nutrients.

Example:

- Studies in **semi-arid regions of India** show that **organic mulching increases soil moisture retention by 25–40%,** leading to **higher crop yields in rainfed wheat and millet systems.**

2. Water Harvesting Structures for Drought Resilience

Rainwater harvesting ensures **water availability during prolonged dry spells,** allowing farmers to **supplement irrigation** and maintain crop growth.

Types of Water Harvesting Structures:

✓ **Farm Ponds:** Small reservoirs that **store excess rainwater** for use in dry periods, improving **crop survival rates by 40–50%.**

✓ **Check Dams:** Low-cost barriers that **slow down water runoff,** increasing groundwater recharge and **prolonging soil moisture retention.**

✓ **Contour Bunding:** Creating ridges along slopes to **prevent soil erosion** and **improve water infiltration.**

Example:

- Research in **Africa's Sahel region** found that farmers using **farm ponds and check dams** had **30% higher crop survival rates** during drought compared to those relying solely on rainfall.

Conclusion: Strengthening Rainfed Farming with Water Conservation Strategies

By integrating **mulching, reduced tillage, and water harvesting structures,** farmers can:

✓ **Retain soil moisture,** ensuring crop survival in dry spells.

✓ **Enhance water infiltration and storage,** reducing drought vulnerability.

✓ **Improve long-term soil health,** supporting **sustainable rainfed agriculture.**

Adopting these **climate-smart water management techniques** will make **rainfed farming systems more resilient,** ensuring **better yields and food security even in water-scarce regions.**

7. Leveraging Climate Information for Decision-Making

In rainfed agriculture, **unpredictable weather patterns** pose a major challenge to **crop productivity and food security.** Farmers often struggle with **erratic rainfall, dry spells, and extreme weather events,** which can lead to **yield losses and economic instability.** Integrating **weather advisory** services and decision support tools into farming practices can mitigate climate risks, enabling smarter, data-driven decision-making.

1. Weather Advisory Services: Enhancing Climate Preparedness

Access to accurate climate forecasts helps farmers make timely and informed decisions about sowing, irrigation, and crop protection.

Key Benefits:

✓ Optimized Sowing Dates: Farmers can adjust planting schedules based on expected rainfall patterns, improving germination rates and early crop establishment.

✓ Water Resource Management: Weather updates help in planning irrigation, ensuring efficient water use during dry periods.

✓ Early Warning for Extreme Events: Alerts about droughts, heavy rains, or heatwaves enable farmers to take preventive measures (e.g., adjusting inputs, using drought-tolerant varieties).

Example:

- Studies in India's semi-arid regions show that farmers who used seasonal climate forecasts increased their yields by 10–20% compared to those relying solely on traditional weather patterns.

2. Decision Support Tools: Smart Farming with Real-Time Guidance

Advancements in mobile technology, AI, and remote sensing have led to the development of decision support systems that provide real-time agronomic recommendations.

Key Features:

✓ Mobile Apps for Farmers: Digital platforms provide personalized advice on fertilization, pest control, and irrigation scheduling.

✓ Satellite-Based Crop Monitoring: Drones and remote sensing track soil moisture, crop health, and pest infestations, enabling timely interventions.

✓ AI-Powered Predictive Analytics: Machine learning models analyze past weather data and predict future climate trends, helping farmers adjust cropping strategies.

Example:

- In Africa, farmers using AI-driven mobile advisory services (e.g., weather-based planting guides) reported a 30% improvement in farm

productivity, reducing input costs and increasing profits.

Conclusion: Transforming Rainfed Agriculture with Digital Solutions

By integrating **weather advisory services and decision support tools**, farmers can:

✓ **Improve climate resilience** through better planning and adaptive strategies.

✓ **Enhance resource efficiency** by optimizing **water, nutrients, and pest control.**

✓ **Reduce yield losses and economic risks**, ensuring **sustainable agricultural productivity.**

Embracing smart technologies in rainfed farming will not only **minimize climate-related vulnerabilities** but also pave the way for **a more sustainable and profitable agricultural future.**

This approach empowers farmers to mitigate the impacts of erratic rainfall, prolonged droughts, and extreme weather events. By integrating **drought-resistant crops, flexible planting strategies, soil conservation practices, and digital climate advisory tools,** rainfed agriculture can become more **productive, stable, and sustainable.** Moreover, promoting **community-based water management, agroforestry systems, and mixed cropping** further strengthens resilience, ensuring that farmers can sustain their livelihoods despite environmental uncertainties.

By adopting **science-backed, climate-resilient farming** techniques, agricultural productivity in rainfed regions can **improve significantly,** contributing to **food security, economic stability, and environmental sustainability** in vulnerable areas.

CHAPTER NINE

WATERSHED MANAGEMENT IN RAINFED AGRICULTURE

9.1 Concept, Objectives, and Principles of Watershed Management

Concept of Watershed Management

Watershed management is a **scientific, holistic, and integrated approach** to conserving, developing, and managing natural resources within a watershed to achieve **sustainable agricultural productivity, water security, and environmental stability**. A watershed is a geographical unit that channels precipitation into streams, rivers, and lakes, influencing water availability and soil fertility. Proper management of watersheds is crucial for **maintaining ecological balance, improving livelihoods, and enhancing climate resilience**, especially in rainfed and drought-prone areas.

Watershed management is especially important for **rainfed agriculture, which accounts for nearly 80% of global farmland and contributes to 60% of global food production** (FAO, 2021). In India alone, **rainfed regions cover 55% of the net cultivated area and support 40% of the country's food production**. However, **climate variability, deforestation, soil**

degradation, and water scarcity threaten the sustainability of these agricultural systems. Research has shown that **integrated watershed management can increase agricultural productivity by 30–70% while reducing water runoff by 40–60%** (ICAR, 2020).

One of the most successful examples of watershed management is the **Sukhomajri watershed project in Haryana, India**, which demonstrated a **300% increase in groundwater levels**, an increase in biomass production, and **higher incomes for local farmers** after implementing soil and water conservation measures. Similarly, the **Watershed Development Programme in Maharashtra** helped increase crop yields by **50–80%** while improving soil fertility and water retention.

Objectives of Watershed Management

Watershed management focuses on achieving multiple objectives related to water conservation, land productivity, and ecosystem sustainability:

1. **Soil and Water Conservation**

Soil and water conservation is a fundamental aspect of watershed management, ensuring sustainable land use, improved agricultural productivity, and enhanced water availability. Watershed-based conservation practices help prevent soil erosion, land degradation, and nutrient depletion while improving water infiltration and retention. Research indicates that integrated watershed management programs have reduced soil loss by 30–60% and improved soil organic matter content by up to 40%. These improvements not only enhance soil fertility and water availability but also contribute to long-term sustainability in agriculture, particularly in rainfed regions where water scarcity is a critical challenge.

One of the most effective methods for soil conservation is contour plowing and terracing, particularly in sloped areas where soil erosion is a major concern. Contour plowing reduces soil loss by 30% and increases moisture retention by 20%, while terracing stabilizes farmland productivity by reducing runoff and sedimentation by 40–60%. Additionally, conservation tillage and mulching techniques help retain soil moisture and reduce evaporation, improving water infiltration by up to 50%. These methods are particularly beneficial in semi-arid and arid regions, where water conservation is essential for sustaining agricultural yields.

Agroforestry and vegetative barriers play a crucial role in soil and water conservation by reducing wind and water erosion. Planting trees and shrubs along farm boundaries and slopes improves soil structure, increases organic carbon levels, and promotes biodiversity. Studies show that agroforestry systems can reduce topsoil loss by 50% and enhance groundwater recharge, providing long-term benefits to farming communities. Similarly, cover cropping and green manuring contribute to soil fertility by preventing erosion and replenishing essential nutrients. Leguminous crops such as pigeon pea and sunn hemp enhance nitrogen content, promoting healthier soil and improved crop productivity.

Rainwater harvesting and groundwater recharge structures such as check dams, farm ponds, percolation tanks, and recharge wells significantly improve water availability in watershed areas. These structures slow down water runoff, allowing more time for infiltration and storage, which helps increase groundwater levels. In Rajasthan, for example, the construction of percolation tanks has led to an increase in groundwater levels by 3–4 meters, providing reliable irrigation for farmers even during dry spells. Watershed-based rainwater harvesting initiatives have also been shown to increase soil moisture by 25–40%, reducing crop failures in water-scarce regions.

Gully plugging and check dams are critical interventions in degraded landscapes where soil erosion is severe. These structures stabilize eroded gullies, slow down water runoff, and prevent sediment loss, ultimately leading to higher soil moisture retention. Studies indicate that gully plugging can reduce sediment yield by up to 70% while improving land productivity. Additionally, micro-irrigation technologies, such as drip and sprinkler systems, enhance water efficiency by ensuring precise water application, reducing wastage by 40–60%. The adoption of soil moisture sensors further improves irrigation efficiency by helping farmers apply water only when necessary.

The overall impact of soil and water conservation measures in watershed management is substantial. By reducing soil erosion and improving water infiltration, these practices increase agricultural productivity by 20–50% in rainfed regions. Improved soil fertility and moisture retention enable farmers to cultivate crops with greater resilience to droughts and erratic rainfall patterns. Watershed-based conservation initiatives also enhance climate resilience, with studies indicating that they can mitigate the impact of droughts and floods by up to 60%.

Incorporating soil and water conservation strategies into watershed management ensures long-term sustainability in agriculture, improves farmer livelihoods, and protects natural ecosystems. By integrating scientific conservation techniques with community-driven initiatives, watershed-based interventions contribute to enhanced food security, climate adaptation, and resource-efficient farming practices.

1. Sustainable Water Resource Utilization

Sustainable water resource utilization is a cornerstone of effective watershed management, aiming to enhance groundwater recharge, minimize runoff, and ensure year-round water availability. Given the increasing pressure on freshwater resources due to climate change, population growth, and agricultural expansion, sustainable water management strategies are essential for securing water supply and improving agricultural productivity. Watershed-based approaches focus on optimizing water use efficiency, reducing wastage, and implementing conservation measures to maintain ecological balance while supporting local communities.

One of the most effective strategies for sustainable water utilization is **rainwater harvesting**, which involves capturing and storing rainwater for future use. Various rainwater harvesting structures, such as check dams, percolation tanks, farm ponds, and recharge wells, have been shown to significantly increase water availability in dryland regions. Studies indicate that properly designed water harvesting structures can increase water storage capacity by 40–50% in semi-arid areas, reducing dependency on erratic monsoon rains. In Rajasthan and Maharashtra, community-based watershed programs have demonstrated an increase in groundwater levels by 3–5 meters due to the implementation of check dams and percolation tanks.

Groundwater recharge enhancement is another crucial aspect of sustainable water resource utilization. Groundwater depletion is a severe issue in many regions due to excessive extraction for irrigation and domestic use. Watershed management techniques, such as constructing infiltration trenches, recharge pits, and subsurface dykes, promote groundwater replenishment by facilitating the percolation of rainwater into aquifers. Case studies from Karnataka and Andhra Pradesh reveal that these interventions have led to a 30–60% improvement in groundwater availability, benefiting both drinking water supply and irrigation.

Efficient irrigation techniques play a vital role in reducing water wastage and maximizing the productivity of available resources. The adoption of **micro-irrigation technologies**, such as drip and sprinkler irrigation, significantly enhances water-use efficiency. Research suggests that drip irrigation systems can reduce water consumption by 40–60% while increasing crop yields by 20–50%. In Gujarat, farmers adopting drip irrigation for vegetable cultivation reported a 50% reduction in water usage while achieving higher productivity. Similarly, precision irrigation techniques, guided by soil moisture sensors and remote sensing technology, allow farmers to apply water only when needed, preventing over-irrigation and conserving resources.

Watershed-based afforestation and agroforestry initiatives contribute to sustainable water management by improving soil structure, reducing surface runoff, and enhancing groundwater recharge. Trees and deep-rooted plants act as natural sponges, facilitating water infiltration and preventing soil erosion. Agroforestry models incorporating trees such as Acacia, Moringa, and Prosopis have been shown to improve water retention and reduce surface runoff by 25–40%. In addition, vegetative buffers and grassland restoration help stabilize riverbanks, preventing siltation of water bodies and ensuring long-term water availability.

Community-led watershed management programs have proven to be highly effective in achieving sustainable water resource utilization. Participatory water governance, where local communities are involved in decision-making and water conservation initiatives, fosters a sense of ownership and ensures better management of resources. The **Sukhomajri Watershed Project** in Haryana is a notable example, where villagers adopted soil and water conservation measures, leading to a 30% increase in groundwater levels and a threefold rise in agricultural productivity. Similar success stories from Maharashtra's **Hiware Bazar watershed project** highlight how collective action in water conservation can lead to the revival of dried-up wells and improved water security.

Water budgeting and crop planning are essential tools in ensuring long-term sustainability in watershed-based water management. By aligning cropping patterns with available water resources, farmers can reduce the risk of overexploitation. **Deficit irrigation strategies**, which involve applying water only during critical crop growth stages, have been shown to save up to 30% of water while maintaining yields. Research in semi-arid regions has demonstrated that alternating low-water-consuming crops with high-demand crops in rotational systems can optimize water use and enhance sustainability.

In conclusion, sustainable water resource utilization within watershed management frameworks ensures the conservation and efficient use of available water resources. By integrating rainwater harvesting, groundwater recharge, micro-irrigation, afforestation, community participation, and scientific water budgeting techniques, watershed management initiatives can significantly improve water security in drought-prone and water-scarce regions. These approaches not only mitigate the impacts of climate variability but also promote long-term agricultural sustainability and rural livelihood resilience.

3. Enhancing Agricultural Productivity

Agricultural productivity in rainfed and semi-arid regions is often constrained by erratic rainfall, soil degradation, and water scarcity. Watershed-based interventions play a crucial role in mitigating these challenges by improving soil moisture retention, enhancing groundwater recharge, and promoting sustainable farming practices. Studies have shown that comprehensive watershed management strategies can increase crop yields by 30–80%, particularly in drought-prone areas, by optimizing water and soil resource use.

One of the key benefits of watershed-based approaches is the improvement of **soil moisture availability**, which directly influences crop growth and productivity. **Soil and water conservation techniques**, such as contour bunding, terracing, and mulching, help reduce surface runoff and enhance water infiltration. Research in semi-arid regions of India has demonstrated that contour bunding can reduce soil erosion by 40% and improve crop yields by 50%, particularly for staple crops like sorghum and millet. Similarly, mulching with crop residues has been found to conserve up to 20–30% more soil moisture, leading to higher yields in water-deficient conditions.

Drought-resilient farming is another critical advantage of watershed-based interventions. By integrating **crop diversification, agroforestry, and water-efficient irrigation techniques**, farmers can reduce dependency on a single crop and build resilience against climate variability. Studies in Ethiopia and India have highlighted that diversified cropping systems incorporating legumes, oilseeds, and drought-tolerant cereals can enhance farm incomes by 60% while maintaining soil fertility. **Agroforestry models,** such as integrating trees like Acacia and Moringa with food crops, have been shown to improve microclimatic conditions, reduce evaporation losses, and enhance nutrient cycling.

Water availability is a major limiting factor in dryland agriculture, and watershed programs facilitate **better water resource management** to improve productivity. **Micro-irrigation systems,** such as drip and sprinkler irrigation, have been successfully adopted in watershed projects to maximize water-use efficiency. Case studies from Maharashtra and Rajasthan indicate that **drip irrigation reduces water consumption by 40–60% while increasing yields by 30–50%** in crops like vegetables, cotton, and pulses. **Rainwater harvesting structures,** such as check dams and farm ponds, have also played a significant role in ensuring water availability during dry spells. Research has shown that well-managed check dams can increase groundwater recharge by 40%, benefiting both agriculture and domestic water supply.

Furthermore, **integrated nutrient management (INM)** within watershed projects has led to substantial improvements in soil fertility and crop yields. The use of **biofertilizers, organic compost, and judicious chemical fertilizers** ensures long-term soil health and reduces input costs. Studies indicate that combining farmyard manure with nitrogen-fixing crops like pigeon pea and cowpea can increase soil nitrogen levels by 20–30%, leading to higher yields and sustainable soil productivity.

Community-led watershed programs have also demonstrated significant success in enhancing agricultural productivity. In **the Hiware Bazar watershed project in Maharashtra,** farmers reported a **300% increase in crop productivity** due to the combined impact of water conservation, soil improvement, and diversified farming systems. Similarly, in the **Sukhomajri Watershed Project,** integrated watershed management practices led to **a threefold increase in crop production** and improved water availability for irrigation.

In conclusion, watershed-based interventions provide a **holistic solution for enhancing agricultural productivity** by improving soil moisture retention, optimizing water use, promoting crop diversification, and maintaining soil fertility. These approaches not only **increase farm yields and incomes** but also ensure **long-term sustainability and resilience** in semi-arid and drought-prone regions. By implementing watershed management strategies on a wider scale, governments and agricultural stakeholders can significantly boost food security and rural livelihoods while safeguarding natural resources.

4. Livelihood and Rural Development

Watershed management plays a crucial role in improving **livelihoods and rural development** by enhancing natural resource sustainability, increasing agricultural productivity, and generating employment opportunities. In many rural areas, especially those dependent on rainfed farming, water scarcity and land degradation limit agricultural potential and income generation. Integrated watershed projects address these issues by optimizing land and water use, promoting sustainable farming practices, and creating employment through conservation and afforestation activities.

One of the primary ways **watershed management supports livelihoods** is through **employment generation in afforestation, agroforestry, and soil conservation.** Many watershed programs include activities like **tree planting, contour bunding, gully plugging, and farm pond construction**, all of which require local labor. A study on watershed programs in **Rajasthan and Madhya Pradesh** found that implementing soil and water conservation measures created **100–150 workdays per hectare annually**, significantly benefiting landless and marginal farmers. **Afforestation initiatives** within watershed projects further boost employment while restoring degraded lands, improving biodiversity, and providing additional sources of income from timber, fuelwood, and non-timber forest products.

Agroforestry and diversified farming systems also contribute to **sustainable income generation** in rural communities. Integrating trees like **Moringa, Acacia, and Prosopis** with crops enhances soil fertility, reduces erosion, and provides multiple sources of income through fruit, fodder, and medicinal plants. Studies in **semi-arid regions of India** have shown that **agroforestry-based watershed interventions** can **increase farmers' incomes by 40–60%** through the sale of tree products, livestock fodder, and improved crop yields. Additionally, integrating livestock with watershed-based agriculture ensures **better pasture availability**, increasing milk and meat production, which further supports household incomes.

Optimizing land and water use through watershed projects significantly enhances agricultural income. Research in Maharashtra's watershed development programs shows that farmers **increased their annual incomes by 50%** due to improved water availability and higher crop productivity. **Water harvesting structures like check dams, percolation tanks, and farm ponds** have led to **a 30–50% increase in groundwater recharge**, enabling farmers to cultivate a second crop season (Rabi cropping) instead of relying solely on the monsoon (Kharif season). This shift has helped smallholder farmers diversify their incomes and improve household food security.

Moreover, **micro-enterprise development linked to watershed management** has played a pivotal role in empowering rural communities. The availability of **better irrigation facilities** encourages **horticulture, vegetable cultivation, and floriculture**, which are high-value agricultural activities. Women-led self-help groups (SHGs) in watershed areas have successfully engaged in **value-added processing of farm produce**, such as making organic fertilizers, dairy production, and processing minor forest products like honey and medicinal plants. Studies in **Karnataka and Tamil Nadu** reveal that watershed-linked micro-enterprises have **boosted rural incomes by 30–40%**, particularly for women and landless laborers.

Community participation in watershed programs has also strengthened **social capital and rural governance**. Successful watershed projects adopt a **bottom-up approach**, involving local communities in planning, implementation, and maintenance. Case studies from the **Sukhomajri and Ralegan Siddhi watershed projects** highlight that **community-driven watershed management** has led to equitable water distribution, reduced conflicts over resource use, and increased self-reliance in rural areas.

Watershed management serves as a **transformative tool for rural development and livelihood enhancement**. By creating employment, improving agricultural income, promoting agroforestry, and encouraging micro-enterprises, these programs uplift rural communities while ensuring environmental sustainability. Scaling up watershed-based interventions can significantly **reduce rural poverty, enhance food security, and build climate resilience** in vulnerable regions.

5. Mitigating Climate Change Impacts

Climate change poses significant challenges to agriculture, water resources, and rural livelihoods, particularly in rainfed and drought-prone regions. **Watershed management serves as an effective strategy to mitigate climate change impacts** by enhancing water security, reducing soil degradation, and promoting carbon sequestration. By regulating water flow, increasing vegetative cover, and improving land-use practices, watershed-based interventions help reduce **the vulnerability of ecosystems and communities** to extreme climatic events such as droughts, floods, and erratic rainfall patterns.

One of the primary ways **watershed management mitigates climate risks** is by **regulating water flow and improving groundwater recharge**. Climate change has increased **the frequency and intensity of extreme weather events**, causing prolonged droughts and devastating floods. **Integrated watershed development projects focus on rainwater harvesting, construction of check dams, percolation tanks, and contour bunding**, which reduce surface runoff and **increase groundwater levels by 30–50%** in dryland areas.

For example, **watershed projects in Rajasthan and Maharashtra** have demonstrated **a 25–40% reduction in the severity of drought impacts** by improving water storage and soil moisture retention. In flood-prone areas, **watershed management reduces waterlogging** by constructing drainage channels, protecting riverbanks, and promoting agroforestry practices that **stabilize soil and prevent excessive runoff**. Studies in **eastern India's flood-affected regions** have shown that well-managed watersheds **reduce flood intensity by 20–35%** by slowing down water flow and increasing soil infiltration rates.

Watershed management also plays a critical role in **climate change mitigation by promoting carbon sequestration**. Tree planting, agroforestry, and sustainable soil conservation practices help absorb atmospheric **carbon dioxide (CO_2), reducing greenhouse gas (GHG) emissions**. Research indicates that **agroforestry systems in watershed projects sequester an average of 2–5 tons of carbon per hectare per year**, contributing to climate mitigation efforts.

Afforestation and reforestation within watershed programs not only **act as carbon sinks but also restore degraded lands**. Projects in **semi-arid regions of Africa and India** have shown that **integrating native tree species with farmland increases soil organic carbon by 15–30% over a decade**, improving soil fertility and moisture-holding capacity. Additionally, conservation agriculture practices such as **zero tillage, cover cropping, and mulching** reduce soil erosion, enhance microbial activity, and store more carbon in the soil.

Watershed management also promotes **climate-smart agricultural practices** that enhance resilience to changing climatic conditions. Techniques such as **drought-resistant cropping systems, mixed farming, and rotational grazing** optimize water use and maintain soil health. Studies in **Madhya Pradesh and Andhra Pradesh** indicate that watershed-based interventions have **increased crop yields by 25–50%** by improving soil moisture retention and nutrient availability.

Furthermore, **community-driven watershed initiatives** strengthen rural resilience by encouraging **participatory planning and resource management**. Farmers who engage in **climate-adaptive farming techniques** under watershed programs report **lower yield losses (by 30–40%)** during drought years compared to those relying on traditional practices.

Watershed management is a **proactive approach to mitigating climate change impacts**, reducing the vulnerability of rural communities to extreme weather conditions, and **enhancing environmental sustainability**. By **regulating water resources, promoting carbon sequestration, and adopting climate-resilient farming methods**, watershed programs **not only safeguard livelihoods but also contribute to long-term ecological stability**. Expanding such initiatives across vulnerable regions can significantly **enhance global climate adaptation and mitigation efforts**.

Principles of Watershed Management

Effective watershed management is founded on **key principles that ensure sustainability, ecological balance, and long-term economic benefits**. These principles guide the planning, implementation, and maintenance of watershed programs, ensuring that both natural resources and local communities' benefit from improved land and water management strategies:

1. **Integrated Resource Management**

Integrated Resource Management (IRM) is a holistic approach that combines **soil conservation, water harvesting, afforestation, and agricultural development** to ensure the sustainable use of natural resources within a watershed. This multidisciplinary strategy enhances environmental stability, improves agricultural productivity, and mitigates resource degradation. By integrating agriculture, forestry, and hydrology, IRM ensures efficient resource utilization and long-term sustainability.

Soil conservation plays a vital role in IRM, as soil erosion, nutrient depletion, and compaction are major challenges in watershed areas. Techniques such as **contour farming, terracing, cover cropping, and conservation tillage** help prevent soil erosion by up to 60%, improving water infiltration and moisture retention. These practices maintain soil fertility and structure, ensuring long-term agricultural productivity. Additionally, the use of **organic matter, green manuring, and mulching** enhances soil health and reduces nutrient loss, making farming systems more resilient to climatic variability.

Water harvesting and efficient utilization are essential in watersheds, particularly in rainfed and semi-arid regions. **Rainwater harvesting structures like check dams, percolation tanks, and farm ponds** have been shown to **increase water availability by 40–50%** in dryland areas, reducing dependence on erratic rainfall. **Drip and sprinkler irrigation systems** further enhance water-use efficiency, cutting water consumption by up to 70% compared to conventional methods. Additionally, **groundwater recharge techniques**, such as infiltration trenches and recharge wells, help replenish aquifers, ensuring long-term water security for both agriculture and domestic use.

Afforestation and agroforestry contribute significantly to watershed stability by **reducing surface runoff, preventing floods, and sequestering carbon**. Trees and vegetation improve water retention, enhance soil fertility, and provide alternative income sources for rural communities through **timber, fuelwood, and non-timber forest products**. Studies indicate that agroforestry systems can sequester **2–5 tons of carbon per hectare annually**, making them an effective strategy for climate change mitigation. Additionally, tree-based farming systems provide **fodder for livestock**, reducing pressure on natural grasslands and preventing overgrazing.

Integrated agriculture and livestock management optimize resource utilization within watersheds. **Diversified cropping systems**, such as intercropping and crop rotation, enhance soil fertility, prevent pest outbreaks, and increase farm productivity. Integrating **livestock with crop farming** allows for efficient nutrient recycling, as manure serves as an organic fertilizer, improving soil health. **Silvopastoral systems**, which combine trees, forage crops, and livestock, provide sustainable fodder sources, reducing degradation of grazing lands and enhancing livestock productivity.

Hydrological and ecological balance is a fundamental aspect of IRM, ensuring a stable relationship between rainfall, soil moisture, and groundwater recharge. Strategies such as **riparian buffer zones, micro-watershed planning, and wetland restoration** maintain water quality, reduce sedimentation, and support biodiversity conservation. By preserving natural ecosystems within watersheds, these measures help regulate water flow, reduce flood risks, and sustain agricultural activities.

In conclusion, **Integrated Resource Management** offers a sustainable solution to managing land, water, and biological resources efficiently. By combining **soil conservation, water harvesting, afforestation, and agricultural development**, IRM enhances **agricultural resilience, boosts water security, and supports rural livelihoods**. Its implementation ensures that **watershed ecosystems remain productive and ecologically balanced**, providing long-term benefits to both farming communities and the environment.

2. Water Conservation and Harvesting

Water conservation and harvesting are essential components of **watershed management**, ensuring sustainable water availability for agriculture, domestic use, and ecosystem preservation. In **rainfed and arid regions**, where erratic rainfall and prolonged dry spells pose significant challenges, implementing **efficient water storage and recharge structures** is critical. Techniques such as **check dams, farm ponds, percolation tanks, and recharge wells** help capture runoff, enhance groundwater levels, and improve soil moisture retention, thereby reducing water scarcity and stabilizing agricultural productivity.

One of the most effective **water harvesting techniques** is the construction of **check dams**, which slow down surface runoff, allowing water to percolate into the ground. Studies indicate that **check dams increase groundwater recharge by 40–50%** in semi-arid zones, helping maintain water tables and ensuring year-round water availability. Additionally, **percolation tanks**, which are shallow reservoirs designed to retain rainwater and enhance infiltration, have been shown to **increase soil moisture levels by 20–30%**, benefiting crops and vegetation in downstream areas.

Farm ponds are another crucial water conservation measure in watershed programs. These small reservoirs collect and store rainwater, providing supplemental irrigation during dry periods. Research shows that **farm ponds can increase crop yields by up to 30% in rainfed areas,** as they allow farmers to irrigate critical growth stages, preventing drought-induced crop failures. **Lined farm ponds,** which minimize seepage losses, further improve water retention and ensure efficient utilization of harvested rainwater.

Rainwater harvesting systems, such as rooftop rainwater collection and bunds in agricultural fields, help farmers maximize rainfall utilization. In dryland regions, **contour bunding and graded trenches** effectively capture runoff, prevent soil erosion, and improve groundwater recharge. These structures **reduce runoff by 50–60%,** enhancing soil moisture and promoting better crop establishment.

The implementation of **water conservation and harvesting techniques** through **community-led watershed programs** has demonstrated remarkable success in **rejuvenating degraded lands and improving rural livelihoods.** In states like **Rajasthan, Maharashtra, and Telangana,** large-scale watershed initiatives have led to increased groundwater levels, revived dried-up wells, and transformed barren lands into productive agricultural fields. The **Hivre Bazar watershed project in Maharashtra,** for instance, increased water availability by **over 50%,** enabling farmers to shift from drought-prone crops to higher-value horticultural and cash crops.

Beyond agriculture, **water harvesting structures also support afforestation and biodiversity conservation,** ensuring a balanced ecosystem. By **enhancing groundwater recharge, stabilizing water availability, and reducing dependency on erratic rainfall,** water conservation strategies contribute to **climate resilience, food security, and long-term agricultural sustainability** in watershed areas.

3. Soil Conservation and Fertility Management

Soil conservation and fertility management are fundamental to **sustainable watershed development,** as they protect against soil degradation, enhance agricultural productivity, and maintain ecological balance. In **rainfed and hilly regions,** soil erosion and nutrient loss are major concerns, reducing land fertility and affecting water retention. Effective **soil conservation practices,** such as **contour farming, terracing, mulching, and conservation tillage,** help mitigate these challenges by preventing soil runoff, improving moisture retention, and replenishing soil nutrients.

Contour farming, a widely adopted soil conservation technique, involves plowing along the natural contours of the land rather than perpendicular to the slope. This method **reduces surface runoff by 30–50%** and allows rainwater to infiltrate the soil, preventing erosion. Studies indicate that **contour bunding and ridge planting** increase soil moisture retention by **15–25%**, making them particularly beneficial in dryland and sloping terrains.

Terracing, commonly used in mountainous and hilly regions, involves creating stepped fields along slopes to slow water flow and minimize soil loss. Research has shown that **bench terraces reduce soil erosion rates by 50–80%**, enhancing soil depth and moisture availability for crops. **Stone bunds and vegetative barriers**, which act as physical barriers to slow down runoff, further support **sediment deposition and organic matter accumulation**, boosting soil fertility.

Mulching, another crucial practice, involves covering the soil with organic or synthetic materials to prevent moisture evaporation, suppress weeds, and improve soil structure. Studies have demonstrated that **mulching enhances soil moisture retention by 25–40%**, significantly benefiting crops during dry spells. **Straw, crop residues, and biodegradable films** are commonly used as mulch materials, reducing soil temperature fluctuations and increasing microbial activity, which improves nutrient cycling.

Conservation tillage, which includes **zero-tillage and minimum tillage techniques**, minimizes soil disturbance, preserving soil organic matter and microbial diversity. Research has found that **zero-tillage can enhance soil water retention by up to 35%**, reducing drought stress and improving root growth. Additionally, conservation tillage contributes to **carbon sequestration**, making it an effective strategy for climate change mitigation in agricultural landscapes.

Agroforestry and cover cropping further enhance soil conservation and fertility management. **Leguminous cover crops**, such as cowpea and clover, fix atmospheric nitrogen, improving soil fertility naturally. Studies indicate that **integrating agroforestry into watershed programs can increase soil organic carbon by 20–30% over time**, enhancing long-term soil health and productivity.

Successful watershed projects have demonstrated the effectiveness of soil conservation techniques in restoring degraded lands. For instance, in

Sukhomajri, Haryana, and Ralegan Siddhi, Maharashtra, large-scale soil conservation efforts, including **check dams, contour bunds, and afforestation**, have **revived groundwater tables, reduced soil erosion, and improved agricultural yields by over 60%**.

By integrating **soil conservation and fertility management practices**, watershed programs ensure **long-term agricultural sustainability, improved water use efficiency, and enhanced resilience to climate change**. These strategies not only protect natural resources but also promote **food security, farmer livelihoods, and environmental sustainability** in vulnerable ecosystems.

4. **Community Participation and Stakeholder Involvement**

Community participation is a **key principle** in successful watershed management, ensuring that conservation efforts are **locally driven, sustainable, and economically beneficial**. By actively involving **farmers, local communities, non-governmental organizations (NGOs), and government agencies**, watershed projects can effectively address **soil and water conservation, sustainable agriculture, and rural livelihoods**. Studies indicate that **watershed projects with strong community participation result in 30% higher economic benefits** compared to those implemented solely through external interventions.

A participatory approach allows **local farmers and stakeholders to take ownership** of conservation initiatives, leading to better **implementation, maintenance, and long-term impact**. Traditional top-down approaches often fail because they do not account for **local knowledge, resource constraints, and social dynamics**. However, when communities are actively engaged, they contribute their **expertise, labor, and financial resources**, ensuring that interventions are **context-specific and widely accepted**.

One of the most effective models of community-driven watershed management is the **Self-Help Group (SHG) and Village Watershed Committee (VWC) approach**. In this model, local committees oversee **soil and water conservation measures, afforestation, and agricultural improvements**. Case studies from **Andhra Pradesh, Maharashtra, and Rajasthan** show that participatory watershed projects have **increased crop yields by 30–50% and improved groundwater recharge by 40%**, leading to enhanced **agricultural sustainability and income generation**.

Additionally, **NGOs and government agencies** play a crucial role in **capacity building, funding, and technical support.** Organizations like **WOTR (Watershed Organization Trust) and NABARD (National Bank for Agriculture and Rural Development)** have successfully facilitated **community-led watershed projects** in India, providing training in **water harvesting, sustainable land management, and agroforestry.** These projects have shown that when farmers are **empowered with knowledge and resources**, they are more likely to **adopt best practices**, such as **contour bunding, mulching, and micro-irrigation**, improving overall watershed health.

Moreover, **women's participation** in watershed programs has demonstrated significant benefits, particularly in resource management and income diversification. In regions where women are involved in **SHGs for water conservation and afforestation**, households have reported **better access to irrigation, increased fodder availability, and improved soil fertility.** Studies show that **women-led watershed initiatives in Gujarat and Madhya Pradesh have contributed to a 20% increase in household incomes,** demonstrating the importance of **inclusive decision-making.**

Overall, integrating **community participation** into watershed management fosters **collective responsibility, economic upliftment, and ecological sustainability.** By ensuring that all stakeholders are actively engaged in **planning, execution, and monitoring,** watershed projects can achieve **greater impact, long-term success, and resilience against climate change.**

5. Equitable Resource Distribution

Ensuring **equitable access** to water, land, and agricultural resources is a fundamental principle of effective **watershed management**, particularly for **small farmers, marginalized communities, and women.** Many rural areas depend on rainfed agriculture, where resource distribution is often unequal, limiting the opportunities for **smallholder farmers to access irrigation, quality soil, and improved farming technologies.** A well-structured watershed management program addresses these disparities by promoting **fair resource distribution, inclusive participation, and targeted interventions** to uplift vulnerable groups.

One of the significant aspects of **equitable watershed management** is the recognition of **land tenure rights and community-based water-sharing**

mechanisms. In regions where small and marginal farmers lack **secure land ownership**, they often face difficulties in accessing **government subsidies, irrigation systems, and credit facilities.** Participatory watershed programs, particularly those implemented in **India, Africa, and Latin America**, have demonstrated that **landless farmers and tenant cultivators can benefit significantly from soil and water conservation initiatives** when given equitable access to common resources.

Furthermore, **women's participation in watershed programs has seen a notable rise,** bringing about transformative changes in rural economies. Studies show that **women's involvement in watershed projects in India has increased by 35% (World Bank, 2019)**, leading to **higher crop productivity, improved household food security, and greater financial independence.** Traditionally, women play a crucial role in **water collection, livestock management, and household farming,** yet they are often excluded from **decision-making and resource allocation.** Inclusive watershed programs promote **gender-sensitive approaches** by facilitating **women-led Self-Help Groups (SHGs), access to microfinance, and agricultural training programs.** In many successful watershed projects, such as those in **Madhya Pradesh and Maharashtra,** women-led initiatives have led to **better irrigation management, increased fodder availability, and diversified income sources** through agroforestry and allied activities.

Equity in watershed management also involves ensuring that **smallholder and tribal farmers** receive adequate support for **adopting climate-resilient farming techniques.** Many watershed initiatives focus on **community irrigation schemes, check dams, and percolation tanks,** ensuring that even the most resource-poor farmers can **benefit from improved groundwater recharge and enhanced soil fertility.** Case studies from **Andhra Pradesh and Rajasthan** indicate that **watershed programs have reduced water conflicts by 50%** through **fair allocation of water resources and participatory governance models.**

Additionally, **government and NGO-led initiatives** work toward integrating **livelihood diversification** as a core component of watershed management. Programs like **Mahatma Gandhi National Rural Employment Guarantee Act (MGNREGA)** in India have provided **wage employment to rural laborers through watershed-related activities,** such as **soil conservation, afforestation, and water harvesting projects.** This approach has not only **strengthened rural livelihoods** but has also led to **higher community involvement and better management of watershed resources.**

By ensuring **fair and inclusive access** to water and land, watershed programs help **reduce socio-economic disparities, empower marginalized communities, and build climate-resilient farming systems.** When **small farmers, women, and indigenous groups** actively participate in watershed planning and implementation, the results lead to **stronger rural economies, improved food security, and sustainable resource management** for future generations.

Conclusion

Watershed management is a **scientific, ecological, and socio-economic strategy** designed to ensure the **sustainable use of land, water, and biological resources,** particularly in **rainfed and drought-prone regions.** As water scarcity and land degradation continue to pose major challenges to global agriculture, **integrated watershed management** has emerged as a vital solution for enhancing **water security, soil health, and rural livelihoods.**

Scientific research and **successful case studies from India, Africa, and Latin America** have demonstrated that watershed-based interventions can **increase water availability, prevent soil erosion, and improve crop productivity.** Studies indicate that **integrated watershed development programs have led to a 30–80% increase in agricultural yields** by enhancing **moisture retention, groundwater recharge, and soil fertility.** By adopting a **multi-disciplinary approach** that combines **hydrology, agronomy, forestry, and community** development, watershed management plays a crucial role in **climate adaptation and resilience building.**

A key aspect of **sustainable watershed management** is **soil and water conservation,** which involves **terracing, contour farming, check dams, and percolation ponds** to prevent **runoff and nutrient loss.** Research shows that **such conservation measures can reduce soil loss by 30–60% and improve organic matter content,** ensuring **long-term agricultural sustainability.** Additionally, **water harvesting structures, such as farm ponds and recharge wells, have been found to increase groundwater levels by 40–50% in arid and semi-arid regions,** providing **year-round irrigation support.**

Beyond environmental benefits, **watershed management significantly enhances rural livelihoods.** Community-driven watershed programs create employment opportunities through **afforestation, agroforestry, and land restoration projects,** helping smallholder farmers diversify their income sources. Case studies from **Maharashtra and Andhra Pradesh in India** show that watershed projects have **increased annual farm incomes by 50%** by optimizing **land and water use.** Additionally, **women's participation in watershed initiatives has grown by 35%,** leading to **greater financial inclusion and empowerment in rural communities.**

By integrating **scientific techniques with participatory planning,** watershed management fosters **equity in resource distribution, resilience against climate change, and long-term environmental sustainability.** As climate variability intensifies, investing in **watershed-based interventions** will be essential for ensuring **food security, water availability, and sustainable agricultural growth** in vulnerable regions worldwide.

9.2 Components of Effective Watershed Management

Watershed management is a comprehensive approach that integrates physical, biological, and socioeconomic factors to ensure the sustainable use and conservation of natural resources within a defined watershed area. It focuses on maintaining the balance between water availability, soil health, agricultural productivity, and the overall well-being of local communities. Given the increasing pressures of climate change, population growth, and land degradation, effective watershed management has become essential for ensuring long-term water security, soil conservation, and ecological stability.

A well-structured watershed management strategy takes into account key physical elements such as topography, land use patterns, soil characteristics, and hydrology to design interventions that optimize water retention and minimize erosion. Biological components, including vegetation cover, agroforestry, and biodiversity conservation, play a crucial role in maintaining ecological balance and enhancing soil fertility. Equally important are the socioeconomic aspects, which emphasize community involvement, equitable resource distribution, and sustainable livelihoods, ensuring that watershed programs address both environmental and human development goals.

Numerous studies have shown that integrated watershed development programs have significantly improved water recharge, reduced soil loss, and increased agricultural yields in rainfed regions. For instance, watershed projects in India's semi-arid regions have led to a 40–50% increase in groundwater availability and improved crop productivity by up to 80%. Similarly, initiatives in sub-Saharan Africa have demonstrated how community-driven watershed management can enhance food security and resilience against droughts and floods.

By implementing a holistic approach that combines physical, biological, and socioeconomic components, watershed management contributes to climate resilience, sustainable agriculture, and rural development. When effectively planned and executed, it provides a long-term solution to the challenges of water scarcity, land degradation, and rural poverty, making it a crucial strategy for ensuring environmental and economic sustainability.

1. Physical Components

Physical components of watershed management play a fundamental role in preserving land, water, and soil resources to enhance watershed health and productivity. These components focus on engineering and natural interventions that help mitigate land degradation, improve water conservation, and ensure sustainable agricultural practices.

Soil and Water Conservation Structures

The implementation of soil and water conservation structures such as contour bunds, terraces, check dams, and farm ponds is crucial in reducing soil erosion, increasing water infiltration, and minimizing surface runoff losses. Contour bunding and terracing slow down water flow on sloped lands, allowing more time for water to percolate into the soil. Check dams and farm ponds collect surface runoff, preventing water loss and facilitating groundwater recharge. Research indicates that integrating soil conservation measures can reduce soil erosion by 30–60% while improving groundwater recharge by up to 40%, leading to enhanced soil fertility and improved agricultural productivity in rainfed regions.

Water Harvesting Systems

Water harvesting techniques play a key role in ensuring water availability throughout the year, particularly in semi-arid and arid regions where rainfall is erratic. Structures such as percolation tanks, rainwater harvesting systems, and subsurface dams help capture and store rainwater, making it available for irrigation, livestock, and domestic use during dry periods. Case studies from dryland regions in India show that these interventions have increased water storage capacity by nearly 50%, ensuring better water security for communities dependent on rainfed agriculture. Additionally, efficient rainwater harvesting reduces dependence on external water sources and mitigates the impact of droughts and dry spells.

Land Use Planning

Effective land use planning is essential for optimizing resource utilization while minimizing environmental degradation. Proper classification and zoning of land for agriculture, forestry, settlements, and conservation help maintain ecological balance and prevent over-exploitation of resources. By implementing sustainable land management practices, watershed projects can ensure long-term productivity while reducing risks such as soil erosion, deforestation, and unregulated urban expansion. Integrated land-use planning strategies have been successful in promoting sustainable farming, afforestation, and eco-restoration in degraded watersheds.

By integrating these physical components, watershed management strategies can significantly improve soil and water conservation, enhance agricultural productivity, and promote long-term ecological stability. These interventions not only benefit farmers and rural communities but also contribute to broader environmental sustainability by reducing land degradation, improving groundwater recharge, and mitigating the adverse effects of climate change.

2. Biological Components

Biological measures in watershed management focus on vegetation management, agroforestry, and biodiversity conservation to improve ecosystem resilience, soil fertility, and water retention. These interventions play a crucial role in stabilizing landscapes, mitigating climate change impacts, and ensuring sustainable agricultural productivity in rainfed and degraded areas.

Afforestation and Agroforestry

Afforestation and agroforestry are effective biological strategies for restoring degraded lands and enhancing watershed sustainability. Planting trees, shrubs, and perennial vegetation helps stabilize the soil, reduce evaporation losses, and improve carbon sequestration. Research has shown that afforestation projects in watershed areas can significantly increase soil organic matter, improve infiltration rates, and reduce surface runoff. Agroforestry systems, which integrate trees with agricultural crops, provide multiple benefits such as fuelwood, fodder, timber, and additional income for farmers. For instance, studies have demonstrated that agroforestry models improve soil moisture retention by up to 20–30%, making them valuable in drought-prone regions. Additionally, deep-rooted trees in agroforestry systems contribute to groundwater recharge by allowing water to percolate into deeper soil layers.

Grassland Development and Silvipasture Systems

Grassland management plays a vital role in preventing soil erosion, enhancing fodder availability, and improving livestock productivity. Establishing pasturelands and silvipasture systems—where trees and grasses are grown together—supports sustainable livestock farming while preventing overgrazing, which is a leading cause of land degradation in many arid and semi-arid regions. Managed grazing and rotational grazing techniques further help in maintaining the health of grasslands, ensuring long-term sustainability. Research indicates that well-managed pasturelands can reduce erosion rates by 30–50% and enhance soil carbon sequestration, making them an essential component of watershed management.

Crop Diversification and Sustainable Farming Practices

Diversifying crops in rainfed areas strengthens ecosystem resilience and reduces the risks associated with erratic rainfall patterns. Introducing drought-tolerant and high water-use efficiency crops ensures stable yields even in unfavorable weather conditions. Studies have shown that intercropping systems—such as sorghum and pigeon pea or maize and cowpea—can improve water retention in the soil and reduce climate vulnerability. Additionally, incorporating nitrogen-fixing legumes into crop rotations enhances soil fertility by naturally enriching nitrogen levels, reducing the dependence on chemical fertilizers.

Biological measures in watershed management help improve soil fertility, control erosion, and enhance water conservation. By promoting afforestation, grassland restoration, and sustainable cropping systems, these interventions contribute to the long-term ecological and economic sustainability of watersheds, ensuring better livelihoods for rural communities and improved resilience to climate change..

3. Socioeconomic Components

A successful watershed program must integrate social and economic considerations to ensure community participation, equitable resource distribution, and long-term sustainability. Socioeconomic interventions not only improve livelihoods but also enhance the effectiveness of watershed management strategies by fostering local ownership and collective responsibility. Research and case studies from various regions highlight the crucial role of community involvement, employment generation, and inclusive development in sustaining watershed projects.

Community Participation and Ownership

Community participation is a cornerstone of successful watershed management. Engaging local stakeholders—farmers, NGOs, government agencies, and policymakers—ensures that watershed interventions align with local needs and resources. Studies indicate that watershed projects with strong community involvement achieve 30% higher economic benefits compared to top-down approaches. When communities actively participate in planning, implementation, and maintenance, they develop a sense of ownership, leading to long-term sustainability. Participatory watershed programs also promote knowledge sharing and traditional water conservation practices, further enhancing resource efficiency.

Livelihood Enhancement and Rural Employment

Watershed programs contribute significantly to rural employment and income generation. Initiatives such as soil conservation, afforestation, agroforestry, and water harvesting create diverse job opportunities in agriculture, livestock rearing, and agro-based industries. In regions like Maharashtra and Rajasthan, watershed-based rural employment schemes have increased farm incomes by 50%, reducing seasonal migration and enhancing food security. Additionally, the promotion of high-value crops, organic farming, and allied activities such as beekeeping and fisheries within watershed areas has further improved economic resilience among rural communities.

Equitable Resource Access and Inclusive Development

Ensuring fair and just distribution of water, land, and financial resources is essential for the success of watershed programs. Smallholder farmers, women, and marginalized groups often face challenges in accessing critical resources. Effective watershed policies focus on empowering these vulnerable communities by providing access to irrigation facilities, microfinance support, and capacity-building programs. Research shows that women's participation in watershed programs has improved by 35% in several regions, leading to increased economic empowerment and household income stability. Women's involvement in self-help groups (SHGs) and decision-making processes has also strengthened the social fabric of rural communities.

Incorporating socioeconomic elements into watershed management ensures that interventions go beyond ecological conservation to improve livelihoods and social equity. Community participation, livelihood enhancement, and inclusive development create a strong foundation for sustainable watershed management, fostering resilience against environmental and economic challenges. By prioritizing these aspects, watershed programs can transform rural economies, promote climate resilience, and achieve long-term sustainability.

An effective watershed management strategy integrates physical, biological, and socioeconomic components to create a sustainable and resilient ecosystem. This comprehensive approach ensures that water resources, land use, and environmental conservation efforts are aligned to maximize ecological and economic benefits. By incorporating advanced scientific techniques, traditional knowledge, and active community engagement, watershed management becomes a powerful tool for addressing climate change, improving agricultural productivity, and strengthening rural livelihoods.

Climate variability poses a significant challenge to water security and agricultural sustainability. Watershed management plays a critical role in mitigating these impacts by promoting water conservation, afforestation, and sustainable land-use practices. Techniques such as check dams, contour bunding, and agroforestry improve water retention, reduce soil erosion, and enhance carbon sequestration. Studies indicate that watershed-based interventions can reduce the effects of droughts and floods, stabilizing local microclimates and protecting vulnerable communities from extreme weather events.

Sustainable agricultural development is a key goal of watershed management. Implementing soil and water conservation practices increases soil fertility, optimizes moisture availability, and enhances crop yields. Research shows that watershed-based interventions can boost agricultural productivity by 30–80%, particularly in semi-arid and drought-prone regions. Integrated nutrient and pest management, along with agroforestry practices, further support resilient farming systems, ensuring food security and economic stability for farming communities.

Watershed development projects generate employment opportunities through afforestation, water conservation, and agro-based industries. Case studies from regions like Maharashtra and Rajasthan reveal that watershed initiatives have led to a 50% increase in farmers' annual income. Additionally, equitable resource distribution, particularly for smallholder farmers and marginalized communities, ensures that economic benefits are shared inclusively. Women's participation in watershed programs has also improved significantly, fostering greater economic empowerment and social cohesion.

As global water and land resources face increasing stress, adopting a holistic watershed management approach is essential for long-term environmental and economic sustainability. Integrated watershed management not only conserves natural resources but also strengthens rural economies, enhances biodiversity, and builds climate resilience. Governments, policymakers, and local communities must work together to scale up successful watershed initiatives, ensuring that future generations have access to vital resources for sustainable development.

9.3 Community Involvement in Watershed Programs

The Role of Local Participation and Empowerment

Community participation is a cornerstone of successful watershed management, ensuring that conservation and resource management efforts are sustainable and effective in the long run. Watershed programs that actively involve local stakeholders—such as farmers, self-help groups, women's collectives, and village institutions—achieve better environmental, social, and economic outcomes. Empowering communities with knowledge, decision-making authority, and financial support fosters a sense of ownership, which is essential for long-term sustainability.

Historically, traditional societies practiced community-led water conservation through systems such as the Phad irrigation system in Maharashtra, the Johad system in Rajasthan, and the Tank system in South India. These methods were collectively managed by local farmers, ensuring efficient water distribution and long-term sustainability. However, modernization and centralized governance led to a decline in community involvement in natural resource management. Reviving participatory watershed management can bridge this gap and enhance the effectiveness of modern conservation efforts.

Involving local communities in watershed management fosters a bottom-up approach, ensuring that interventions align with local needs and challenges. Participatory watershed programs improve the efficiency of soil conservation, water harvesting, and afforestation activities. Studies indicate that watershed projects with strong community involvement result in a 30–50% increase in water availability and a 20–40% rise in agricultural productivity compared to top-down approaches. Empowering communities also enhances social equity by ensuring fair access to water and land resources, particularly for smallholder farmers, women, and marginalized groups. Research indicates that in India, watershed development projects have increased women's participation in agriculture by 35%, improving household incomes and food security.

Despite its benefits, community participation in watershed management faces several challenges. Lack of awareness, inadequate financial support, and weak institutional frameworks often hinder effective engagement. However, with the rise of self-help groups, participatory rural appraisal techniques, and decentralized governance policies, communities can play a more proactive role in managing their water and land resources.

A well-implemented, community-driven watershed management approach leads to sustainable resource use, climate resilience, and improved rural livelihoods. By integrating traditional knowledge with scientific interventions, community-led watershed programs can play a vital role in combating water scarcity, land degradation, and rural poverty. Governments, NGOs, and research institutions must work collaboratively to strengthen grassroots participation and empower local communities to take charge of their natural resources for long-term sustainability.

Importance of Local Participation in Watershed Management

1. **Improved Resource Management**

Local communities possess valuable traditional knowledge about land, water, and crop management, which can complement scientific interventions to create more effective and sustainable watershed management strategies. Indigenous practices, such as contour farming, traditional rainwater harvesting systems, and natural soil fertility enhancement methods, have been refined over generations and adapted to local climatic and geographical conditions. Integrating these traditional techniques with modern watershed interventions ensures that management plans are not only technically sound but also practical, socially acceptable, and culturally relevant.

Community-led watershed projects have demonstrated significant improvements in environmental sustainability and agricultural productivity. Studies indicate that participatory watershed management has led to a 30–50% increase in water conservation efficiency by enhancing groundwater recharge, reducing runoff, and improving soil moisture retention. This, in turn, has resulted in higher agricultural yields, increased crop diversification, and greater resilience to climate variability. For example, villages implementing community-driven watershed initiatives have reported improved water availability throughout the year, reducing dependence on erratic monsoon rainfall and enabling multiple cropping cycles.

When communities actively engage in watershed programs, they develop a sense of ownership and responsibility, ensuring long-term maintenance of conservation structures such as check dams, percolation tanks, and farm ponds. Local participation also fosters social cohesion and collective action, leading to more equitable resource distribution, particularly benefiting smallholder farmers and marginalized groups. By empowering local stakeholders with decision-making authority, financial support, and capacity-building initiatives, community-driven watershed management can enhance food security, strengthen rural economies, and contribute to long-term ecological balance.

2. Sustainability of Watershed Initiatives

When local people are directly involved in planning, implementing, and maintaining watershed structures such as check dams, farm ponds, and recharge wells, the likelihood of long-term success increases significantly. Community participation ensures that interventions are tailored to the specific needs of the region, leading to better resource utilization and sustainability. Farmers and villagers, who are the primary beneficiaries of watershed programs, develop a sense of ownership when they actively contribute to decision-making and execution. This involvement enhances the durability and efficiency of conservation measures, ensuring that structures are maintained and utilized effectively over time.

Research indicates that community-managed watershed programs have a 40% higher success rate compared to externally controlled projects. This is because local stakeholders are more invested in the upkeep and monitoring of conservation structures, reducing the risks of neglect and mismanagement. When villagers take responsibility for maintaining check dams, farm ponds, and recharge wells, these structures function efficiently for longer periods, continuously replenishing groundwater and providing water security for agricultural and domestic use.

Additionally, community-led watershed initiatives often encourage collective decision-making, fostering collaboration among farmers, local governing bodies, and development agencies. This participatory approach ensures that resource distribution is equitable and benefits all sections of the community, particularly smallholder farmers and marginalized groups. Furthermore, locally driven projects promote skill development and employment opportunities, as people receive training in soil and water conservation techniques, sustainable farming practices, and watershed management strategies. By empowering communities with the knowledge and resources to manage their watersheds effectively, participatory programs contribute to long-term agricultural sustainability, climate resilience, and rural development.

3. Equitable Distribution of Benefits

Ensuring equitable access to water, land, and financial resources is essential for improving the livelihoods of smallholder farmers and marginalized communities. In many rural areas, these groups face challenges such as limited access to irrigation, insecure land tenure, and financial constraints that hinder agricultural productivity. Watershed management programs that prioritize inclusive participation help bridge these gaps by implementing policies that ensure fair distribution of resources. By actively involving small farmers, women, and socially disadvantaged groups, these programs create opportunities for sustainable income generation and improved living conditions.

In India, watershed programs with strong community engagement have led to a 35% increase in women's participation in agricultural decision-making. Traditionally, women in rural areas have had limited roles in land and water management despite being heavily involved in farming activities. However, participatory watershed programs have provided women with access to training, financial support, and leadership roles in resource planning. This has resulted in improved household incomes, better food security, and enhanced resilience to climate variability.

Furthermore, community-led watershed initiatives empower marginalized groups by promoting cooperative water-sharing arrangements, microfinance opportunities, and capacity-building programs. These efforts ensure that economic benefits reach all community members, reducing rural poverty and enhancing social equity. By fostering inclusivity in watershed management, programs not only improve resource efficiency but also strengthen the social fabric of rural communities, making them more resilient to environmental and economic challenges.

4. Employment Generation and Skill Development

Watershed management programs play a crucial role in rural economic development by creating employment opportunities in various sectors, including land conservation, afforestation, irrigation infrastructure, and agro-based industries. These projects generate jobs in activities such as constructing check dams, soil conservation structures, and rainwater harvesting systems, providing both skilled and unskilled labor opportunities for rural communities. The increased availability of water and improved soil conditions also lead to higher agricultural productivity, which, in turn, supports livelihoods and reduces migration to urban areas.

Skill development programs integrated into watershed projects further enhance the economic potential of rural populations. Training initiatives in sustainable agriculture, water conservation techniques, and agro-processing equip farmers with the knowledge and skills needed to adopt modern, climate-resilient farming methods. These programs help farmers optimize resource use, increase crop yields, and explore alternative income sources such as agroforestry, dairy farming, and value-added agricultural products.

Additionally, watershed programs encourage entrepreneurship by facilitating access to microfinance, cooperatives, and self-help groups. Many successful watershed initiatives have led to the establishment of small-scale businesses related to seed production, organic farming, and food processing, contributing to rural economic diversification. By strengthening local economies and promoting sustainable livelihoods, watershed management projects not only improve environmental resilience but also foster long-term economic growth and poverty reduction in rural areas.

Strategies to Strengthen Community Involvement

1. Formation of Village Watershed Committees (VWCs)

Village Watershed Committees (VWCs) play a crucial role in ensuring the success and sustainability of watershed management programs. These community-based organizations serve as a bridge between local stakeholders and implementing agencies, facilitating participatory decision-making and effective resource management. By actively involving farmers, women's groups, and local leaders, VWCs ensure that watershed activities align with the specific needs and priorities of the community.

One of the key functions of VWCs is planning and overseeing watershed activities at the grassroots level. This includes identifying priority areas for intervention, coordinating the construction of soil and water conservation structures, and monitoring the long-term impact of watershed initiatives. By engaging community members in these processes, VWCs enhance transparency, accountability, and local ownership, increasing the likelihood of project success.

Training and capacity-building programs for VWCs further strengthen their ability to manage watershed resources efficiently. These programs provide knowledge on sustainable land and water management, financial planning, and conflict resolution, equipping local leaders with the skills needed to oversee watershed development activities. Studies have shown that watershed programs with well-trained VWCs achieve higher success rates in soil conservation, water recharge, and livelihood enhancement, as community members take greater responsibility for maintaining and protecting their natural resources.

By empowering VWCs and fostering participatory governance, watershed management programs can achieve long-term sustainability, ensuring that rural communities continue to benefit from improved water availability, soil fertility, and agricultural productivity.

2. Participatory Rural Appraisal (PRA)

Engaging communities in mapping their water resources, identifying challenges, and proposing solutions is essential for designing effective and locally relevant watershed management plans. When local stakeholders actively participate in assessing their water availability, land conditions, and environmental concerns, watershed initiatives become more accurate, practical, and sustainable.

Community-led resource mapping allows villagers to visually document existing water bodies, soil types, and land use patterns. This participatory approach helps identify critical areas facing water scarcity, erosion, or degradation, ensuring that interventions address actual needs rather than relying on generalized assumptions. For example, farmers can pinpoint regions where groundwater depletion is severe or where rainwater harvesting structures would be most beneficial.

By involving the community in problem identification, watershed programs foster a sense of ownership and responsibility among local residents. When people recognize their role in resource management, they become more committed to maintaining water conservation structures, preventing land degradation, and adopting sustainable agricultural practices.

Moreover, encouraging local participation in solution-building leads to innovative, context-specific strategies. Farmers, livestock owners, and women's groups bring valuable traditional knowledge that complements scientific watershed management techniques. Their insights on rainfall patterns, soil moisture retention, and indigenous water-saving methods can enhance the effectiveness of watershed development projects.

Ultimately, community engagement in mapping and planning ensures that watershed management aligns with local realities, resulting in more efficient resource utilization, stronger social cohesion, and improved environmental sustainability.

3. Microfinance and Self-Help Groups (SHGs)

Providing financial assistance and credit facilities is essential for empowering small-scale farmers and women entrepreneurs to adopt sustainable farming practices and water conservation technologies. Limited financial resources often prevent marginalized communities from investing in efficient irrigation systems, soil conservation measures, and climate-resilient farming techniques. By offering targeted financial support, watershed programs can significantly enhance agricultural productivity, resource efficiency, and rural livelihoods.

Microfinance institutions, government subsidies, and agricultural credit programs play a crucial role in making capital accessible to smallholder farmers. With financial backing, farmers can install drip irrigation, construct farm ponds, or adopt rainwater harvesting techniques, reducing their dependence on erratic rainfall. Studies have shown that access to credit for water-saving technologies can improve water-use efficiency by 30–50% in dryland farming systems.

Women entrepreneurs, particularly in rural areas, benefit immensely from financial assistance, as they often face greater challenges in accessing credit due to land ownership constraints and social barriers. By facilitating loans and grants for women-led agricultural enterprises, watershed programs can enhance their participation in sustainable farming, agro-processing, and value-added activities such as organic farming and dairy production. Research indicates that when women have financial independence, household nutrition, education levels, and overall community development improve.

Beyond direct financial aid, capacity-building programs that teach financial literacy and business management further empower farmers and entrepreneurs. Training sessions on budgeting, loan utilization, and investment strategies help maximize the benefits of financial assistance, ensuring long-term economic stability.

Ultimately, integrating financial support into watershed management initiatives not only strengthens climate resilience and food security but also promotes inclusive development by enabling disadvantaged groups to actively participate in sustainable agriculture.

4. Awareness and Capacity-Building Programs

Educating local farmers on watershed conservation, soil health management, and climate-resilient agriculture is crucial for ensuring the long-term sustainability of watershed programs. Knowledgeable farmers are better equipped to implement sustainable land and water management practices, which enhance agricultural productivity, improve environmental health, and build resilience against climate change.

Training programs on watershed conservation emphasize the importance of protecting water resources through soil conservation techniques, afforestation, and rainwater harvesting. Farmers learn how check dams, contour bunding, and vegetative barriers can reduce soil erosion and increase groundwater recharge. Studies show that well-informed farmers adopt conservation measures more effectively, leading to a 30–50% improvement in water retention and soil stability in watershed areas.

Soil health management is another critical aspect of farmer education. Overuse of chemical fertilizers and poor land management practices degrade soil fertility, reducing crop yields over time. By educating farmers about integrated nutrient management (INM), composting, and organic farming techniques, watershed programs help improve soil structure, microbial activity, and nutrient availability. Research indicates that farms adopting sustainable soil management practices experience a 20–40% increase in crop productivity while reducing input costs.

Climate-resilient agriculture training enables farmers to adapt to erratic rainfall patterns, prolonged droughts, and extreme weather events. By promoting drought-resistant crop varieties, agroforestry, mixed cropping, and conservation tillage, these educational initiatives help communities sustain agricultural production even under challenging climatic conditions. Case studies from rainfed regions suggest that farmers who adopt climate-smart techniques can reduce yield losses by up to 40% during drought years.

Community-led farmer field schools, extension services, and digital advisory platforms play a vital role in disseminating knowledge and building technical skills. Interactive learning approaches, such as demonstration plots and peer-to-peer training, encourage farmers to experiment with new practices and integrate them into their farming systems.

By investing in farmer education, watershed programs create a foundation for self-reliant, environmentally responsible agricultural communities. Empowered with knowledge, farmers become active participants in watershed conservation efforts, ensuring the long-term success and sustainability of watershed management initiatives.

Community involvement is not just a component but a driving force behind the success of watershed programs. Effective watershed management depends on the active participation of local communities in planning, implementation, and maintenance efforts. When communities take ownership of watershed initiatives, they contribute traditional knowledge, ensure long-term sustainability, and foster environmental stewardship.

Local knowledge is a valuable asset in watershed programs, as indigenous farming and water conservation practices have been developed over generations to suit specific ecological conditions. By integrating these traditional techniques with modern watershed management strategies, programs can become more effective and contextually relevant. Studies indicate that community-driven watershed projects have demonstrated a 30–50% improvement in water conservation efficiency and agricultural productivity compared to top-down approaches.

Empowering marginalized groups, including smallholder farmers and women, is another critical factor in successful watershed initiatives. Ensuring equitable access to water, land, and financial resources enables vulnerable populations to enhance their livelihoods and contribute to sustainable resource management. In India, watershed programs with strong community participation have increased women's involvement in agricultural decision-making by 35%, leading to improved household income and food security.

Participatory decision-making ensures that watershed interventions align with local needs and priorities. Village Watershed Committees (VWCs) and self-help groups play a pivotal role in mobilizing community members, overseeing resource allocation, and managing conservation efforts. Training and capacity-building initiatives further empower local stakeholders, enabling them to take charge of watershed governance. Research shows that watershed programs with active community leadership have a 40% higher success rate compared to externally controlled projects.

Beyond conservation, watershed programs generate employment opportunities in land rehabilitation, afforestation, irrigation infrastructure, and agro-based industries. Skill development initiatives equip farmers and rural workers with knowledge in sustainable agriculture, water conservation, and entrepreneurship, fostering economic growth in watershed regions. Financial support mechanisms, such as microcredit facilities and government incentives, further enable communities to invest in water-saving technologies and climate-resilient farming practices.

By fostering a sense of collective responsibility, community-led watershed management initiatives create long-lasting environmental and economic benefits. Strengthening community-driven approaches will be crucial in addressing future water scarcity challenges and ensuring sustainable development in rural landscapes. Through continued education, empowerment, and participatory governance, watershed programs can serve as a model for integrated resource management, benefiting both people and ecosystems for generations to come.

9.4 Factors Affecting Watershed Success

Expanding on this, watershed management programs must adopt a holistic approach that integrates environmental conservation, advanced technical strategies, and strong policy frameworks. Environmental factors such as climate, topography, and soil characteristics determine the natural capacity of a watershed to retain water and sustain agricultural activities. Technical aspects, including soil conservation methods, water harvesting structures, and modern monitoring tools like Geographic Information Systems (GIS), play a crucial role in optimizing watershed functions. Additionally, policy measures that promote participatory governance, financial support, and regulatory oversight ensure the sustainability of watershed projects.

A key challenge in watershed management is climate variability, which affects rainfall patterns, water availability, and soil erosion risks. Programs must incorporate adaptive strategies such as drought-resistant cropping, afforestation, and water conservation technologies to mitigate climate-related vulnerabilities. Moreover, successful implementation depends on the availability of skilled professionals, adequate funding, and community engagement. When local stakeholders actively participate in planning, execution, and maintenance, the long-term impact of watershed programs is significantly improved.

Ultimately, a well-coordinated approach that addresses these environmental, technical, and policy-related challenges will lead to more resilient watersheds, improved agricultural productivity, and enhanced livelihoods for rural communities. By integrating traditional knowledge with modern scientific advancements, watershed management can provide sustainable solutions to water and land resource challenges in the face of global environmental change.

Environmental Factors

Technical aspects are fundamental to the effectiveness of watershed management, as they determine how efficiently water and soil resources are conserved and utilized. The design and implementation of soil and water conservation structures, such as check dams, farm ponds, percolation tanks, and recharge wells, directly influence groundwater recharge and water availability. Advanced techniques like remote sensing and Geographic Information Systems (GIS) aid in watershed planning by identifying critical areas for intervention and monitoring land-use changes over time. Additionally, sustainable agricultural practices, including conservation tillage, crop rotation, and precision irrigation, help optimize resource use while maintaining soil health and productivity.

The adoption of innovative water harvesting methods is also crucial in regions facing erratic rainfall and prolonged dry spells. Techniques such as micro-catchment water harvesting and subsurface dams have been proven effective in improving moisture retention in dryland ecosystems. Similarly, bioengineering approaches, such as vegetative barriers and live check dams using fast-growing tree species, contribute to stabilizing degraded lands while enhancing biodiversity. When technical interventions are well-planned and aligned with the natural characteristics of a watershed, they significantly improve resilience to climate variability and environmental degradation.

However, technical solutions alone are not sufficient for ensuring long-term watershed success. Capacity building and knowledge transfer among local communities are essential for the proper maintenance and operation of watershed structures. Training programs focused on sustainable land and water management equip farmers and other stakeholders with the skills needed to implement best practices effectively. By integrating traditional knowledge with modern scientific advancements, watershed programs can achieve more sustainable and lasting impacts, ultimately enhancing agricultural productivity, water security, and ecosystem health.

Technical Factors

olicy support plays a crucial role in the success of watershed management programs by providing the necessary regulatory framework, financial incentives, and institutional backing. Effective policies promote integrated watershed development by aligning conservation efforts with rural development goals. Government initiatives, such as subsidies for water-saving technologies, afforestation programs, and incentives for sustainable agriculture, encourage community participation and adoption of best practices. Additionally, policies that facilitate decentralized governance, such as participatory watershed committees and self-help groups, empower local communities to take ownership of watershed projects.

Institutional coordination among government agencies, non-governmental organizations (NGOs), research institutions, and local stakeholders is vital for ensuring efficient implementation. Watershed programs that integrate multi-sectoral approaches—combining agriculture, forestry, water resources, and rural livelihoods—tend to yield more sustainable outcomes. For example, policies that promote integrated water resource management (IWRM) help balance water use between agriculture, domestic needs, and industry, reducing conflicts and ensuring equitable distribution.

Despite the importance of policy frameworks, challenges such as bureaucratic delays, inconsistent funding, and weak enforcement mechanisms can undermine watershed initiatives. In some cases, a lack of coordination between different agencies leads to overlapping responsibilities and inefficient resource allocation. Strengthening institutional frameworks, ensuring long-term financial commitment, and fostering collaboration among stakeholders can significantly enhance the impact of watershed programs. Furthermore, policies that encourage public-private partnerships and community-driven development ensure that watershed management remains adaptive and sustainable in the face of evolving environmental and socio-economic challenges.

Policy-Related Factors

Effective policies and institutional support play a crucial role in ensuring the long-term success of watershed management programs. Governments, international organizations, and non-governmental agencies provide essential funding, technical expertise, and regulatory frameworks that guide sustainable watershed development. Well-structured policies not only promote conservation but also empower local communities to participate actively in resource management, thereby fostering long-term environmental and economic sustainability.

One of the key policy initiatives in watershed management is the promotion of **participatory governance**. Policies that encourage community-led approaches, such as the formation of **Village Watershed Committees (VWCs), Water User Associations (WUAs), and self-help groups**, enhance local ownership and ensure that interventions are tailored to community needs. Research shows that watershed programs with strong community participation have a significantly higher success rate, as local stakeholders are more committed to maintaining conservation structures and adopting sustainable practices. In India, for example, the **Integrated Watershed Management Programme (IWMP)** has emphasized decentralized planning and implementation, allowing village institutions to take an active role in managing natural resources.

Financial incentives and subsidies are also vital policy tools that encourage farmers to adopt sustainable watershed management practices. Governments often provide financial support for water-saving technologies, soil conservation measures, and afforestation projects. For instance, subsidies for micro-irrigation systems such as **drip and sprinkler irrigation** have improved water efficiency in semi-arid regions, reducing dependency on erratic rainfall. Additionally, financial assistance for constructing check dams, farm ponds, and percolation tanks helps increase groundwater recharge and improve water availability for agriculture.

Another important policy consideration is the **integration of watershed management with broader rural development programs**. Watershed-based initiatives are often linked with employment generation schemes such as **Mahatma Gandhi National Rural Employment Guarantee Act (MGNREGA) in India,** which provides rural households with guaranteed wage employment in land and water conservation activities. This not only strengthens watershed infrastructure but also boosts rural incomes and food security. Similarly, policies that promote **sustainable agriculture, agroforestry, and climate-resilient farming techniques** contribute to long-term watershed sustainability by reducing pressure on land and water resources.

However, despite these policy interventions, challenges persist. **Fragmented policies, lack of coordination between agencies, and inadequate enforcement of environmental regulations** often hinder effective watershed management. In many cases, overlapping responsibilities between agricultural, water resources, and forestry departments lead to inefficiencies in program implementation. Moreover, weak monitoring and evaluation frameworks result in poor accountability and limited assessment of long-term impacts.

To address these challenges, policymakers must focus on **strengthening inter-agency collaboration, enhancing policy coherence, and ensuring long-term financial support** for watershed initiatives. Establishing **dedicated watershed management authorities** at regional and national levels can help streamline efforts and improve program effectiveness. Additionally, integrating **digital monitoring tools such as Geographic Information Systems (GIS), remote sensing, and real-time data analytics** can improve decision-making and ensure better tracking of watershed development outcomes.

By addressing these environmental, technical, and policy-related factors, watershed management programs can achieve their objectives of conserving water resources, improving agricultural sustainability, and enhancing rural livelihoods. An integrated and adaptive approach that considers ecological, technological, and governance aspects will be essential for the long-term resilience of watersheds in the face of climate change and growing water demands.

CHAPTER TEN

FUTURE PROSPECTS AND INNOVATIONS IN RAINFED AGRICULTURE

10.1 Emerging Technologies in Rainfed Farming

Rainfed farming, which depends solely on natural precipitation, is highly vulnerable to climate change, erratic rainfall, and soil degradation. These challenges make it difficult for farmers to maintain stable yields and ensure food security. However, the adoption of emerging technologies in precision agriculture, remote sensing, and weather forecasting is transforming rainfed farming systems, making them more resilient, productive, and sustainable. By leveraging data-driven insights, farmers can optimize resource use, reduce production risks, and improve decision-making, ultimately enhancing agricultural sustainability.

Precision agriculture utilizes advanced tools such as GPS-guided equipment, soil sensors, and variable rate technology (VRT) to apply inputs like fertilizers and irrigation more efficiently. This site-specific approach minimizes resource wastage, improves soil health, and enhances productivity, even in rainfed regions where water availability fluctuates. The adoption of precision farming in dryland agriculture has been shown to increase yields by 10–30% while reducing input costs.

Remote sensing technologies, including satellite imagery, drones, and GIS-based mapping, provide real-time data on soil moisture, vegetation health, and climate conditions. These technologies help farmers monitor crop stress, detect early signs of drought, and implement targeted interventions. For example, multispectral satellite imagery can identify areas experiencing water stress, allowing farmers to take timely action such as mulching or supplementary irrigation where feasible.

Weather forecasting tools play a crucial role in mitigating risks associated with rainfall variability. Advances in meteorological modeling and artificial intelligence (AI)-based weather prediction systems have improved the accuracy of short- and long-term forecasts. Farmers can use mobile-based weather advisory services to determine optimal planting times, anticipate dry spells, and plan contingency measures. Studies indicate that access to timely weather forecasts can reduce yield losses by up to 20% in rainfed regions by enabling better farm planning.

The integration of these emerging technologies empowers farmers to **adapt to changing climatic conditions, optimize water and nutrient use, and improve overall farm profitability**. Governments, research institutions, and private sector initiatives are increasingly investing in digital agriculture and smart farming solutions to support rainfed agricultural communities. Moving forward, the widespread adoption of these innovations will be critical in ensuring the long-term sustainability and productivity of rainfed farming systems.

1. Precision Agriculture

Precision agriculture integrates cutting-edge technologies to optimize farm productivity, minimize resource wastage, and reduce environmental impacts. By leveraging real-time data and automation, farmers can make more informed decisions about soil management, irrigation, and input application, significantly improving the efficiency and sustainability of rainfed farming systems.

GPS-Guided Machinery and Variable Rate Technology (VRT)

Global Positioning System (GPS)-enabled tractors and drones play a crucial role in precision farming by ensuring accurate seed placement, irrigation, and fertilization. By mapping field variability, GPS-based equipment optimizes input application, reducing overlaps and wastage. **Variable Rate Technology (VRT)** further refines input management by applying fertilizers, pesticides, and water based on the specific needs of different field zones. This targeted approach enhances nutrient use efficiency, improves crop health, and minimizes chemical runoff. Studies indicate that adopting precision agriculture can **reduce input costs by 20–30%** while significantly increasing yields, making it an essential tool for sustainable rainfed farming.

Soil Moisture Sensors and Smart Irrigation

Soil moisture sensors are instrumental in guiding irrigation decisions, ensuring water is applied only when necessary. These sensors measure soil water levels in real time, allowing farmers to optimize irrigation schedules and prevent over- or under-watering. **Automated irrigation systems**, such as drip and sprinkler irrigation, can be integrated with sensor data to precisely deliver water based on plant requirements, improving **water use efficiency by 25–40%**. This is particularly beneficial for rainfed farming, where erratic rainfall patterns can lead to drought stress. By reducing unnecessary water use, smart irrigation technologies help conserve precious water resources while enhancing crop resilience in water-scarce regions.

Drone Technology in Crop Monitoring

Drones equipped with **multispectral and thermal imaging cameras** provide high-resolution data on crop health, soil conditions, and pest infestations. These aerial monitoring tools help farmers detect early signs of **nutrient deficiencies, disease outbreaks, and water stress**, enabling timely interventions to protect yields. Drone-based surveillance can cover large areas quickly and cost-effectively, offering a major advantage over traditional field scouting methods. Research indicates that drone-assisted crop monitoring can **reduce yield losses by 10–20%** by facilitating precise and timely agronomic actions.

By integrating these advanced tools, precision agriculture enhances the adaptability of rainfed farming to climate uncertainties, improves input efficiency, and promotes sustainable land use practices. Expanding access to these technologies through government support, digital advisory services, and capacity-building programs can help smallholder farmers maximize productivity and resilience in unpredictable climatic conditions.

2. Remote Sensing and GIS in Rainfed Farming

Remote sensing technologies and Geographic Information Systems (GIS) have revolutionized modern agriculture by providing real-time monitoring, predictive analytics, and decision-support tools. These technologies enable farmers, researchers, and policymakers to better understand environmental dynamics, optimize resource management, and enhance agricultural sustainability, particularly in rainfed regions where climate variability poses significant challenges.

Satellite Imaging and Normalized Difference Vegetation Index (NDVI)

Satellite-based imaging, particularly **NDVI (Normalized Difference Vegetation Index)**, is widely used to assess **crop vigor, monitor plant health, and detect drought stress**. By analyzing variations in vegetation reflectance, NDVI helps identify early signs of water deficiency, pest infestation, or nutrient deficiencies, allowing for timely corrective measures. Additionally, **microwave soil moisture mapping** provides crucial data on water availability at different soil depths, assisting farmers in irrigation planning and drought preparedness. Research indicates that integrating remote sensing technologies with farm management practices can **enhance water conservation by 30–50%**, improving crop resilience in water-scarce regions.

GIS-Based Decision Support Systems

GIS technology plays a pivotal role in **mapping soil fertility, water resources, and land-use patterns**, aiding in agricultural planning and watershed management. By overlaying multiple data layers, GIS helps identify **potential rainwater harvesting sites**, enabling farmers to **enhance water storage and improve groundwater recharge**. Furthermore, GIS-based models are valuable in monitoring **soil erosion risks, optimizing watershed development strategies, and planning afforestation projects**. These spatial tools allow decision-makers to **prioritize conservation efforts** and design region-specific interventions for sustainable rainfed agriculture.

Unmanned Aerial Vehicles (UAVs) for Precision Monitoring

Unmanned Aerial Vehicles (UAVs), or **drones**, have emerged as a game-changing tool for **real-time assessment of crop conditions**. Equipped with **high-resolution multispectral and thermal sensors**, UAVs can detect **pest infestations, disease outbreaks, and soil moisture variations** at an early stage, facilitating prompt interventions. The ability to rapidly survey large areas makes drones especially beneficial for **monitoring extensive rainfed farms**, reducing the need for labor-intensive field scouting. Studies show that UAV-assisted **precision monitoring can increase productivity in rainfed systems by 15–25%** by enabling targeted input applications and reducing losses due to pests and diseases.

By integrating remote sensing, GIS, and UAV-based technologies, rainfed farming systems can become more **data-driven, climate-resilient, and**

resource-efficient. Expanding access to these technologies through farmer training programs, digital advisory services, and public-private partnerships can help bridge the technological divide and unlock their full potential for sustainable agricultural development.

3. Weather Forecasting and Climate Advisory Tools

Accurate weather forecasting and climate advisory services play a vital role in helping farmers **anticipate climate risks, optimize farm operations, and mitigate losses** due to unpredictable weather patterns. In rainfed farming, where productivity is highly dependent on natural precipitation, these technologies offer **real-time insights into rainfall patterns, temperature fluctuations, and pest risks**, enabling farmers to make proactive and informed decisions.

Agro-Meteorological Services

The integration of **weather stations, AI-driven climate models, and mobile-based advisory services** has significantly improved the accuracy of localized weather forecasts. **Short-term and seasonal climate predictions** allow farmers to adjust sowing schedules, irrigation timing, and pest control measures, reducing the adverse impact of extreme weather events. Studies indicate that **farmers who rely on weather forecasts experience 10–20% lower yield losses,** as they can adapt to erratic rainfall, avoid crop failures, and optimize input application.

Artificial Intelligence and Big Data Analytics

Artificial Intelligence (AI) and **Big Data analytics** enhance weather prediction by **analyzing historical and real-time meteorological data.** AI models can detect climate trends, forecast droughts, and predict rainfall variations with greater accuracy. By integrating **satellite imagery, soil data, and climate records,** Big Data platforms provide **precision insights into crop water requirements, disease risks, and temperature fluctuations.** These tools enable **adaptive farm planning,** allowing farmers to **adjust cropping patterns** and adopt climate-resilient practices to reduce losses from weather uncertainties.

Internet of Things (IoT) in Rainfed Farming

The **Internet of Things (IoT)** is revolutionizing rainfed farming through **real-time environmental monitoring.** IoT-enabled **soil moisture sensors, temperature probes, and humidity detectors** continuously collect data on field conditions, helping farmers make data-driven decisions. These sensors are connected to **cloud-based platforms,** which integrate **IoT data with weather forecasting models** to provide farmers with personalized recommendations for irrigation, fertilization, and disease prevention. By optimizing resource allocation, IoT technology enhances **crop resilience, minimizes input wastage, and boosts overall farm efficiency**.

Future Prospects and Challenges

Despite the transformative potential of these emerging technologies, several challenges hinder their widespread adoption in rainfed farming:

- **High Initial Costs**: Precision farming tools, IoT devices, and AI-based analytics require significant investment, making them less accessible for smallholder farmers.
- **Limited Connectivity in Rural Areas**: Many rainfed regions lack **internet access and mobile network infrastructure**, restricting farmers' ability to receive digital advisory services.
- **Need for Capacity Building**: Farmers require **training programs and technical support** to effectively utilize digital tools and integrate them into traditional farming practices.
- **Integration with Traditional Knowledge**: Ensuring that **scientific advancements align with indigenous agricultural wisdom** is crucial for practical and culturally relevant applications.

Moving forward, **public-private partnerships, government incentives, and community-driven digital literacy programs** will be essential to overcoming these challenges and expanding access to smart agricultural technologies. By integrating **emerging innovations with sustainable farming practices**, rainfed agriculture can become more **climate-resilient, productive, and resource-efficient**, securing food and livelihoods for millions of smallholder farmers.

Emerging technologies in rainfed farming are transforming traditional agricultural practices by enhancing productivity, optimizing water use, and improving resilience to climate change. The integration of precision agriculture, remote sensing, and weather forecasting tools enables farmers to make data-driven decisions that minimize risks associated with erratic rainfall, soil degradation, and pest outbreaks. These innovations have demonstrated significant improvements in crop yields, resource efficiency, and overall farm profitability.

Precision agriculture techniques, such as GPS-guided machinery, variable rate technology (VRT), and smart irrigation systems, help optimize input application, reducing costs and environmental impacts. Remote sensing technologies, including satellite imaging, UAVs, and GIS-based decision support systems, provide real-time monitoring and analysis of agricultural conditions, allowing for better land and water management. Additionally, weather forecasting tools powered by AI and IoT-enabled climate monitoring devices help farmers anticipate and prepare for extreme weather events, reducing yield losses and improving farm resilience.

Despite these advancements, several challenges hinder the widespread adoption of emerging technologies in rainfed farming. High initial investment costs for precision farming equipment and digital tools remain a significant barrier, particularly for smallholder farmers in developing regions. Limited access to reliable internet connectivity and digital infrastructure in remote agricultural areas further restricts the effectiveness of these innovations. Additionally, the successful implementation of these technologies requires extensive farmer training and capacity-building programs to bridge the knowledge gap and ensure that farmers can fully utilize digital solutions.

To maximize the benefits of emerging technologies, policymakers, researchers, and agribusiness stakeholders must work together to promote inclusive and sustainable digital transformation in agriculture. Governments and international organizations should invest in subsidized technology access, rural digital infrastructure, and farmer education programs to ensure equitable adoption. Public-private partnerships can play a crucial role in making precision farming tools more affordable and accessible, particularly in developing economies. Moreover, integrating modern technological solutions with traditional agricultural knowledge will enhance the practicality and effectiveness of these interventions.

In the long run, investing in technology-driven solutions for rainfed agriculture will be essential for ensuring global food security and environmental sustainability. As climate change continues to threaten rainfed farming systems, embracing innovations that improve resource efficiency, mitigate climate risks, and enhance productivity will be key to building a resilient and sustainable agricultural future.

10.2 Climate-Resilient Agriculture

Climate change poses significant challenges to rainfed farming, which depends entirely on natural precipitation for crop production. The increasing frequency of extreme weather events, such as unpredictable rainfall patterns, prolonged droughts, intense heat waves, and floods, threatens agricultural productivity, soil health, and water availability. These climatic uncertainties make rainfed farming highly vulnerable, leading to yield instability, food insecurity, and economic hardships for millions of smallholder farmers worldwide.

To mitigate these risks and build long-term agricultural sustainability, Climate-Resilient Agriculture (CRA) strategies must be adopted. CRA integrates a combination of sustainable farming practices, technological innovations, and policy interventions to enhance productivity while reducing vulnerability to climate variability. By implementing techniques such as drought-tolerant crop varieties, efficient water management systems, precision agriculture tools, and soil conservation methods, farmers can adapt to changing climatic conditions and maintain stable yields.

Furthermore, CRA emphasizes the role of scientific advancements and digital technologies in predicting weather patterns, optimizing resource use, and providing timely advisory services to farmers. Equally important is the involvement of policymakers, extension services, and local communities in promoting climate adaptation strategies that are practical, scalable, and economically viable. Strengthening institutional support, improving access to financial resources, and encouraging knowledge-sharing among farmers will be essential for ensuring the successful adoption of climate-resilient agricultural practices.

By integrating innovative solutions with traditional wisdom, CRA can help rainfed farming systems withstand climate shocks while improving food security, rural livelihoods, and environmental sustainability. Investing in climate adaptation strategies today will be crucial in ensuring a more resilient agricultural future in the face of climate change.

1. Climate-Smart Cropping Systems

Adopting climate-resilient crops and improved cropping techniques is essential for mitigating the adverse effects of climate change on rainfed farming. By selecting drought-tolerant varieties, diversifying cropping systems, and employing conservation practices, farmers can enhance productivity, optimize resource use, and increase resilience against erratic weather patterns.

Drought-Tolerant and Heat-Resistant Crops

Developing and promoting climate-resilient crop varieties is a crucial strategy for sustaining agricultural productivity in regions prone to extreme temperatures, droughts, and floods. Advances in plant breeding, genetic engineering, and biotechnology have led to the development of crop varieties that can withstand harsh environmental conditions while maintaining high yields.

- **Drought-tolerant maize, pearl millet, and sorghum** are well-suited for arid and semi-arid regions, requiring less water while producing stable yields.
- **Heat-resistant wheat and chickpea varieties** are designed to endure high temperatures, preventing yield losses caused by heat stress.
- **Flood-resistant rice varieties**, such as "Scuba rice," can survive prolonged submergence during heavy rainfall events, ensuring food security in flood-prone areas.
- **Salt-tolerant crops**, including certain varieties of barley, rice, and quinoa, help farmers cultivate land affected by soil salinity, a growing issue due to rising sea levels and poor irrigation management.

Intercropping and Crop Diversification

Diversifying cropping systems improves farm resilience by reducing dependency on a single crop, stabilizing yields, and enhancing soil fertility.

- **Intercropping**, the practice of growing two or more crops together, improves nutrient cycling, reduces the spread of pests and diseases, and optimizes land use. For example, maize-legume intercropping improves nitrogen fixation, reducing the need for synthetic fertilizers.
- **Crop diversification**, which involves cultivating different crops in a given area, helps spread risks associated with climate variability. Farmers can rotate cereals with pulses, oilseeds, or vegetables to maintain soil health and ensure continuous food supply.
- **Agroforestry systems**, which integrate trees and shrubs with crops or livestock, provide additional income sources, reduce soil erosion, and improve microclimatic conditions for crops.

Conservation Agriculture

Conservation agriculture enhances soil health, improves water retention, and minimizes land degradation, making farming systems more climate-resilient.

- **Minimum tillage (no-till farming)** reduces soil disturbance, preserving soil structure and moisture while preventing erosion. Studies have shown that no-till farming can increase soil organic matter by 15–30% over time.
- **Crop residue retention** involves leaving harvested plant residues on the soil surface, improving water infiltration, suppressing weeds, and reducing soil temperature fluctuations.
- **Crop rotation**, alternating different crops each season, disrupts pest cycles, replenishes soil nutrients, and enhances biodiversity. Rotating nitrogen-fixing legumes with cereal crops improves soil fertility while reducing dependency on synthetic fertilizers.

By integrating climate-resilient crop varieties with sustainable cropping techniques, farmers can build adaptive farming systems capable of withstanding climate-related challenges while ensuring long-term productivity and food security.

2. Water Management Strategies

Water scarcity and unpredictable rainfall patterns pose significant challenges to rainfed farming. Efficient water management strategies are essential for optimizing water use, enhancing moisture retention, and ensuring sustainable agricultural production under climate stress. By adopting rainwater harvesting techniques, advanced irrigation methods, and integrated watershed management approaches, farmers can improve water availability and resilience to droughts.

Rainwater Harvesting

Rainwater harvesting techniques help capture and store excess rainfall, reducing dependence on erratic precipitation and ensuring water availability during dry periods.

- **Farm ponds**: Small, excavated water storage structures that collect and store rainwater for supplementary irrigation. Research shows that farm ponds can increase crop yields by 20–30% in rainfed areas.
- **Percolation tanks**: Shallow reservoirs that enhance groundwater recharge by allowing rainwater to infiltrate the soil, improving water table levels.
- **Check dams**: Small barriers constructed across seasonal streams to slow down water flow, reduce erosion, and promote groundwater recharge. Studies indicate that check dams can improve water availability by

40–50% in semi-arid regions.

- **Contour bunding and trenches**: Structures built along field contours to reduce runoff, increase soil moisture retention, and prevent soil erosion.

Micro-Irrigation Systems

Micro-irrigation technologies optimize water application, ensuring that crops receive the right amount of moisture without wastage.

- **Drip irrigation**: Delivers water directly to plant roots through a network of pipes, reducing evaporation and improving water use efficiency by up to 90%.
- **Sprinkler irrigation**: Simulates rainfall by distributing water evenly across fields, improving soil moisture retention while minimizing runoff.
- **Subsurface irrigation**: A system that delivers water underground through buried pipes, reducing evaporation losses and enhancing water absorption by plant roots.

Watershed Management

Integrated watershed management promotes sustainable water conservation and equitable distribution across agricultural landscapes.

- **Soil and water conservation measures**: Implementing techniques such as terracing, vegetative barriers, and agroforestry to prevent land degradation and improve water retention.
- **Reforestation and afforestation**: Increasing tree cover in watershed areas enhances infiltration, stabilizes soil, and maintains water balance.
- **Community-based water governance**: Encouraging participatory approaches where local communities manage and maintain watershed structures to ensure long-term sustainability.

By integrating rainwater harvesting, efficient irrigation methods, and watershed management strategies, farmers can enhance their adaptive capacity, reduce water stress, and sustain crop production in rainfed agricultural systems.

3. Soil Health Management

Healthy soils are the foundation of sustainable agriculture, particularly in rainfed farming systems where water availability and soil fertility are key constraints. Enhancing soil health improves water retention, boosts nutrient cycling, and strengthens resilience to climate stress, ultimately supporting higher yields and long-term agricultural sustainability.

Organic Matter Addition

Increasing soil organic matter enhances soil structure, moisture-holding capacity, and microbial diversity, leading to improved nutrient availability and plant health.

- **Compost and farmyard manure**: Organic amendments such as decomposed plant material and livestock waste enrich soil with essential nutrients, improving crop productivity and reducing dependency on chemical fertilizers.
- **Green manure**: Incorporating nitrogen-fixing plants like sunn hemp and dhaincha into the soil enhances fertility and organic carbon content.
- **Biofertilizers**: Beneficial microbial inoculants, such as Rhizobium and Azotobacter, promote biological nitrogen fixation, reducing the need for synthetic fertilizers.

Mulching

Applying organic or synthetic mulches helps regulate soil temperature, conserve moisture, and suppress weed growth.

- **Crop residue mulching**: Leaving harvested crop residues on the field reduces soil erosion, enhances water infiltration, and minimizes surface evaporation.
- **Biodegradable mulches**: Using materials like straw, wood chips, or biodegradable plastic sheets protects soil from excessive heat and maintains optimal moisture levels.
- **Live mulching**: Growing low-height cover crops alongside main crops prevents moisture loss and enriches soil fertility.

Agroforestry and Cover Cropping

Integrating trees and diverse plant species into cropping systems enhances soil conservation and boosts productivity.

- **Agroforestry systems**: Planting trees such as Gliricidia, Moringa, or leguminous species alongside crops prevents soil degradation, improves carbon sequestration, and provides additional income sources.

- **Cover cropping**: Growing leguminous cover crops like clover, cowpea, or vetch between growing seasons improves nitrogen levels, suppresses weeds, and prevents soil erosion.
- **Alley cropping**: Planting rows of trees or shrubs between crops protects against wind erosion, enriches soil with organic matter, and stabilizes the microclimate.

By implementing soil health management strategies such as organic matter addition, mulching, and agroforestry, farmers can enhance soil fertility, improve water conservation, and build resilience against climate-induced stress in rainfed farming systems.

4. Livelihood Diversification and Risk Reduction

Diversifying income sources plays a crucial role in enhancing the adaptive capacity of rural communities to climate change. In rainfed regions, where agricultural outputs are highly dependent on unpredictable rainfall and vulnerable to extreme weather events, relying solely on seasonal cropping can be risky. Integrating supplementary livelihood options strengthens household income, reduces vulnerability, and ensures long-term sustainability of farming systems.

- **Agro-Based Enterprises**: Encouraging farmers to engage in value-added activities like beekeeping, mushroom cultivation, vermicomposting, and small-scale food processing helps optimize resource use and generate year-round income. These enterprises require relatively low investment and can be easily adopted alongside existing farming practices. They also reduce post-harvest losses and increase the market value of farm produce.
- **Livestock Integration**: Incorporating dairy, poultry, goatery, or fish farming into crop-based systems provides an additional and steady source of income. Livestock also contribute organic manure, which enhances soil fertility and reduces the need for chemical fertilizers. Integrated farming systems have been shown to improve farm productivity and resilience by diversifying outputs and spreading risk.
- **Climate Insurance**: Weather-based crop insurance offers a financial safety net to farmers in case of climate-induced losses such as drought, floods, or unseasonal rains. These schemes are increasingly being adopted in India and other developing countries to ensure that farmers are compensated promptly when adverse weather conditions impact crop yields. By reducing the economic uncertainty of farming, climate insurance encourages continued investment in agriculture and adoption of climate-

resilient practices.

Overall, income diversification strategies empower rural households to withstand climate shocks, reduce economic dependence on a single activity, and enhance the sustainability of agricultural livelihoods in vulnerable rainfed ecosystems.

5. Use of Digital Technologies and Early Warning Systems

Technological advancements are playing an increasingly vital role in building resilience in rainfed agriculture by equipping farmers with timely, accurate, and actionable information. These tools not only enhance decision-making but also help reduce the risks and uncertainties associated with climate variability.

• **Weather Forecasting and Advisory Services**: Access to real-time weather data and short- to medium-term forecasts empowers farmers to make informed decisions regarding the timing of sowing, irrigation, fertilization, and harvesting. Mobile-based advisory services, offered through SMS or smartphone applications, disseminate localized climate information and agronomic tips, enabling proactive responses to changing weather patterns. Studies have shown that farmers who use weather advisories experience fewer losses and improved yields during abnormal seasons.

• **Remote Sensing and GIS**: Satellite-based remote sensing and Geographic Information Systems (GIS) provide high-resolution data on soil moisture, crop health, vegetation cover, and rainfall distribution. These tools are essential for monitoring land and water resources over time, assessing the impacts of climate change, and planning interventions such as drought preparedness or replanting strategies. By identifying vulnerable zones, remote sensing supports more targeted and efficient resource use.

• **Decision Support Systems (DSS)**: Artificial Intelligence (AI)-powered platforms and Big Data analytics combine climate forecasts with local agronomic and economic data to offer customized recommendations. These systems assist farmers in selecting appropriate crop varieties, estimating irrigation needs, and managing pests and diseases. DSS tools also help policymakers and extension workers design region-specific adaptation strategies, making them integral to climate-resilient planning.

By leveraging these emerging technologies, rainfed farming systems can transition from reactive to proactive management, increasing productivity, reducing crop failure risks, and contributing to sustainable agricultural development in the face of climate change.

6. Policy Support and Institutional Interventions

Government policies and institutional frameworks are fundamental to scaling up and sustaining climate-resilient agriculture, particularly in vulnerable rainfed regions. By creating an enabling environment, these support systems help bridge gaps in resources, knowledge, and infrastructure—ensuring that farmers can effectively adapt to climate risks.

• **Subsidies and Incentives**: Financial support mechanisms, such as subsidies for solar-powered pumps, precision agriculture equipment, micro-irrigation systems, and certified climate-resilient seeds, significantly lower the barriers to adoption. These incentives make it economically viable for smallholder farmers to invest in sustainable technologies. For example, programs like India's Pradhan Mantri Krishi Sinchayee Yojana (PMKSY) and Sub-Mission on Agricultural Mechanization (SMAM) promote efficient water use and climate-smart mechanization.

• **Farmer Training and Extension Services**: Institutional support through agricultural extension programs enhances farmers' capacity to adopt adaptive practices. Training sessions, field demonstrations, and digital literacy initiatives help farmers understand and implement techniques like conservation agriculture, integrated pest management, and weather-informed planning. Public-private partnerships and NGOs also play a key role in delivering tailored knowledge and tools at the grassroots level.

• **Community-Based Adaptation Initiatives**: Local institutions such as Village Climate Resilience Committees, Watershed Associations, and Self-Help Groups (SHGs) facilitate decentralized planning and implementation of adaptation measures. These participatory structures ensure that interventions reflect local ecological and socioeconomic contexts. By encouraging bottom-up governance, community-based approaches foster ownership, inclusivity, and long-term sustainability of climate adaptation efforts.

Together, these policy instruments and institutional interventions lay the groundwork for building resilient agricultural systems. Coordinated efforts between governments, research organizations, and local communities are essential to mainstream climate resilience in agricultural planning and secure food systems in the face of ongoing climate change.

Building climate resilience in rainfed agriculture demands an integrated approach that combines scientific innovation, sustainable land and water management, and robust institutional frameworks. Climate-smart practices—such as adopting resilient crop varieties, efficient irrigation techniques, and soil health conservation—equip farmers to adapt to increasing climate variability. The use of digital tools, including weather forecasting, remote sensing, and decision support systems, further empowers farmers with timely information for informed decision-making.

Equally important is the role of policy and community engagement. Collaborative efforts among policymakers, researchers, extension agencies, and farming communities are critical to scaling up successful models and ensuring inclusivity. Strengthening institutional capacity, providing financial incentives, and fostering participatory governance will be key to transforming vulnerable rainfed systems into resilient, productive, and sustainable landscapes.

Investing in climate-resilient agriculture today will not only safeguard rural livelihoods but also ensure long-term food security and environmental sustainability for future generations.

10.3 Policy Recommendations and Future Directions

Sustainable development of rainfed farming systems hinges on the formulation of robust policy frameworks and focused research strategies tailored to the distinctive challenges of these agro-ecosystems. These regions often face erratic rainfall, limited infrastructure, degraded soils, and heightened vulnerability to climate change—necessitating a holistic, integrated approach to development. Policies must not only promote the adoption of resource-efficient technologies, such as micro-irrigation and drought-resilient crop varieties, but also encourage active community participation and localized decision-making to ensure long-term sustainability. Simultaneously, research must prioritize region-specific innovations—addressing soil, water, and climate variability—and facilitate the development of scalable, cost-effective solutions that enhance both productivity and resilience. By aligning policy and research efforts, rainfed farming can transition from a risk-prone livelihood to a climate-resilient and sustainable pillar of rural development.

1. Strengthening Institutional and Policy Support

- **Integrated Rainfed Agriculture Mission**: Establish comprehensive national and state-level missions dedicated to the sustainable development of rainfed areas. These missions should integrate core components such as watershed development, water-use efficiency, soil health restoration, and climate-resilient agricultural practices. A convergence of existing schemes under a unified framework would ensure better coordination, monitoring, and impact assessment, while also addressing regional disparities in resource allocation and implementation.

- **Subsidies for Climate-Smart Technologies**: Introduce targeted financial incentives and credit support for the adoption of climate-resilient technologies among smallholder farmers. This includes subsidies for micro-irrigation systems (drip and sprinkler), drought- and heat-tolerant crop varieties, precision farming tools like soil moisture sensors, and solar-powered pumps and machinery. Special emphasis should be given to making these technologies affordable and accessible to women farmers and marginalized communities.

- **Decentralized Governance**: Strengthen decentralized and participatory governance structures by empowering grassroots institutions such as Village Watershed Committees (VWCs), Farmer Producer Organizations (FPOs), and self-help groups (SHGs). These bodies should play a central role in planning, implementing, and monitoring rainfed development programs, ensuring that interventions are context-specific and locally accepted. Capacity-building initiatives and digital tools can further enhance the effectiveness and accountability of these institutions.

2. Enhancing Research and Development
Region-Specific Crop Breeding

Strategic investment in crop improvement is essential for enhancing resilience and productivity in rainfed regions. Collaboration among public research institutions, agricultural universities, and private sector breeding programs should focus on developing high-yielding, short-duration, and abiotic stress-tolerant varieties adapted to specific agro-ecological zones. Special emphasis should be placed on:

- **Drought-tolerant pulses**, such as chickpea and pigeon pea;
- **Heat- and salinity-tolerant cereals**, like millets and sorghum;
- **Oilseeds suited for marginal soils**, like sesame and niger;
- **Revival of indigenous and underutilized crops**, which offer both climate resilience and nutritional security.

Digital Agriculture Innovations

Harnessing digital technologies can transform rainfed agriculture into a more productive, data-driven, and adaptive system. Public-private partnerships should be scaled up to develop and deploy tools based on:

- **Artificial Intelligence (AI)** for predictive analytics and decision support;
- **Internet of Things (IoT)** for real-time monitoring of soil moisture, crop health, and weather conditions;
- **Big Data platforms** to synthesize diverse data sources into localized crop advisories.

  Government programs should focus on ensuring rural connectivity, creating farmer-friendly mobile apps in local languages, and strengthening digital literacy through extension networks.

Soil and Water Resource Inventories

A sound understanding of the resource base is foundational for sustainable rainfed farming. Policymakers should prioritize the creation of **geospatial resource inventories** using GIS and remote sensing technologies in combination with on-ground surveys. These should cover:

- **Soil fertility and texture** maps to inform nutrient management strategies;
- **Land capability and erosion risk zones** for prioritizing conservation practices;
- **Groundwater recharge potential and surface water availability** to guide irrigation planning.

  These dynamic, location-specific databases must be integrated into district and watershed-level planning processes to support evidence-based interventions.

3. Capacity Building and Knowledge Dissemination

Farmer Training and Extension Services

Capacity building is critical for the successful adoption of sustainable and climate-resilient practices in rainfed agriculture. Strengthening **Krishi Vigyan Kendras (KVKs)**, agricultural universities, and state extension agencies can help scale up farmer outreach. Key actions include:

- Regular **training modules on climate-smart practices**, integrated nutrient and pest management, and water-efficient technologies;
- Incorporation of **digital tools**, such as mobile apps, drones, and automated weather stations into hands-on demonstrations;
- Promotion of **farmer-to-farmer learning** and participatory extension models to enhance adoption at scale.

Climate Literacy Campaigns

Creating awareness and understanding of climate change impacts is essential for proactive adaptation at the grassroots level. Dedicated campaigns should:

- Use **local languages and culturally relevant materials** to communicate risks and solutions;
- Establish **Farmer Field Schools (FFSs)** as interactive platforms for practical learning on soil, water, and crop management under climate stress;
- Disseminate **climate advisories via SMS, community radio, and WhatsApp groups**, ensuring inclusive access for women and smallholder farmers.

Public–Private Partnerships (PPPs)

Collaborative models are necessary to bridge technological, infrastructural, and market gaps in rainfed areas. Policy should support:

- **Technology dissemination** through agri-tech startups and cooperatives, providing access to sensors, mobile platforms, and weather tools;
- **Value-chain development** for rainfed crops (e.g., millets, pulses, oilseeds), linking production to processing, branding, and marketing;
- Creation of **resilient supply chains** through aggregation models like Farmer Producer Organizations (FPOs), supported by digital traceability and market analytics.

4. Financial and Market Access
Credit and Insurance Support

Access to timely and affordable credit is vital for smallholder farmers to invest in sustainable technologies and practices. Policy measures should:

- **Expand institutional credit coverage** in rainfed regions through simplified loan procedures, crop-specific lending models, and inclusion of tenant and women farmers;
- Promote **weather-indexed insurance schemes** and **climate risk financing mechanisms** to protect farmers from losses due to erratic rainfall, droughts, or floods;
- Integrate **insurance with digital platforms** for claim processing and grievance redressal, ensuring transparency and timely payouts.

Market Reforms

Efficient market access is critical to improving farm incomes in rainfed systems. Reform strategies should aim to:

- **Upgrade rural market infrastructure**, including storage, grading, and cold chains to reduce post-harvest losses;
- Strengthen **aggregation mechanisms** such as Farmer Producer Organizations (FPOs) and cooperatives to enhance bargaining power and reduce transaction costs;
- Introduce **price stabilization measures** and **minimum support prices (MSPs)** for underutilized and climate-resilient rainfed crops like millets, pulses, and oilseeds.

Incentivizing Diversification

Promoting livelihood diversification reduces dependence on monsoon-driven crops and enhances household resilience. Key approaches include:

- **Support for agroforestry models** that integrate trees with crops and livestock, improving soil health, biodiversity, and carbon sequestration;
- **Incentives for allied activities** such as dairy farming, poultry, mushroom cultivation, and beekeeping, especially through rural entrepreneurship programs;
- Encourage **value-added enterprises and processing units** to create rural employment, reduce migration, and increase farm profitability.

5. Future Research Directions
Research Priorities for Sustainable Rainfed Farming
Climate Resilience Metrics

Establishing robust and standardized indicators is essential for tracking the effectiveness of climate-resilient agricultural practices in rainfed regions. These metrics should:

- Evaluate key parameters such as yield stability, water productivity, soil health, and carbon sequestration;
- Include **social and economic indicators**, such as income diversification, access to resources, and community-level adaptive capacity;
- Enable policy feedback loops by integrating data into planning tools used at district and state levels for climate-smart agriculture initiatives.

Long-Term Impact Assessments

To ensure evidence-based policymaking, long-duration studies should be prioritized to assess the sustained benefits and unintended consequences of various interventions. These assessments should:

- Examine the **long-term ecological and economic impacts** of watershed development, agroecological practices, and livelihood diversification models;
- Use **mixed-methods approaches** (quantitative and qualitative) to capture system-wide changes, including environmental restoration and social transformation;
- Inform the design of scalable models and investment priorities for different agro-ecological zones.

Social Equity and Gender Studies

Ensuring inclusivity in rainfed farming development requires deeper understanding of social structures and disparities. Research should focus on:

- **Gender roles in resource access, decision-making, and labor allocation**, particularly in tribal and marginalized communities;
- **Land tenure systems and their implications** for the adoption of conservation practices and access to institutional support;
- Strategies to **mainstream women, youth, and vulnerable groups** in value chains, financial syste

The transformation of rainfed agriculture into a resilient and productive system is not merely an agricultural imperative—it is a national priority for achieving inclusive and sustainable development. This transition demands a synergistic approach combining **forward-looking policies, region-specific research,** and **community-driven implementation strategies.**

By fostering an **enabling ecosystem** that promotes innovation in digital and climate-smart technologies, strengthens institutional capacities, and ensures equitable access to resources and services, governments and stakeholders can unlock the full potential of rainfed regions. Investing in **knowledge dissemination, market reforms,** and **climate adaptation tools** will empower smallholder farmers to overcome the challenges posed by climate variability and resource constraints.

Ultimately, the path to sustainable rainfed agriculture lies in **collaborative action**—where policymakers, researchers, civil society, and farmers co-create solutions that safeguard livelihoods, ensure food security, and preserve natural ecosystems. With the right vision and commitment, India and other rainfed-dependent countries can build **climate-resilient rural economies** that thrive for generations to come.